George Reynolds

The Story of the Book of Mormon

Vol. 4

George Reynolds

The Story of the Book of Mormon
Vol. 4

ISBN/EAN: 9783337296957

Printed in Europe, USA, Canada, Australia, Japan

Cover: Foto ©Thomas Meinert / pixelio.de

More available books at **www.hansebooks.com**

THE STORY

OF THE

BOOK OF MORMON.

By ELDER GEORGE REYNOLDS.

Author of "The Myth of the Manuscript Found;" "Are we of Israel?"
Treatise on "The Book of Abraham;" "Dictionary of the Book
of Mormon;" "Concordance of the Book of Mormon."

"Truth shall spring out of the earth; and righteousness shall
look down from heaven."—*Psalm, LXXXV, 11.*

FOURTH EDITION.

PRESS OF
HILLISON & ETTEN CO.
CHICAGO

PREFACE

THE Book of Mormon is the record of God's dealings with the peoples of ancient America, from the age of the building of the Tower of Babel to four hundred and twenty-one years after the birth of Christ. It is the stick of Ephraim, spoken of by Ezekiel: the Bible of the western continent. Not that it supersedes the Bible or in any way interferes with it, any more than the history of Peru interferes with or supersedes the history of Greece; but, on the other hand, in many places it confirms Bible history, demonstrates Bible truths, sustains Bible doctrines, and fulfills Bible prophecy.

For many years we have taken great pleasure in perusing its sacred pages and studying its truths. The more we read it the more we found it contained. Like other inspired records, every time it was opened we discovered new and ofttimes unexpected testimonies of its divinity. From reading it we turned to writing of it; and much that this volume contains has been penned at various intervals, from the days we were in prison for conscience sake, where portions were written, to the present. And now we present it to the reader with the feeling that the work is but commenced; that what remains unsaid is probably as important as what is given, but with the hope that what we have done will not prove ineffectual in spreading the truth, in increasing knowledge concerning God's dealings with mankind, and aiding in the development of the purposes of Jehovah. If this be accomplished we shall feel that great has been our reward.

This volume presents one unique feature, in that it is the first attempt made to illustrate the Book of Mormon; and we have pleasure in realizing that the leading illustrations are the work of home artists. To break fresh ground in such a direction is no light undertaking; the difficulties are numerous, none more so than the absence of information in the Book of Mormon of the dress and artificial surroundings of the peoples whose history it recounts. Each artist has given his own ideas of the scenes depicted, and as so much is left to the imagination, some readers will doubtless praise where others will blame; and the same effort will be the subject of the most conflicting criticism.

Not the least interesting feature of the book will, we believe, be found in the reproductions of portions of certain ancient Aztec historical charts. These have been the subjects of controversy for centuries past; many efforts have been made at their translation; but all such attempts have been ineffectual, and in many cases ludicrous. It required the publication of the Book of Mormon to turn on them the light of divine truth, when their intent at once became apparent. Others, we trust, in time will be discovered which will be added testimonies to its genuineness and divine authenticity, as well as to the sacred mission of the instrument in God's hands in bringing it forth—the youthful Prophet, Joseph Smith.

Geo. Reynolds

December, 1888.

CONTENTS.

INTRODUCTION.

America the first inhabited of all Lands—Its Ancient Peoples—The Garden of Eden—The Antediluvians—The Jaredites—The Nephites and Lamanites.. 15

CHAPTER I.

Ancient Jerusalem—Lehi—His Vision—His Call to Preach to the Jews—They Persecute Him—He is Commanded of God to take his Family into the Wilderness—Their ·Departure—The Return of his Sons to Jerusalem to obtain the Records. They are ill-treated by Laban—His Death—Zoram Accompanies the Brothers into the Wilderness... 18

CHAPTER II.

The Rejoicing Over the Records—Nephi and his Brothers again Return to Jerusalem—They Conduct Ishmael and his Family into the Wilderness—Lehi's Dream—The Tree of Life—The Rod of Iron—The Boturini Manuscript—Nephi's Vision................ 25

CHAPTER III.

Marriages in the Company—The Liahona—The Journey Continued—Nephi Breaks his Bow—Death of Ishmael—They Reach the Ocean—Nephi Builds a Ship—They Cross the Great Waters and Reach the Promised Land.. 35

CHAPTER IV.

The Promised Land—Chili—Its Natural Productions—The Death of Lehi—His Blessing on his posterity—Prophecies of his Ancestor Joseph 44

CHAPTER V.

The Nephites and Lamanites Separate—The Nephites seek a New Home—Nephi Chosen King—He Builds a Temple—Instructs his People in the Arts of Peace—War with the Lamanites—The Sword of Laban—Nephi's Death—Jacob, his Brother, Becomes the Chief Priest—Jacob's Teachings on Marriage............... 47

CHAPTER VI.

The Condition of the Lamanites—Sherem, the First Anti-Christ—His Recantation and Dreadful End...................................... 50

CHAPTER VII.

Enos, the Son of Jacob—The Nephites and Lamanites of his Day—His Testimony and Prophecies.................................... 53

CHAPTER VIII.

Jarom—Omni—Amaron—Chemish—Abinadom—Amaleki — Mosiah—Review of Nephite History for Four Hundred Years............ 55

CHAPTER IX.

Causes that Led to the Migration from the Land of Nephi—The People of Zarahemla—Mulek and his Colony—The Fusion of the Two Nations—Mosiah made King—His Happy Reign.......... 59

CHAPTER X.

The Reign of King Benjamin—The Progress of his People—His Last Great Speech—He Establishes the Church of Christ—All the People Covenant with God—Mosiah II. Anointed King...... 64

CHAPTER XI.

Zeniff Returns to the Land of Nephi—His Treaty with the Lamanites—The Prosperity of the People of Zeniff—The Treaty Broken—War—Peace and Wars Again—The Death of Zeniff—Noah's Wicked Reign—His Wars with the Lamanites—The Prophet Abinadi—His Terrible Message of God's Wrath—He is Martyred—Alma—He Pleads for Abinadi—Is Cast Out—Flees to the Place of Mormon... 69

CHAPTER XII.

The Waters of Mormon—Alma, Helam and Others Baptised Therein—The Church Organized—The King Warned—He Sends Troops—Alma and his People Flee to the Land of Helam—They Build a City 77

CHAPTER XIII.

King Noah's Subjects Rebel—Gideon—The Lamanites Invade Lehi-Nephi—The Nephites Retreat—A Part Surrender—The New Terms of Peace—Noah is Burned to Death—Limhi made King—Noah's Priests Escape—They seize some Lamanite Maidens—Another War—The Nephites Victorious—The King of the Lamanites wounded—Mutual Explanations...................... 80

CHAPTER XIV.

The Bondage of the People of Limhi—An Expedition North—Finding of the Jaredite Records—The Arrival of Ammon—The People of Limhi Escape—The Pursuit—The Amulonites—The People of Alma—They are Brought into Bondage—Their Deliverance 84

CONTENTS.

CHAPTER XV.
Mosiah's Good Reign—The Circumstances of his Advent—He Assembles the People—The Baptism of Limhi—Churches Organized Throughout the Land.. 89

CHAPTER XVI.
The Unbelief of the Youth of Zarahemla—The Younger Alma and the Sons of Mosiah—They Encourage the Persecutions Against the Church—They are Met by an Angel—His Message—Alma's Awful Condition—His Vision and Testimony—The Changed Life of the Young Men... 92

CHAPTER XVII.
The Growth of the People in Zarahemla—They Build Many Cities—Mosiah's Sons Desire to Take a Mission to the Lamanites—Mosiah Inquires of the Lord—The Divine Answer................ 96

CHAPTER XVIII.
Mosiah's Sons Refuse the Kingdom—He Grants the People a Constitution—The People to Elect their Rulers—Alma, the Younger, First Chief Judge... 98

CHAPTER XIX.
The Mission of the Sons of Mosiah to the Lamanites—Their Journey in the Wilderness—Ammon Brought before King Lamoni—The Conflict at the Waters of Sebus—The Miraculous Conversion of Lamoni and his Family—Abish the Waiting Woman..... 100

CHAPTER XX.
Ammon and Lamoni Start for the Land of Middoni—They Meet the Old King—His Rage at Seeing Ammon—He Endeavors to Kill his Son—Aaron and his Brethren Liberated—A Sketch of their Labors and Sufferings—The Conversion of Lamoni's Father and his Household... 106

CHAPTER XXI.
The King Issues a Proclamation—The Results of the Labors of the Sons of Mosiah—The People of Anti-Nephi-Lehi—They Bury their Weapons of War—Are Massacred by the Thousand—They Remove to the Territory of the Nephites, who give them the Land of Jershon 110

CHAPTER XXII.
Review of the Mission of the Sons of Mosiah—Its Importance and Great Length—Its Results to Both Races—The Dates of its Leading Occurrences 114

CHAPTER XXIII.

The Days of the Judges—Their Names and Reigns—The Heresy of Nehor—He Slays Gideon and is Executed—Amlici's Rebellion—The Battle of Amnihu—The Conflict at the Crossing of the Sidon—A Third Battle 117

CHAPTER XXIV.

Alma Resigns the Chief Judgeship—Nephihah Chosen—Alma Ministers in Zarahemla, Gideon, Melek and Ammonihah—Condition of the Last Named City—It Rejects the Message Alma Bears—An Angel Meets Him—Amulek—The Lawyer Zeezrom—The Great Controversy—Zeezrom Converted and Cast Out—The Martyrdom of the Believers—Alma and Amulek in Prison—Their Deliverance 124

CHAPTER XXV.

Zeezrom Sick with Fever—His Miraculous Recovery—The Destruction of Ammonihah—The Invasion of the Land of Noah—Zoram, the Nephite Commander, Seeks the Mind of the Lord—It is Given—Its Results—The War Ended—Alma's Ministrations..... 131

CHAPTER XXVI.

Korihor, the Anti-Christ—His False Teachings and Blasphemy—He is Taken before Alma—Is Struck Dumb—His Miserable End—The Heresy Rooted Out.. 135

CHAPTER XXVII.

Zoram and the Zoramites—Their Peculiar Heresy—The Land of Antionum—The Rameumptom—Alma's Mission to these People—Those Who Receive His Teachings Persecuted—They Flee to Jershon 139

CHAPTER XXVIII.

Another War—Moroni the Leader of the Nephites—The Tactics of the Lamanites—Zerahemnah—The Battle at Riplah—Defeat of the Lamanites 144

CHAPTER XXIX.

Alma's Charge to His Sons—He Transfers the Records to Helaman—He Leaves This World—Zeezrom's Latter Days—Helaman's Ministrations 147

CHAPTER XXX.

Amalickiah—His Apostasy and Treason—Moroni's Title of Liberty—The Nephites Respond to His Call—Lehonti—He is Poisoned by Amalickiah—The King of the Lamanites Treacherously Slain—Amalickiah Marries the Queen and is Proclaimed King—A Disastrous Lamanite Raid 149

CHAPTER XXXI.

A Few Years of Peace—Teancum—The Contention Between Lehi and Morianton—Amalickiah's Terrible Invasion—His Success—He is Stopped at Bountiful by Teancum—Teancum Slays Amalickiah—Ammoron Made King of the Lamanites.......................... 156

CHAPTER XXXII.

Jacob the Zoramite—His Characteristics—The Strategy by Which Mulek Was Taken—The Fierce Battle between Jacob and the Nephite Forces—Jacob's Death 159

CHAPTER XXXIII.

The War in the South-west—Antipus—Helaman and His Two Thousand Sons—Their Valor and Faith—The Repulse of the Lamanites 162

CHAPTER XXXIV.

The Relief of Manti—The Overthrow of the Kingmen—Pachus Slain—The Struggle at Moroni—Teancum Slays Ammoron, but at the Cost of His Own Life—Teancum's Noble Character.............. 167

CHAPTER XXXV.

Peace Once More—The Results of the War—The Labors of Helaman—Shiblon Receives the Records—Hagoth, the Ship-builder—Another War—Moronihah—Pahoran's Death—Contention Regarding the Chief Judgeship—Paanchi's Rebellion—The Gadianton Bands—Assassination of Pahoran II.—Another Lamanite Invasion..... 171

CHAPTER XXXVI.

Pacumeni Slain—Helaman Chosen Chief Judge—The Conspiracy to Slay Him—Kishkumen Killed—The Prosperity of the Nephites under Helaman 175

CHAPTER XXXVII.

The Sons of Helaman—Nephi's Righteous Rule—The Lamanites Again Invade Zarahemla—They Drive the Nephites into the Northern Continent—The Ministrations of Nephi and Lehi—The Manifestations of God's Power in the City of Nephi—Aminadab—The Conversion of the Lamanites—Universal Peace............ 177

CHAPTER XXXVIII.

Growth of Evil amongst the Nephites—The Increase of the Gadianton Robbers—Nephi's Announcement of the Murder of the Chief Judge—The Discovery—Nephi Arrested—He is Proven Innocent—God's Covenant with Him—Increase of Iniquity—A Terrible Famine—The Welcome Rain—The Trend to Death.............. 184

CONTENTS.

CHAPTER XXXIX.

Samuel, the Lamanite—His Mission and Prophecies—The Vain Attempt to Destroy Him—He Returns to His Own Country........ 189

CHAPTER XL.

Nephi Translated—His Son Nephi—Time of the Savior's Coming—The Conspiracy to Slay the Believers—The Revelation to Nephi—The Promised Signs Appear—Increase of the Gadianton Robbers—War—Lachoneus Gathers all the People to One Land—The End of the Struggle..................................... 193

CHAPTER XLI.

The Last Chief Judge Murdered and the Republic Overthrown—The Signs of the Savior's Death Appear—A Terrible Storm—The Universal Darkness—The Unparalleled Destruction—The Terror of those Hours.. 197

CHAPTER XLII.

The Voice from Heaven—The Savior Testifies of Himself—Silence Throughout the Land—How oft would Christ have Gathered His People—The Darkness Departs........................... 202

CHAPTER XLIII.

Christ Appears in the Land Bountiful—The Testimony of the Father—Jesus Calls Twelve Disciples—His Teachings to Them and to the Multitude 205

CHAPTER XLIV.

The Fulfillment of the Mosaic Law—"Other Sheep Have I"—The Ten Tribes—The Events of the Latter Days.................... 208

CHAPTER XLV.

The Savior Heals the Sick—He Blesses the Children of the Nephites—Angels Minister unto them................................. 210

CHAPTER XLVI.

The Sacrament Administered—The Savior's Teachings Regarding it—He Confers on His Disciples the Power to Give the Holy Ghost—He Ascends into Heaven............................ 213

CHAPTER XLVII.

Jesus Returns and Renews His Teachings—He Administers the Sacrament—He Explains the Teachings of the Prophets—The Words of Malachi 216

CHAPTER XLVIII.

The Savior Continues His Ministrations—He Raises a Man from the Dead—The Labors of the Twelve—The Name of the Church—The Three who should Remain.............................. 220

CHAPTER XLIX.

The Long Continued Era of Peace and Righteousness—Death of Nephi—His Son Amos—Amos the Second.................... 223

CHAPTER L.

The Commencement of the Apostasy—It Grows in Intensity—The Persecution of the Disciples—Lamanites Again—Re-appearance of the Gadianton Bands—War—Ammaron Hides the Records.... 226

CHAPTER LI.

The Last Long Series of Wars—Mormon—The Final Conflict at Cumorah—The Last of the Nephites......................... 229

CHAPTER LII.

The Historians of the Nephites—The Plates of Nephi—List of their Custodians—Their Lengthened Years......................... 232

CHAPTER LIII.

The Women of the Book of Mormon—Their Condition and Position—Abish—Isabel—Marriage—Amulek—Moroni's Title of Liberty—The Mothers of the Ammonites—Two Extremes................ 237

CHAPTER LIV.

Domestic Life Among the Nephites—Household Duties—Dress—Ornaments—Homes—Food—Manufactures—Transportation 241

CHAPTER LV.

Agriculture Among the Nephites—Grains—Stock Raising—Irrigation. 247

CHAPTER LVI.

Science and Literature Among the Nephites—Their Astronomy and Geography—The Learning of Egypt........................... 250

CHAPTER LVII.

The Art of War Among the Nephites—Their Weapons, Armor and Fortifications—Moroni's Line of Defense....................... 255

CHAPTER LVIII.

The Laws of the Nephites—The Roman and Nephite Civilizations—The Laws under the Kings—Position of the Priesthood—Slavery—Criminal Offenses.. 262

CHAPTER LIX.

The Laws under the Judges—The Voice of the People—Elections—Rights of the People—Church and State—The Criminal Procedure 269

CHAPTER LX.

Laws of the Nephites, Continued—The Division into Tribes—The Messianic Dispensation—The Final Convulsion................. 277

CHAPTER LXI.

The Money of the Nephites—Their Coins—Barley the Standard of Value 281

CHAPTER LXII.

Personal Appearance of the Nephites—Their Beauty—Testimony of Remains Found—The Dark-Skinned Lamanites................. 284

CHAPTER LXIII.

Language of the Nephites—The Influence of the Egyptians—Nephite Words — Rameumptom — Liahona — Rabbanah — The Lamanite Tongue—Word Building 287

CHAPTER LXIV.

Nephite Proper Names—Bible Names—Sariah—Nephi—Sam—Melek—Jershon—Isabel—Aha, etc.—Prefixes and Suffixes.............. 294

CHAPTER LXV.

The Lands of the Nephites—Mulek and Lehi—Zarahemla and Nephi—The Wilderness—The Land of First Inheritance—The Journeys Northward—The Waters of Mormon—Lehi-Nephi.............. 300

CHAPTER LXVI.

Nephi in the Hands of the Lamanites—The Lands of Shemlon, Shilom, Helam, Amulon, Ishmael, Middoni, Jerusalem, etc.......... 310

CHAPTER LXVII.

The Lands of the Nephites, Continued—Zarahemla—Jershon—Antionum—Manti—Gideon 314

CHAPTER LXVIII.

Lands of the Nephites, Continued—Minon—Melek—Ammonihah—Noah—Sidom—Aaron—Lehi—Mulek—Bountiful—The South-west Border 318

CHAPTER LXIX.

The Lands of Antum, Teancum, Joshua, David, etc.—Cumorah—The Hills of the Nephites—The River Sidon................. 325

CHAPTER LXX.

Religion of the Nephites—It is Stated by Nephi—The Priesthood and Ordinances Thereof—Baptism—Confirmation—Ordination—The Sacrament—Spiritual Gifts 329

CHAPTER LXXI.

Miracles Among the Nephites—The Miracles of Christ—John and the Three Nephites—Translations 336

CHAPTER LXXII.

The Prophecies Regarding the Savior—Their Completeness and Detail—Names and Titles Given to Christ........................ 341

CHAPTER LXXIII.

Nephite Apostates—The Order of Nehor—Amalekites—Amalickiahites—Amulonites—Abinadi's Prophecy—The Gadiantons.......... 343

CHAPTER LXXIV.

Church Discipline Among the Nephites—Treatment of the Unrepentant—The Word of the Lord Regarding Transgressors—The Testimony of Moroni... 349

CHAPTER LXXV.

The Discovery of the Jaredite Records—Coriantumr—Ether—The Dispersion at Babel—The Journey of the Jaredites—Atlantis....... 352

CHAPTER LXXVI.

Moriancumer—Building the Barges—The Finger of the Lord—The Appearing of the Savior—The Voyage........................... 356

CHAPTER LXXVII.

The Land of Promise—A Monarchy Established—The Kings of the Jaredites from Orihah to Omer—Akish—The Daughter of Jared. 359

CHAPTER LXXVIII.

The Kings of the Jaredites from Omer to Coriantumr—The Material Prosperity of this Race... 361

CHAPTER LXXIX.

The Judgments of God on the Jaredites—The Extinction of the Race—The Hill Ramah—Shiz and Coriantumr—Ether................ 363

BOOK OF MORMON CHRONOLOGY........................... 368

APPENDIX 381

LIST OF ILLUSTRATIONS

	PAGE
The Glorious Appearing of Jesus to the Nephites........*Armitage*	Frontispiece
Ancient Aztec Chart, Showing Lehi's Travels. No. 1....*Boturini*	22
Ancient Aztec Chart, Showing Lehi's Travels. No. 2.....*Boturini*	30
Vision of Nephi .... *Held*	32
Ancient Aztec Chart, Showing Lehi's Travels. No. 3.....*Boturini*	36
Ancient Aztec Chart, Showing Lehi's Travels. No. 4.....*Boturini*	37
Ancient Hieroglyphic Chart ....*Farerri*	43
The First Sacrifice on the Promised Land................*Ottinger*	45
The Jews Led Away to Captivity................................	62
The Land of Helam	79
Discovery of the Records of the Jaredites...............*Ottinger*	85
Baptism of Limhi ....*Ottinger*	91
Wilderness of Hermounts.......................................	122
Moroni Raises the "Title of Liberty"....................*Ottinger*	151
Destruction of Zarahemla ....*Ottinger*	201
Ancient Egyptian Characters	290
Copy of Characters on the Plates from Which the Book of Mormon Was Translated..	291
Appearance of Christ to the Brother of Jared..............*Held*	357
Ether Finishing His Record..............................*Morris*	364

THE
Story of the Book of Mormon.

INTRODUCTION.

AMERICA THE FIRST INHABITED OF ALL LANDS—ITS ANCIENT PEOPLES—THE GARDEN OF EDEN—THE ANTEDILUVIANS—THE JAREDITES—THE NEPHITES AND LAMANITES.

THE story that we are about to relate is a true one. It is the history of the races who lived on this broad land of ours long, long ago. From it we shall learn many lessons of God's great love for man. We shall also learn how oft his love has been spurned, how apt his favored children have been to walk in ways of sin, and how prone to disobey his holy law. It is a story full of light and shade, one which it will be well for all of us to take to heart, for by so doing our faith in God will increase, and we shall be prompted to strive the more earnestly to avoid the evils that others, by their misdeeds, have brought upon themselves and their posterity.

America, the land we love, is, in our Heavenly Father's eyes, choice above all other lands as the home of those of his sons and daughters, whom he has placed upon this earth. For all God's creatures are not here. He has made many worlds and filled them with his children. How many we know not; they are countless to us. The stars, that shine in myriads in the heavens, are nearly all suns like the one that gives us light: the remaining few are worlds like unto this on which we dwell; and ours is one of the very smallest of them all. To the works of God there is no beginning, neither is there any end.

God made America the richest of all lands. He filled its depths with precious minerals; he caused the most lovely trees, and herbs, and flowers to grow upon its surface. In all things he made it most desirable as a home for man. And here he planted the Garden of Eden, and placed our first parents, Adam and Eve, therein. From that garden they were afterwards driven forth when they failed to keep God's law. But they did not leave this continent. Here they still remained; here their sons and daughters were born, until many strong peoples had sprung from them. It was in this land that Cain slew his brother Abel; it was here that Enoch and his city dwelt, that Noah preached to the ungodly, and the ark was built. But when the flood was over and the waters sank, that ark, by the winds and waves, had been carried far away to a new land, until it rested on the Mountains of Ararat. Then for a short time America was without inhabitant.

But not long after the deluge the wicked tried to build a tower that would reach so high that if ever another flood came they might escape the rising waters by ascending it. This is called the Tower of Babel. The Lord was angry with those who attempted to build this tower, for he had promised that he would never again destroy the earth with the waters of a flood. But they did not believe him; and in their unbelief they went to work to construct it. In his anger he confounded their language, that they could not understand each other. Then he scattered them abroad upon the face of the earth. Some few, better than the others, he brought to America. Here he made them a great nation; and they filled the land for many hundreds of years. By and by they grew exceedingly wicked and gathered together in vast armies to war one with another. And they fought so terribly that at last they were all destroyed,—all except one man. These people were called the Jaredites.

By this we see that this continent was a second time left

without inhabitants because of the great wickedness of the people.

After this the Lord brought another people to fill this land. They were a branch of the house of Israel, and we call them the Nephites and Lamanites. They also grew great, prospered, flourished, and fell. Like the Jaredites, at the last, they destroyed each other in war, and there were but few left. But from those few have come the many tribes of Indians that today are found scattered far and wide over both North and South America, and also on some of the outlying islands of the sea.

Thus fell a third race who would not serve God; for he had decreed that the wicked should not inherit this land. To one of his ancient servants he declared, "If iniquity shall abound cursed shall be the land for their sakes; but unto the righteous it shall be blessed for ever." (II. Nephi 1:7.)

North America was the first of all lands to be inhabited; it was here that Adam and Eve dwelt. The Jaredites from the Tower of Babel also first landed here. But the Nephites made their earliest settlements on the western shores of the southern continent, where by degrees they spread north and south, then east and west, until their cities and villages could be seen in every part of the land.

CHAPTER I.

ANCIENT JERUSALEM—LEHI—HIS VISION—HIS CALL TO PREACH TO THE JEWS—THEY PERSECUTE HIM—HE IS COMMANDED OF GOD TO TAKE HIS FAMILY INTO THE WILDERNESS—THEIR DEPARTURE—THE RETURN OF HIS SONS TO JERUSALEM TO OBTAIN THE RECORDS—THEY ARE ILL-TREATED BY LABAN—HIS DEATH—ZORAM ACCOMPANIES THE BROTHERS INTO THE WILDERNESS.

(I. NEPHI CHAP. 1 TO 4.)

OUR story opens in the royal city of Jerusalem, in the first year of the reign of King Zedekiah, or exactly six hundred years before the birth of our Savior. It was then very grand and very beautiful, the capital of the Kingdom of Judah, and the chief city of all Israel. In name it was holy, for the Temple of the Lord was there. Its busy streets were crowded with a mixed multitude. Priests and Levites, who officiated in the ordinances of the law of Moses, worshipers from the other tribes of Jacob, warriors of the armies of Judah, courtiers and attendants on the king, merchants from Egypt, from Tyre and Sidon and from many other parts, artificers in various trades, all these combined to make it wealthy and renowned, a busy mart of trade, a center of civilization, and a sacred city.

Holy it should have been, but the glory of the Lord had departed from his house. Its people had become very wicked. They were filled with pride and greed; they heeded not the law of the Lord; their affections were set upon the things of this world; they served God with their lips only, while their hearts were far from him. He had sent unto them his prophets, but one after another they had rejected these holy men; many they had persecuted, and some they had slain.*

In this city, at that time, dwelt a worthy man named Lehi. He was of the tribe of Manasseh, but had made his home in Jerusalem all his days, though it was a city of the Kingdom of Judah. He was a man who had been prospered of the Lord and had gathered around him considerable wealth. His wife's name was Sariah, and they had four sons and some daughters. The names of the sons, in the order of their ages, were Laman, Lemuel, Sam and Nephi; the number or names of the daughters are nowhere given in the sacred history.

To this good man the word of the Lord came. God raised him up to be a prophet. He sent him with a message to the people of Jerusalem. As a servant of the Lord he had to warn them of many evils that would come upon them if they did not cease from their wicked ways. But they paid no heed to his words; they refused to listen to his warning. Indeed, they became very angry because he told them of their sins, and before long they sought to kill him.

God gave to Lehi many dreams and visions. One day a pillar of fire came and rested on a rock before him; and then he heard and saw many wonderful things. The things which he had seen and heard so overpowered him that he went home to his house at Jerusalem, and threw himself on his bed. Then being overcome by the Holy Spirit he was carried away in a vision. In that vision he saw God sitting upon his throne, surrounded by vast hosts of angels who were singing and praising the Lord. And he saw a holy Being, surrounded by a glory as bright as the sun at noon day, come down out of the midst of heaven. It was the Lord Jesus. Our Savior was followed by twelve others whose brightness exceeded that

---

*See II. Chronicles 36: 14-16.

of the stars. They were Christ's Apostles. These came down and went forth on the face of the earth.

And in the vision the Savior came to Lehi and gave him a book, and bade him read it. In that book was an account of events that had not yet taken place. It was full of the woes that should happen to Jerusalem and her people if they repented not of their sins and follies. It told how that great city should be taken by her enemies and destroyed; how numbers of the inhabitants should perish, while many should be carried captive into Babylon. All of which was fulfilled a few years later. These things with others were what Lehi told the Jews; and as they did not believe his words they became enraged at him and ill treated him. How gracious was our heavenly Father to show such great things to Lehi, and to reveal to him so much with regard to the earthly life of our Lord and Savior, whose coming in the flesh was yet six hundred years in the future.

Before long the Lord was satisfied with what Lehi had said and done. He told him, in a dream, that as the Jews had rejected his message and sought his life, to leave them to the destruction that would surely come upon them. God then directed him to leave Jerusalem and take his family and journey into the wilderness. This Lehi did. He left behind him his gold and other precious things, and only carried with him what was needful for the use of his family during their travels. Like Abraham before him, he went not knowing whither he was going, but went because God had commanded him; and, like Abraham, he was led by Divine power to a blessed land of promise.

When Lehi and his family left Jerusalem they traveled southward to the borders of the Red Sea. There they pitched their tents and rested for a season in a valley near a river which emptied into the sea. In this valley Lehi built an altar, and upon it he offered a sacrifice to the Lord, and gave thanks unto him for his great goodness in bringing them out of the doomed chief city of Judah.

It was while Lehi's little company were camped in this valley, to which he gave the name of the Valley of Lemuel, that the dispositions of the four young men began to show themselves. Laman and Lemuel here commenced to grumble, to complain and to rebel, while Nephi was obedient in all things to the word of God and the wishes of his father. He sought the Holy One in earnest prayer in his own behalf and in that of his brothers, and the Lord made him many precious promises, all of which were, in due time, fulfilled.

While encamped in this valley the Lord, in a dream, commanded Lehi to send his sons back to Jerusalem to obtain certain plates on which was engraven a record of the Jews. They also contained a genealogy or list of Lehi's forefathers. These plates were kept by a rich man named Laban, who held them because, like Lehi, he was a descendant of that Joseph who was sold into Egypt.

When Lehi's elder sons heard this they murmured. They did not want to go back to the city. They said it was a hard thing to do, and they claimed to be afraid of Laban. But Nephi neither feared nor murmured, for he was a man of much faith. On this occasion he said to his father, I will go and do the things which God has commanded, for I know that the Lord gives no commandment to the children of men, save he prepares a way that they may do the thing that he requires of them. When Lehi saw how strong was his son's faith he greatly rejoiced, for he perceived that Nephi had been much blessed of the Lord.

At last all the sons consented to return and get the plates. They took their tents with them, traveled as they came, and in a few days reached Jerusalem. When they arrived they cast lots to decide which of them should first visit Laban. The lot fell upon Laman. As he had no faith in his mission, we can readily understand that he failed to get the records.

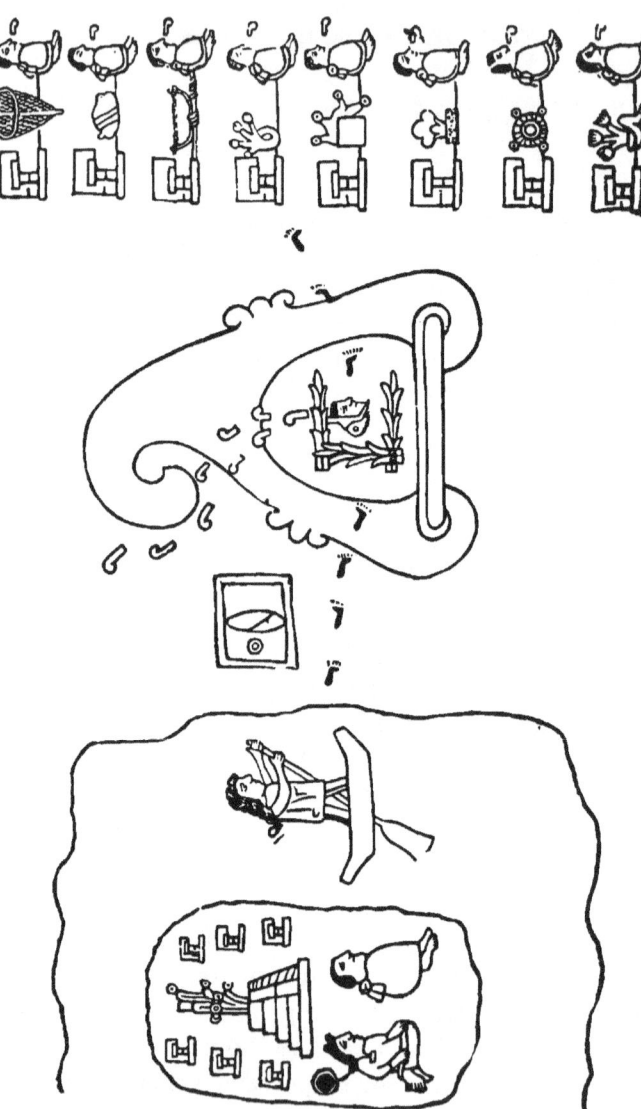

ANCIENT AZTEC CHART SHOWING LEHI'S TRAVELS. NO. 1.

He went to Laban's house, which was a very fine one, and talked with him on the matter. But Laban grew angry, would not let him have the plates, called him a robber, and drove him out of the house. When Laman returned to his brothers they were very sad at hearing how violently Laban had acted. All but Nephi wished to return to their father in the wilderness; but he would not consent. He had come up to Jerusalem to do what God had commanded, and he would not return until he had done it. He said to his brothers, "As the Lord liveth, and as we live, we will not go down unto our father in the wilderness, until we have accomplished the thing which the Lord has commanded us." Brave words from a heart of faith, and by that faith their purpose was accomplished.

Nephi next proposed that they should go to their father's house and collect some of the gold, silver and other precious things which he had left behind, take them to Laban and offer them to him in exchange for the records.

They did all this; still Laban would not let them have the plates. But when he saw how great was the value of the property which they offered him, he coveted it; for he was a wicked man, filled with greed and covetousness. So he thrust the brothers out of his house and kept their property. Not content with this he sent his servants after them to slay them. But the servants did not overtake them, for Nephi and his brothers outran them and hid themselves in a cave in the wilderness outside of the walls of the city.

Laman and Lemuel were now furious at their lack of success. In their anger they said many hard things to Sam and Nephi, and moreover they beat them with a rod. While thus engaged an angel of the Lord stood before them and rebuked them for their cruel treatment of their younger brothers. He further told them to go up to Jerusalem once again, and Laban should be delivered into their hands.

Even though an angel from heaven had appeared to them, Laman and Lemuel still murmured and did not want to go back to the house of Laban. But after some persuasion from Nephi they reluctantly followed him. His faith had made him their leader, which position he ever afterwards held.

Nephi caused his brethren to hide themselves without the walls, and then went forward alone, not knowing exactly where he was going, but suffering himself to be guided by the Spirit of the Lord. It was now night. When near the house of Laban he came across a man lying in a drunken stupor on the ground. It proved to be Laban himself.

The Spirit of the Lord now directed Nephi to slay Laban, telling him that it was better that one man should die than that a nation should dwindle and perish in unbelief. This the Nephites undoubtedly would have done had they not had the law of the Lord with them; and this law was engraved on these plates. As we proceed we shall find that both the Lamanites and the people of Zarahemla sank in sin and dwindled in unbelief from this very cause,—they had no Divine records.

For all that the Spirit thus prompted, still Nephi felt loath to slay Laban, although he had robbed him and his brothers of their father's property and sought to take their lives. But at last he obeyed the voice of the Spirit, and drawing Laban's own sword from its sheath, with it he smote off this wicked man's head.

Nephi next removed Laban's armor from the dead body and put it on his own person; he also took the sword of Laban and girded it around his waist. Then he went to the dead man's house, and, imitating Laban's voice, he commanded the servant who had the keys of the room where the records were kept to go with him and get them. The servant, whose name was Zoram, obeyed, and brought forth the records, for in the darkness, he thought it was his master who was talking to him.

Nephi, still acting as though he was Laban, had Zoram go with him to where his brothers were hid. When Laman,

Lemuel and Sam saw him coming they became greatly afraid, for they did not know him, dressed as he was in the armor of Laban; and he had some little difficulty in making them understand that he was their brother, and that they had no cause for fear. But when Zoram discovered that Nephi was not his master, he also was seized with fear, and would have run away had not Nephi held him. We may be sure Nephi did not want Zoram to return to Jerusalem, lest he should gather a body of men and follow him and his brothers into the wilderness and slay them. So he spake kind and encouraging words to Zoram, who soon consented to make a covenant of friendship with Nephi and go with him to the place where Lehi had pitched his tents. This covenant Zoram most faithfully kept.

CHAPTER II.

THE REJOICING OVER THE RECORDS—NEPHI AND HIS BROTHERS AGAIN RETURN TO JERUSALEM—THEY CONDUCT ISHMAEL AND HIS FAMILY INTO THE WILDERNESS—LEHI'S DREAM—THE TREE OF LIFE—THE ROD OF IRON—THE BOTURINI MANUSCRIPT—NEPHI'S VISION.

(I. NEPHI CHAP. 5 TO 15.)

WHEN Nephi and his companions reached their father's tent in the wilderness their parents were exceedingly glad. Sariah had mourned during their absence because she fancied her sons would never return alive; and with those feelings she had upbraided her husband for sending them away. She charged him with being a visionary man, who was always giving heed to dreams in which she had little faith. All this was changed when her boys got back; then she was willing to acknowledge the inspiration of Heaven in her husband's visions.

The first thing Lehi did when his sons arrived was to offer a sacrifice to the Lord, as a token of his gratitude for their safe return. Next he examined the records, and rejoiced greatly to find that they contained the five books of Moses and a history of the Jews to the commencement of the reign of King Zedekiah. These plates also contained many of the prophecies of the holy prophets, and a genealogy of Lehi's fathers. We may be well assured how grateful Lehi felt to the Lord for placing these sacred records in his hands, so that his people could have the Law of the Lord and the history of their ancestors always in their possession. It is a great stay and a help to any people, who, like Lehi's family, are separated from the rest of mankind and who are building up a new civilization to possess the annals of their forefathers. It tends to keep them from sinking into idolatry, and from corrupting the laws of heaven; it preserves the purity of their language, and connects them with those from whom they have sprung.

But the four young men had to return once again to Jerusalem. God intended to make of Lehi's posterity a great nation. This could scarcely be done unless his sons married. But they had no young maidens with them in the wilderness who would do for wives. So the Lord told Lehi to send his sons to a man named Ishmael, of the tribe of Ephraim, who dwelt in Jerusalem, and desire him and his family to join them on their journey. The reason why God sent them to Ishmael was that he was a good man and had a number of daughters. When Lehi's sons delivered their message the Lord softened Ishmael's heart and he consented to go with them; and soon he and his family were on the way to the valley by the Red Sea where Lehi was encamped.

As they journeyed, however, they had the usual trouble. Laman and Lemuel had another rebellious fit. They induced some of the family of Ishmael to join them, and for a time there was great division in the little company. Nephi, inspired with the Spirit of the Lord, rebuked them for their folly. This so angered them that they bound him with cords, intending in their cruelty to leave him to perish in the wilderness, or to be devoured by wild beasts. But Nephi prayed in great faith to the Lord to give him strength to burst the bands which held him. The Lord answered his prayer and the cords were loosened from his hands and feet. Being now free he again reproved his brethren, which renewed their anger. Once more they sought to take his life, but Ishmael's wife and one of her sons and a daughter so earnestly plead for him that the hearts of the rebels were softened and they ceased their efforts to slay him. By and by, when their anger had cooled down, they felt very sorry for their great wickedness in trying to kill their brother. Then they humbled themselves before him and sought his forgiveness, which he, in the goodness of his heart, at once most gladly granted.

When the company reached the tents of Lehi, after the usual custom they offered burnt offerings and sacrifices to the Lord.

While Lehi dwelt in the Valley of Lemuel he had another remarkable dream. It was like unto this: He dreamed that a man stood before him and bade him follow him. This Lehi did. They traveled for many hours through a dark and dreary waste. When they had thus journeyed for so long a time Lehi began to pray to the Lord to have mercy on him. After he had prayed he beheld a large and spacious field. In it grew a tree whose fruit was very desirable to make one happy. Lehi partook of this fruit. He found it whiter and sweeter than any fruit he had ever before seen or tasted. When he had eaten his heart was filled with great joy, and he was very anxious that his family should partake of it also. So he looked around in the hope of seeing some of them, and in doing so his eyes fell upon a river. Its waters were filthy, and it ran along near the tree upon which the sweet fruit grew. Not far off was the fountain from whence the river sprang; and near by he saw his wife Sariah, and his sons, Sam and Nephi. They stood there hesitating, as if they knew not where to go. Lehi thereupon beckoned, and called them to come to him and taste of the fruit. Then they all three came and partook of it.

Lehi now felt desirous that his two elder sons, Laman and Lemuel, should also partake; but when he called them, they would not come.

Lehi also saw a rod of iron. It extended along the bank of the river and led to the tree by which he stood. And there was a straight and narrow path which ran along by the rod of iron to the tree. This path led into a broad field, so spacious that it might have been a world. He likewise saw vast numbers of people, many of whom were pressing forward to get to the path which led to the tree. Then it seemed that as soon as these people began to walk in the path there arose a great mist of darkness, that many missed their way, wandered off, and were lost. Others, by taking hold of the rod of iron, and clinging thereto, kept in the narrow path, reached the tree and partook of its precious fruit.

Some of those who tasted the fruit appeared to soon grow ashamed; and Lehi, casting his eyes across the river, beheld on the other side a very large and fine building, which stood as if it were in the air high above the earth.

This building was filled with men and women of all ages, whose style of dress was very rich and grand. These people were mocking and ridiculing those who ate of the fruit of the tree. Because of this taunting and derision some felt ashamed, and they fell away into forbidden paths and were lost. Lehi also saw other multitudes groping their way towards the spacious building; and some were drowned in the fountain of filthy water, and others were lost to sight wandering in strange roads.

The interpretation of Lehi's dream is this: The tree which bore the precious fruit, of which Lehi, Sariah, Sam and Nephi ate, was the tree of life. The rod of iron which led thereunto represented the word of God, and whoso will hearken unto the word of God, and will cleave unto it, will never perish, but partake of the fruit of the tree of life. The river of filthy water showed the awful gulf which separates the wicked from the tree of life and from the saints of God. The vast and costly building represented the wicked world, with those who belong thereto.

Lehi further saw that Laman and Lemuel ate not of the fruit of the tree, and it gave him much sorrow.

We present a copy of a portion of an ancient Aztec map or chart. The original map is about twenty feet in length, it was found in Mexico more than a hundred years ago by an Italian gentleman named Boturini.* On a previous page we have inserted a copy of the first part of this map or panorama, which seems to show the departure of Lehi from Jerusalem, his crossing some waters, his journey in the desert, and the names of his family. In the second part we consider is yet more clearly shown Lehi's dream. We can plainly see the tree of life, with its twelve branches, with Lehi near by, the rod of iron that led thereto, Sariah, Sam and Nephi partaking of the fruit; while Laman and Lemuel are not touching it. Then the journey is continued, and we see them all weeping over one man. This we think represents the death of Ish-

---

*Of Boturini, Humboldt observes. "This Milanese traveler had crossed the seas with no other view than to study on the spot the history of the native tribes of America; but in traversing the country to examine its monuments and make researches into its antiquities, he had the misfortune to fall under the suspicion of the Spanish government. After having been deprived of the fruit of his labors, he was sent in 1736 as a state prisoner to Madrid. The king of Spain declared him innocent, but this did not restore to him his property; and this collection * * * lay buried in the archives of the University of Mexico; those valuable relics of the culture of the Aztecs were preserved with so little care that there scarcely exists at present an eighth part of the hieroglyphic records taken from the Italian traveler."

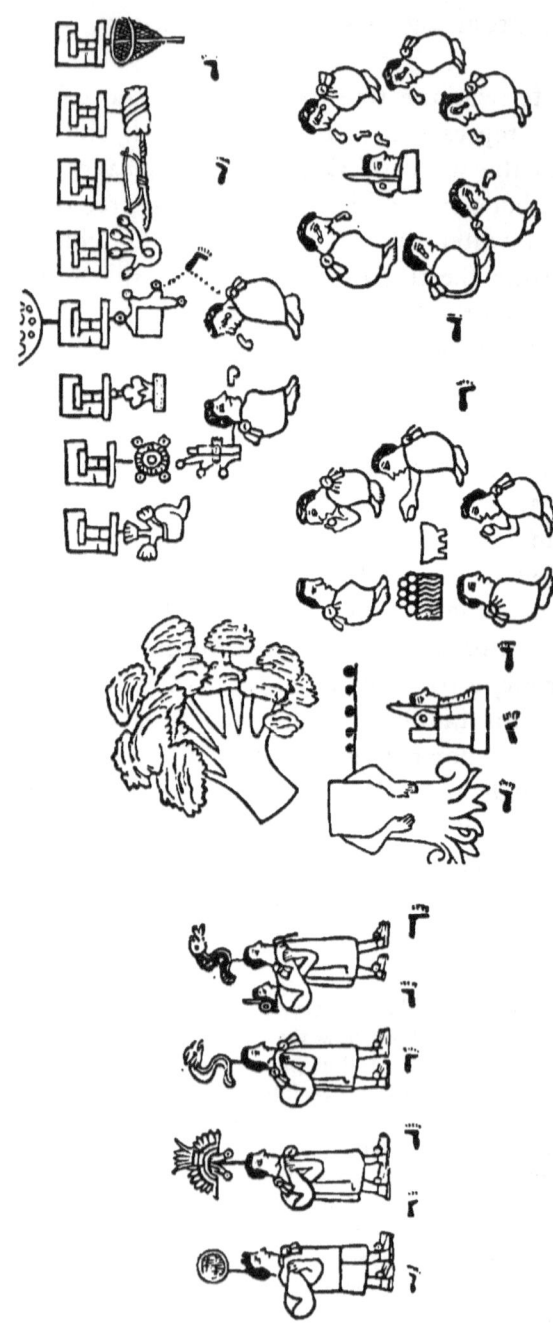

mael, of which we shall speak hereafter. Above again appear the names of the family.*

Nephi was very desirous to have the same dreams as his father; and he prayed earnestly to the Lord that this favor might be granted him. God answered his prayers, and showed him many of the greatest events that would take place in the future history of the world. For while Nephi was pondering these things in his heart he was caught away in the Spirit of the Lord, into an exceedingly high mountain,

---

*The priests of the Roman Catholic Church who visited Mexico at the time of and soon after the Spanish conquest were struck with the great resemblance of so large a number of the customs of the Mexican people to those of the ancient Israelites. To account for these resemblances they invented the theory that the devil had imitated the Lord when he delivered the Hebrews from their bondage in Egypt, by bringing the forefathers of the American races from their original home to this continent with many signs and wonders. Further, that Satan had revealed to these people a spurious or bastard gospel, as near to the true one as was possible, in order to lead their souls to eternal perdition. Based on this theory,—that the devil was the real god of the Indians, Torquemeda, in his "Indian Monarchy," and others, give the following as the translation of the opening portions of this chart:

"Although they were all of the same race and lineage, still they did not all compose a single family, but were divided into four tribes. * * The Azticas, therefore, quitted their country under the guidance of Zacpaltzin and Huitzon, in the first of the first circle; for they commenced the computation of their years from that period; and proceeded some stages on their journey, in which they employed the space of a year, at the end of which they arrived at a place called Hueycolhuacan where they remained three years. In this place (they say) the devil appeared to them in the form of an idol, declaring to them that it was he who brought them out of the land of Aztlan, and that he would accompany them, being their God, to favor them in everything. * * This being the beginning of the devil's proceedings among this people, they marched from one place to another, where there was a large and thick tree where he caused them to stop, at the trunk of which they made a small altar, upon which they placed an idol, for so the devil commanded, and they sat down under its shade to eat, but whilst eating. a loud sound proceeded from the tree, and it rent in the middle. The Azticas, terrified at this sudden accident, considered it a bad omen, and surrendering themselves up to affliction, terminated the repast."

VISION OF NEPHI.

on which he had never before set his foot. There the Spirit, which was in the form of a man, showed him the things which he desired. After the Spirit left him he was shown Jerusalem and other cities, especially Nazareth, and therein a virgin exceedingly white and fair. While gazing upon this scene, he beheld the heavens open, and an angel came down and stood before him, who explained to him the various scenes that were brought before his vision.

The virgin that Nephi saw was named Mary; she was the mother of Jesus. Next the angel showed him the virgin with the babe in her arms. The angel also showed him the Savior; how he should be baptized of John in the Jordan; how he went forth among the people preaching the gospel and doing marvelous works, and how that he was taken and crucified, and thus died for the sins of the world. Nephi further saw how the world fought against the disciples of Christ, and how, in the end, all those who contended against heaven and against God's servants were destroyed.

Furthermore he was shown the land of America filled with a numerous people, who were the seed of his father. He also saw the terrible earthquakes and devastating storms that took place on this land at the time of the crucifixion of the Redeemer.

He saw the Savior visit this land, and how he chose twelve disciples and here established his holy church. He saw the reign of profound peace that continued for three generations, and also the time of awful wickedness that followed this blessed era. And there were shown to him the final wars in which the Nephite nation was destroyed.

Nor was this all. Like a vast panorama, the kingdoms and nations of the Gentiles were presented to his view. He saw a man inspired by the Spirit of God cross the great waters which separated the Gentiles from the land on which the remnants of his father's seed dwelt, and that this man was followed by numerous hosts of others who came out from the nations and occupied the land. He saw the remnants of the seed of his father, the Indians, abused, robbed and massacred by the Gentiles. Then the war of the revolution was shown to him, the triumph of the colonies, and the growth of the people of this land in power, riches and pride.

And again he saw the rise of a great and abominable church which exercised power and dominion over many peoples. It was the great apostate Christian Church which held sway after the true gospel ceased to exist on the earth by reason of the wickedness of mankind. Nephi also saw the coming forth of the Book of Mormon, the establishment of the great Latter-day work, the preaching of the gospel to Gentile and Jew, and the final triumph of God's cause. Indeed he saw to the end of the world and thereafter; but much that he had revealed to him he was told not to write, as the Apostle John would have the same things shown to him in a later day, and John would be instructed of the Lord to write the things which he heard and saw.

CHAPTER III.

MARRIAGES IN THE COMPANY—THE LIAHONA—THE JOURNEY CONTINUED—NEPHI BREAKS HIS BOW—DEATH OF ISHMAEL—THEY REACH THE OCEAN—NEPHI BUILDS A SHIP—THEY CROSS THE GREAT WATERS AND REACH THE PROMISED LAND.

(I. NEPHI CHAP. 16 TO 18.)

WHILE the two families dwelt in the Valley of Lemuel they had a number of marriages. Zoram, Laban's servant, married Ishmael's eldest daughter, and each of Lehi's four sons married one of her sisters. We are not told whether Lehi's daughters were married at this time or not.

Soon after these marriages the voice of the Lord spake unto Lehi by night and commanded him that on the morrow he should resume his journey. When Lehi arose the next morning and went to the door of his tent he saw a strange object lying on the ground before him. It was a brass ball of very fine workmanship. Within this ball were two spindles or needles, one of which pointed the way that the little company should travel in the wilderness.

God had prepared this strange instrument or guide for them. In the days of Moses, when he led the children of Israel out of Egypt, a pillar of cloud by day and of fire by night moved in front of them. This the Hebrews followed. But to Lehi he gave this Liahona, or compass, as the ball was called; and it pointed the way they should travel. It had one strange peculiarity, which was that it worked according to their faith and diligence. When they kept God's law it showed them much more clearly the way they should go than when they were careless or rebellious.

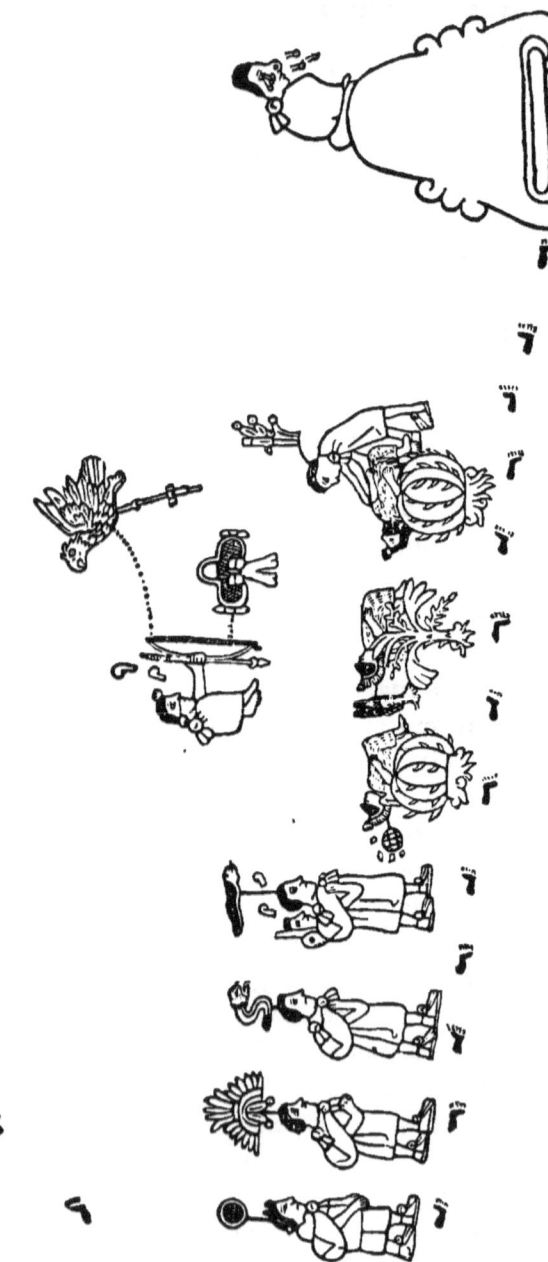

ANCIENT AZTEC CHART, SHOWING LEHI'S TRAVELS. NO. 3.

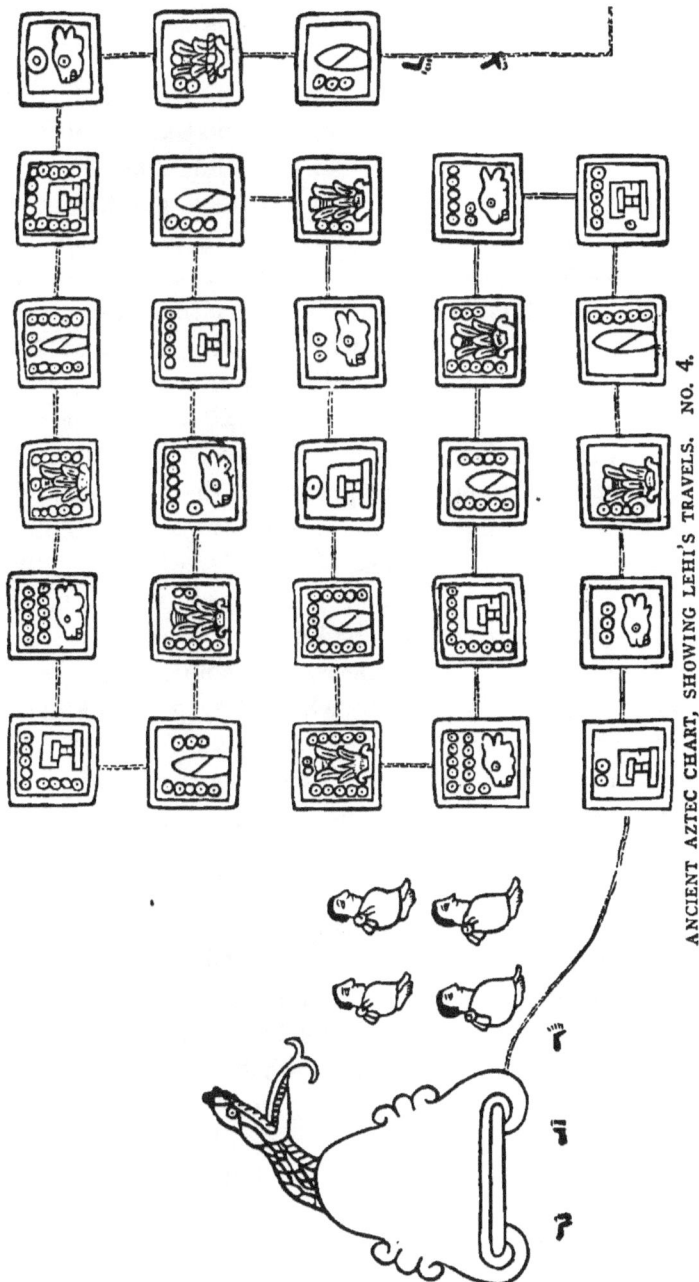

ANCIENT AZTEC CHART, SHOWING LEHI'S TRAVELS. NO. 4.

Some people have confused this ball, because it is called a compass, with the mariner's compass, that sailors use at sea to direct the course of their ships. But there is a great difference between the two. The Liahona pointed the way that Lehi's company should travel, while the needle in the mariner's compass points to the north. The one showed the way Lehi *should* go, the other informs the traveler which way he *is* going. The one was specially prepared by the Lord for Lehi and his companions, and was used through faith only; the other can be used by all men, whether believers in the true God, pagans or infidels. At times, also, writing would miraculously appear on the Liahona, giving directions or reproving for sin, as the company most needed.

According to the command of the Lord the company gathered their provisions, their tents, their seeds and other things and again started on their long and ofttimes wearisome journey. They traveled a little east of south, and after four days again rested at a place to which they gave the name of Shazer. Here they hunted and killed game for food. When they had obtained enough for present use they again started, traveling in very much the same direction, and keeping near the eastern shore of the Red Sea.

About this time a slight accident occurred which gave cause for much trouble and discontent. It would appear that Nephi was the chief hunter of the company. Going out one day to slay beasts for food he broke his bow, which was made of very fine steel. This made his brothers very angry, for they obtained no food, as their bows had lost their springs. Hungry, angry and dejected, they returned to their tents. They were very much fatigued, and, like most men when hungry and tired, they were in bad humor. Even Lehi so far forgot himself, at this time, that he also murmured against the Lord. But Nephi, in this trying hour, retained his trust in God. He did not murmur nor complain, but, after having reasoned with the rest of the family, he went to work, and out of suitable wood he made a bow, and out of a straight stick he cut an arrow. When he had done this he went to his father, who had now humbled himself before the Lord and sought forgiveness, and asked him where he should go to obtain food.

Then the voice of the Lord came to Lehi and he was truly chastened because of his murmuring. The voice said, Look upon the ball. When he looked he was seized with fear because of the things which were written thereon, and the rest of the family also feared and trembled exceedingly when they read the writing.

The writing on the ball also directed Nephi to go to the top of a certain high mountain, and there slay game for food. This he did, and brought it with joy to the tents of his people.

We think it probable that the design near the top of the accompanying Aztec map is intended to represent this incident; as the bird has evidently been shot by an arrow from the hunter's bow. The lower portion seems to show some of the many attempts made by Nephi's brethren to slay him, when they bound him to trees in the wilderness and otherwise abused him. Picture four is evidently a record of the months or years occupied in the journey.

The journey was thus continued for a long time. The company would travel for a few days, then rest and hunt, then again take up the line of march as the compass directed. It generally guided them through the most fertile portions of the desert. Their journeys appear to have been frequently disturbed by the bad conduct of Laman and Lemuel and of those who would heed them. Before long, Ishmael, who was an aged man, died, at a place which they named Nahom. This was a cause of great grief to his children, and a fresh excuse for Laman and his following to murmur. They complained that they had been led into that strange land to die of want and fatigue, and desired to go back to Jerusalem. So hard hearted had Laman by this time become that, with others, he formed a plot to murder his own father and his brother Nephi. But the voice of the Lord came to them, chastened them severely for their sins, and reproved them with such power that their hearts were softened and they repented. After this the Lord again blessed them.

From this time the compass changed the course of their travel and they journeyed almost directly eastward. This must have taken them across the peninsula of Arabia to its eastern coast.

It took them eight years to make the journey, during which time a number of children were born, including two sons to Lehi's wife. These he called Jacob and Joseph. As they went the Lord strengthened them, that they endured their privations and labors without fatigue. He would not permit them to make much fire to prepare their food, but rendered it sweet to them without cooking.

They had great joy when they came to the sea. They gave to it the name of Irreantum, which word means many waters. The land on the coast they called Bountiful, because of its much fruit and wild honey. While they rested on the sea shore the Lord gave Nephi a new command. It was that he should build a ship to carry the company across the ocean. As we may suppose, Nephi's brothers made all kinds of fun of him when they found he was about to try to build a ship. But this did not affect him. He knew that God never told a man to do a thing that he did not give him power to do. It was so in this case. The Lord revealed to Nephi all that was necessary, and the building of the ship began.

At first Nephi's brothers would not help him in the least. They treated him as the people did Noah when he was building the ark. They called him a fool, and mocked him, and then threatened to throw him into the sea. But the power of God was so strong upon Nephi that had his brothers attempted to carry out their threat they would have withered before him like a dried reed. As it was, when he stretched forth his hand towards them they felt a shock, which made their whole frames quiver. This convinced them that God was with their brother, for no man could have such power unless God was with him. After this they went to work and helped Nephi build the ship; and a good ship it was, the Lord having directed the way in which it should be fashioned.

When the vessel was finished the Lord told Lehi and his people to go on board. They took with them fruit, meat, honey, and other food in abundance, with many other things needful for their comfort; also seeds to plant in the soil of the promised land. Then they all embarked—men, women and children—beginning at the eldest, down to the least. A favorable wind sprang up and they were swiftly carried towards the promised land. First they crossed the Indian Ocean, then the South Pacific Ocean, and after many days reached the west coast of South America. They landed at a point near where the city of Valparaiso, in Chili, now stands.

But we must not forget to tell you that on the voyage they had another of those ever-recurring outbreaks. Laman, some of the sons of Ishmael and others, at one time, grew very merry. By and by they became boisterous and rude. They danced and sang and talked improperly. Nephi reproved them. This opened the old sore. They said they would not have him for their ruler, but would do as they pleased. Then they seized and bound him, hands and feet, so tightly that he suffered a great deal. The result was that the Lord was angry and the compass ceased to work. A heavy storm arose, a head wind drove them back upon the waters, the waves threatened to engulf them, and they were all in danger of being drowned. For three days the rebels continued stubborn in their anger; during that time they would not loose Nephi, and every one who plead for him or spoke in his favor was threatened with like tortures. At last, however, the danger grew so threatening that they released him;

but his legs and arms had swollen so greatly by reason of the way in which he had been tied that he could scarcely use them. Notwithstanding his great weakness and suffering, as soon as he was loosed he took the compass, and in his hands it began to work. Then the wind fell, the storm ceased, and there came a great calm. And Nephi took charge of the ship and guided it without further trouble, to the promised land.*

---

*On the opposite page we present a reduced copy of a hieroglyphic drawing in the British Museum, representing the journey of the forefathers of the Mexicans from Asia to this continent. The original was first given to the world by the famous Italian traveler Gumelli Farerri in his book entitled "Giro del Mondo." Clavigero, Humboldt and others have endeavored to explain the meaning of this drawing. You will notice a palm tree near a hieroglyphic which much resembles that supposed to represent Jerusalem in the commencement of the Boturini manuscript. This is said to signify the house of God; here the journey began. Near by is a bird, which stands for Asia. The tradition runs thus: Huitziton was a person of great authority amongst the Aztecs, in Asia, who for some reason not remembered, persuaded his countrymen to change their country. While he was thus meditating, a bird was heard singing in a bush ti hui, ti hui, which means "let us go." "Do you hear that?" said Zacpaltzin, "it is the warning voice of the secret Deity to leave this continent and to find another." Therefore they started, with those they could persuade to go with them, traveling by Tlapalan, translated, the country of the Red Sea, and after long journeys reached the land where the hieroglyphics leaves them.

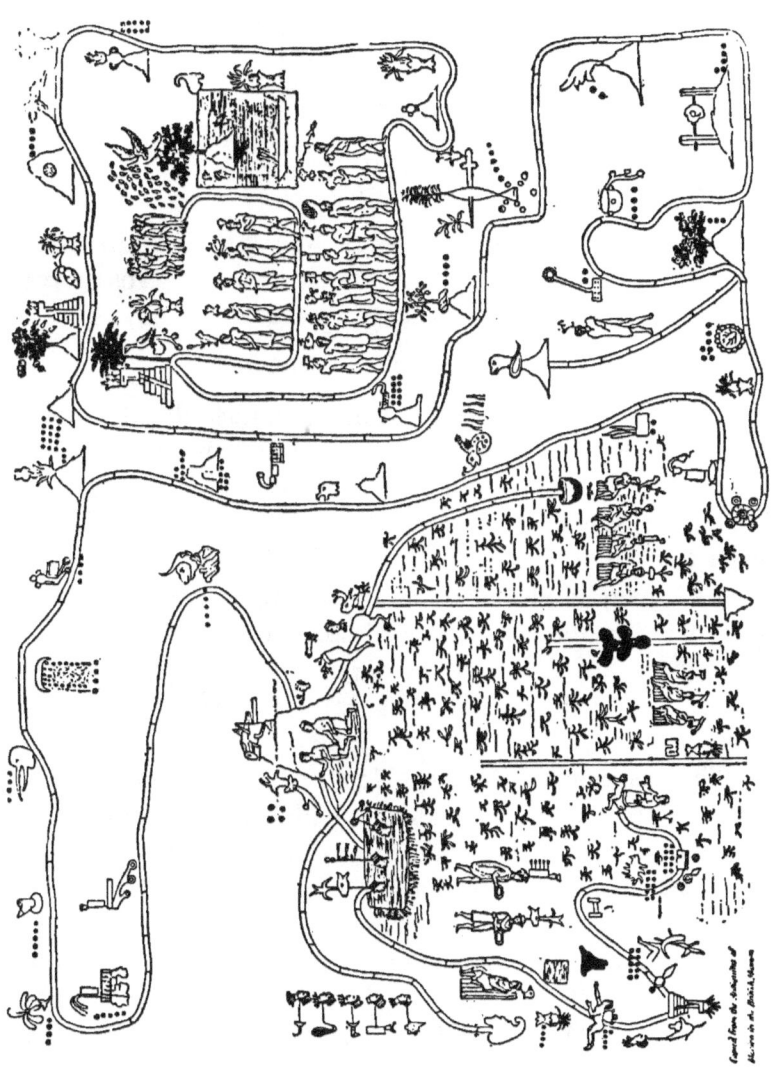

CHAPTER IV.

THE PROMISED LAND—CHILI—ITS NATURAL PRODUCTIONS—THE DEATH OF LEHI—HIS BLESSING ON HIS POSTERITY—PROPHECIES OF HIS ANCESTOR JOSEPH.

(I. NEPHI CHAP. 18 TO II. NEPHI CHAP. 4.)

WHEN the little colony, which numbered, we imagine, from sixty to eighty souls, landed on the promised land they pitched their tents and soon after began to till the ground. From their sowing they reaped abundant crops. They explored the wilderness around them, and found beasts of the forest of many kinds; also the ox, the horse, the goat and the wild goat. In the rocks they discovered ores of gold, silver and copper. Of the gold ore Nephi was commanded of the Lord to make plates on which to keep the records of his people.

The description given by Nephi of the region where the colony landed exactly corresponds with what we know of the country now called Chili; and it was on its coast, the Prophet Joseph Smith informs us, that the Nephites landed, and there they established their first homes. Chili is favored with one of the finest and healthiest climates in the world. The soil is exceedingly fertile, and the productions of both hemispheres seem to thrive equally well there. The most delicious fruit grows in abundance—the apple, peach, grape, strawberry, etc. Its forests are magnificent, and furnish many kinds of beautiful wood. The grass in its rich meadow pastures, is often so tall and luxuriant as to hide the cattle grazing amongst it. Chili also possesses valuable mines, especially of gold, silver, copper and coal

The people of Lehi were so few in number that they were a quiet and solemn race, with few amusements, but with

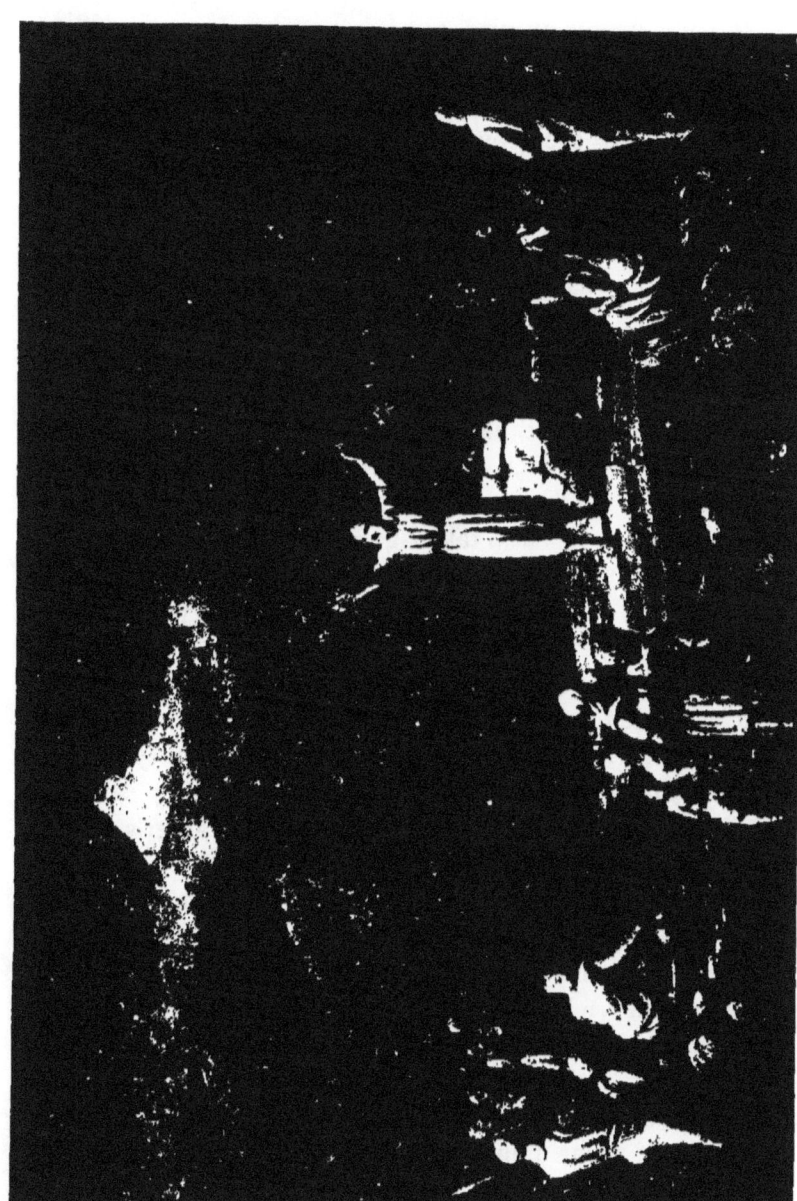

THE FIRST SACRIFICE ON THE PROMISED LAND.

an oppressing sense of the vastness of the land which they occupied, and of their own insignificance. Nor was there entire peace amongst them, for Laman and Lemuel, with others, were still fractious and turbulent.

In course of time Lehi felt that his earthly life was near its close, for he was aged and in failing health. So he called to him his sons and daughters and the other members of his colony, and blessed them in the same manner as his forefather Jacob blessed his family before he died. Lehi also prophesied many things that should happen to his posterity after him, for he was possessed of much of the Spirit of the Lord. After he had done this he died and was buried.

Lehi appears to have taken great pleasure in the knowledge that he was a descendant of that Joseph who was sold by his brethren, and afterwards carried into Egypt. In the blessing that he pronounced upon his own son Joseph, Lehi quotes largely from the prophecies of the former Joseph; prophecies which are nowhere given us, except in the Book of Mormon. From them we learn that this mighty son of Jacob was greatly favored of the Lord in having revealed to him much that related to the future of his father's house, especially to his own posterity. He saw the days of Moses and the work that that prophet performed; he saw Lehi's day and his work, and, more interesting to us than all, he saw the establishment of the kingdom of God in our day. He was told that the prophet whom the Lord would raise up to be the leader of God's people in the latter days would be of his seed, and the name of this prophet, and that of his father also, would be the same as his—that is, it would be Joseph. Many other events of great moment that are even now taking place, were also made manifest to him by the Lord.

CHAPTER V.

THE NEPHITES AND LAMANITES SEPARATE—THE NEPHITES SEEK A NEW HOME—NEPHI CHOSEN KING—HE BUILDS A TEMPLE—INSTRUCTS HIS PEOPLE IN THE ARTS OF PEACE—WAR WITH THE LAMANITES—THE SWORD OF LABAN—NEPHI'S DEATH—JACOB, HIS BROTHER, BECOMES THE CHIEF PRIEST—JACOB'S TEACHINGS ON MARRIAGE.

(II. NEPHI CHAP. 5 TO JACOB, CHAP. 4.)

SCARCELY was Lehi buried than fresh trouble arose. Laman and Lemuel, with their friends, would not be led by Nephi. They asserted that they were the elder brothers and theirs was the right to rule. They would not recognize Nephi's authority, though they knew that God had appointed him to be their leader. So, by the command of Heaven, the two parties separated. Nephi, and those who would listen to him, moved away, and left those who clung to Laman in possession of their first home.

Those who went with Nephi were his own family, Zoram, Sam, Jacob and Joseph, and their families, and some others whose names the Book of Mormon does not give. Henceforth those who belonged to this branch of Lehi's house were known as Nephites, after Nephi, their leader; while those who remained with Laman were called Lamanites.

The condition of the Lamanites was now pitiable; they had cut themselves off from the presence of the Lord, the Priesthood was withdrawn from them, the records and scriptures were beyond their grasp. Hatred and malice reigned supreme in their souls; they had no inclination for the arts of peace; they were restless, cunning and idle, whilst they sought in the wilderness the food necessary to sustain life. Already the curse of God was falling upon them. Lest they should appear pleasant to Nephite eyes, their fair and beautiful skins grew dark and repulsive, their habits became loathsome and filthy, and the same skin of darkness came upon the children of all those who intermarried with them.

The Nephites called the new country in which they made their homes the land of Nephi. There, Nephi by the wish of the people, became their king, though this step was contrary to his own feelings. So greatly was he beloved by his subjects that when he died the people called the next king, Nephi the second, the next, Nephi the third, and so on. All the kings were thus called Nephi, in the same way as all the monarchs of ancient Egypt were Pharaohs, and the emperors of modern Russia are Tzars.

One of the first things that Nephi and his people did in their new home was to build a temple. This showed great faith and courage on the part of so small a community. And their faith and courage triumphed, for the temple was finished. It was built after the manner of Solomon's Temple in Jerusalem, but it was not so large, so costly, or so grand. Yet it was a magnificent edifice to be erected by a people so few in number. Here the Nephites offered burnt offerings according to the law of Moses, which they strictly observed; and Nephi consecrated Jacob and Joseph to be priests, to officiate therein.

Nephi not only built a temple, but he taught his people to be industrious and thrifty, honest and virtuous. He caused them to build dwellings and other edifices, and to work in wood, iron, copper, brass, steel, silver and gold; for there was a great abundance of precious ores in the land in which they now dwelt.

Nephi still retained possession of the sword of Laban; and, taking it as a pattern, he made many swords for his people to use in their own defense should they be attacked by the Lamanites. This precaution proved a very wise one, for in less than forty years from the time that Lehi left Jerusalem the Lamanites had followed up the Nephites and commenced war upon them. But the Lamanites were not successful, for Nephi, wielding the sword of Laban with his own hands, led his people to battle and drove back the invaders.

When fifty-five years had passed away Nephi handed the small plates which he had made to his brother Jacob, that he might keep the sacred records thereon. Sometime after, how long we are not told, Nephi anointed another man to be king over his people; and then, having grown old, he died.

Great was the love of the people for Nephi. He had been their prophet, priest and king; father, friend and guide; protector, teacher and leader; next to God, their all in all. He labored diligently all the days of his life to teach the people to serve God, to believe in Christ, to keep the laws of heaven, and to be and to do all that God's holy law required. In all these labors his brother Jacob nobly aided him.

When Nephi died Jacob became the chief religious teacher of the people. He was a man of much faith and diligence, and received the word of the Lord from time to time in great fullness, as the church needed.

We know but little of what occurred among the Nephites in Jacob's time. The people, however, appear in some respects to have fallen into sin. They had grown in worldly pride, and devoted far too much of their time and energies to the search for wealth. By reason of their isolated position, and because the Jews, their forefathers, had abused the principle of plural marriage, the people of Lehi had been commanded that each man should have but one wife. Some of them did not heed this special law, but took other wives, not only without God's sanction, but entirely contrary to his express command. Indeed they committed other grievous sins, excusing themselves therefor by quoting the actions of King David, and Solomon, his son. At this the Lord was greatly displeased, and he instructed Jacob to reprove them sharply. This he did in the temple. He re-affirmed the law that the Nephites of that age should have only one wife; but added, in the name of the Lord of Hosts, that if he (God) wanted to raise up a holy seed to himself, he would command his people. This we have reason to believe, from reading the Book of Mormon, he afterwards did, though we find therein no direct statement on the matter.

CHAPTER VI.

THE CONDITION OF THE LAMANITES—SHEREM, THE FIRST ANTI-CHRIST—HIS RECANTATION AND DREADFUL END.

(JACOB, CHAP. 3 TO 7.)

WHILST the early Nephites were polygamists, and, unfortunately for them, unrighteous ones, the Lamanites were monogamists, which form of marriage they appear to have ever after retained.

One phase of Lamanite character, originating, doubtless, in their Israelitish ancestry, is worthy of our praise. It was the great strength of their domestic affections, their love for their wives and their kindness to their families. As we shall have to refer so often to their vices, we must, in justice to them, here insert the description of their virtues given by Jacob, the son of Lehi. He says, "Behold, their husbands love their wives, and their wives love their husbands; and their husbands and wives love their children; and their unbelief and their hatred towards you, is because of the iniquity of their fathers." Nor is there anything in this incompatible with the ferocity of their character or their bloodthirstiness in war. In the earlier ages of the Lamanite nationality, rigid chastity was observed by the men as well as by the women. Indeed, it may be said that while they manifested most of the prominent vices of semi-barbarous people, they also possessed the virtues that such races, uncorrupted by a more luxurious mode of life, generally show. Nor would it be consistent, nor historically true, to give one general description and apply it to the whole Lamanite race, for as their numbers increased the state of society amongst them grew more complex, and we read of different grades of civilization in their midst.

It must not be forgotten that the Lamanites occupied a much wider extent of country than did the Nephites. In this vast area were found people who dwelt in cities and cultivated the arts to the extent generally found amongst races of the same grade and characteristics. Whilst others, degraded in life and habits, roamed in the wilderness, building no houses, forming no permanent abiding places, but wandering from place to place, and depending for food and clothing upon the animals they caught in the chase, the fishes that abounded in the waters, and whatever they could steal from the hated Nephites, or indeed of their somewhat more highly civilized fellow-countrymen.

It was in the days of Jacob that the first Nephite Anti-Christ appeared. His name was Sherem. He openly and unblushingly taught that there would be no Christ and that there was no necessity for an atonement. He was a type of many who came after, and a well fitted instrument for his evil work. Bland in manners, fluent of speech, much given to flattery, and withal, well versed in the learning of the Nephites, he, by his sophistries, led many astray. His success fired his zeal and filled him with conceit. He actually sought to convert to his views Jacob, the prophet and presiding priest of the church, a man rich in wisdom, and the recipient of many divine revelations; one indeed who had ofttimes seen angels and heard the voice of the Lord.

In the interview that occurred between these two widely differing men, Sherem charged that Jacob had changed the law of Moses, which was the right way, into the worship of a being whom Jacob said should come many hundred years hence. He added, "Now behold, I, Sherem, declare unto you, that this is blasphemy; for no man knoweth of these things; for he cannot tell of things to come." Thus he denied prophecy, styled good evil, and exalted error in the place of truth.

Jacob, being filled with the Spirit of God, confounded his arguments, brought forward the testimony of the scriptures, and proved that the very law of Moses, on which he lay so much stress, was from beginning to end but the type and foreshadowing of the more perfect law of the Christ who should come.

Beaten in his arguments, Sherem fell back upon that almost universal refuge of the false teacher. He defiantly called for a sign. A sign was given him. The power of God came upon him and he fell stricken to the ground. For many days he was nourished, but ineffectually. He himself perceived that death was approaching, and with this perception gathered in his soul all the fears and horrors of an apostate's doom. But before his death he called the people to him and confessed his iniquity. He denied the things he had taught, he "confessed the Christ and the power of the Holy Ghost, and the ministering of angels." He avowed that he had been deceived by the power of the devil, and bitterly bewailed his condition; as the fear that he had committed the unpardonable sin, in denying the Savior, weighed his soul down to hell. Having made these small amends for his past iniquities, he could say no more, and gave up the ghost.

When the people who had gathered to hear his last words, witnessed the terrors of his death, they were softened in their hearts, the power of God rested upon them, and they fell to the earth. The corrupt weeds he had sown in their hearts had withered, the truth had been vindicated, the cause of the Savior extolled, and peace and the love of God were restored again among the people. Thus was this apostasy eradicated, and God glorified; the Nephites of that generation from that time searching the scriptures and cleaving unto the truth.

When Jacob grew old he gave the sacred records to the keeping of his son Enos.

CHAPTER VII.

ENOS, THE SON OF JACOB—THE NEPHITES AND LAMANITES OF HIS DAY—HIS TESTIMONY AND PROPHECIES.

(BOOK OF ENOS.)

IN THE days of Enos the struggle still continued between the Nephites and Lamanites. The latter seem to have made it the business of their lives to harass and annoy their more peaceful brethren. Their hatred was fixed. They swore in their wrath that if it were possible they would destroy the Nephites, and also their records, that they might no longer be compelled to listen to their warnings, or be annoyed by their appeals for peace and friendship.

The picture that Enos draws of the degradation into which the Lamanites had fallen at this early day is a very pitiable one. He says they were led by their evil nature that they became wild and ferocious, and a blood-thirsty people, full of idolatry and filthiness, feeding upon beasts of prey, dwelling in tents, and wandering about in the wilderness with a short skin girdle about their loins, and their heads shaven; and their skill was in the bow, and in the cimeter, and the axe. And many of them did eat nothing save it was raw meat. This last named practice they seem to have inherited from their fathers in the wilderness.

On the other hand, the Nephites at this time were a rural, pastoral people, rich in grain and fruits, flocks, and herds. They were industrious in their habits, and committed but few serious offenses. They observed the law of Moses, but were lacking in faith, hard to understand gospel principles, wayward and stiff-necked. The terrors of the word had to be sounded in their unwilling ears more often than the gentler strains of gospel invitation.

Enos was one of the most zealous servants of the Lord who ministered and prophesied to the early Nephites. As the son of Jacob, he succeeded his father in the sacred offices of priest and historian. He appears to have inherited his father's faith, gentleness and devotion. Of his personal life we have no particulars, but it is evident that he was a very aged man at the time of his death. His father Jacob was the elder of the two sons born to Lehi in the Arabian wilderness, between the years 600 and 590 before Christ; let us place the event about 594 B. C. Enos, in closing his record, states that one hundred and seventy-nine years had passed since Lehi left Jerusalem. Supposing Enos was born when Jacob was thirty years old, it would make his age one hundred and forty-three years at the date of his writing. But we have no direct statement either of his birth or the exact time of his death; all we know is that when he left this earth he gave the records and the other sacred things into the hands of his son Jarom.

One incident in the life of Enos is given us which is very interesting. It affords a deep insight into the purity and strength of his character. On one occasion when he went into the forest to hunt, his whole soul was filled with thoughts of the prophecies and teachings of his devout father, and he greatly hungered for more light regarding eternal things. In this fitting frame of mind, surrounded by the solitudes of the forest, he bowed before the Lord, and in prayers long and fervent, sought his face. All day long he raised his voice to heaven, and when the night came he did not cease. At last his steadfast faith and godly yearnings prevailed. There came a heavenly voice of comfort to his heart, saying:

Enos, thy sins are forgiven thee, thou shalt be blessed.

Lord, how is it done? he anxiously asked.

The answer came: Because of thy faith in Christ, whom thou hast never before heard nor seen. And many years pass away before he shall manifest himself in the flesh; wherefore, go to, thy faith hath made thee whole.

Enos continued struggling with the Lord for promises in behalf of both the Nephites and Lamanites. He received many precious assurances of things yet to be; amongst others, that the Lord would preserve the holy records and bring them forth unto the Lamanites in his own due time. Of these things Enos gladly testified to the people, prophesying of the mighty events yet in the future, and bearing record of that which he had both seen and heard.

CHAPTER VIII.

JAROM—OMNI—AMARON—CHEMISH—ABINADOM—AMALEKI —MOSIAH—REVIEW OF NEPHITE HISTORY FOR FOUR HUNDRED YEARS.

(BOOKS OF JAROM AND OMNI.)

THE days of the prophet Jarom were neither few nor unimportant. During the sixty years that he had charge of the holy things (B. C. 422 to B. C. 362) the Nephites may be said to have grown from a powerful tribe to a wealthy, though not as yet very numerous, nation. Indeed, their numbers were far from being equal to those of the wild and blood-thirsty Lamanites. The latter, like their descendants of today, spent their time almost exclusively in the chase of wild animals and in war; yet, notwithstanding their vigorous and repeated onslaughts, the age of Jarom was to the Nephites one of marked progress in the arts of peace.

They ceased to be entirely a pastoral people. They gave much attention to the adornment of their homes and public buildings with fine and curious work in wood and metal. Agriculture and manufacture received a new impetus by the invention of various labor-saving machines, implements and tools. Their safety from successful attack from the Lamanites was also measurably secured by the introduction of more perfect weapons of war, and the development of a rude system of fortification, sufficient, however, to protect their cities and settlements from the means of attack at the command of their foes.

Though the Nephites of this age were stiff-necked and perverse, requiring the constant warnings of prophets to keep them from backsliding, yet the pervading tone of their society was simple and unaffected, and the people were generally industrious, honest and moral. They neither blasphemed nor profaned the holy name of the Deity, they kept sacred the Sabbath day, and strictly observed the law of Moses. Their prophets, priests and teachers not only instructed them in this law, but also expounded the intent for which it was given, and while so doing, directed their minds to the coming of the Messiah, in whom they taught the people to believe as though he had already come. These pointed and constant teachings preserved the Nephites from destruction, by softening their hearts and bringing them to repentance, when war, wealth or pride had exerted its baneful influences.

Shortly before Jarom died he delivered the sacred plates to his son Omni. Omni kept them for about forty-four years and then handed them to his son Amaron; who in turn transferred them to his brother Chemish. Chemish, when his end drew near, placed them in the hands of his son Abinadom, who afterwards gave them in charge of his son Amaleki.

It is very little that we know of the history of the Nephites from the death of Jarom to the time of Amaleki, a period of about one hundred and fifty years. The political records of the nation were engraved on other plates, which were kept by the kings, and as there was little that the ecclesiastical historians felt it necessary to write beyond what Nephi and Jacob had written, their records are very short. From what little we can glean from these writings it is evident that during this era the Nephites had frequent wars with the Lamanites, in many of which they suffered severely. The Lord permitted these wild sons of the wilderness to be a constant scourge to the people of Nephi when they turned away from him; and we fear that the seasons were not unfrequent when they had to be reminded of their duty in this terrible way. It also seems probable that, to avoid the constant incursions of the warriors of the house of Laman, the Nephites had more than once forsaken their homes and retired farther northward into the wilderness. We judge this from the fact that in the days of Amaleki, the land of Nephi appears to have been in or near the region we call Ecuador, a country far distant from the place where Lehi's colony first landed; and it is scarcely consistent with the narrative of the Book of Mormon to believe that Nephi and his little band, when they first separated from their brethren, made a journey of so many hundreds of miles before they established their homes. Then the very fact that the Lamanites almost immediately began to harass them in the new land which they occupied is strong evidence that their first removal was not so distant but that these enemies could, without great difficulty, reach them, a thing that would have been almost impossible if they had gone directly to the far distant region of Ecuador.

We now come to the days of the first Mosiah. But before relating the story of his life and reign we will briefly summarize what we know of the history of the Nephites during the first four hundred years of their national existence.

They were governed by kings who were the direct descendants of Nephi. These kings were, as a rule, righteous men and wise rulers. The law of Moses was strictly observed, and other good and just laws were enacted to regulate those matters which the Mosaic laws did not touch.

The Nephites multiplied greatly, and also grew exceedingly rich in the wealth of this world; while their artisans and mechanics were very expert in the arts and manufactures. They also spread abroad on the face of the land of Nephi and were much scattered.

The Lamanites followed them from the land of their first possession, and were constantly harassing them by incursions and invasions, which led to numerous and bloody wars. These were sometimes very disastrous to the Nephites.

Spiritually, the Nephites had many seasons of faithfulness to God when they listened to and obeyed the words of his prophets; and, unfortunately, they had also many seasons of apostasy, at which times the judgments of God fell upon them; the Lamanites being often used by him as a sharp instrument to bring them to repentance and reformation.

CHAPTER IX.

CAUSES THAT LED TO THE MIGRATION FROM THE LAND OF NEPHI—THE PEOPLE OF ZARAHEMLA—MULEK AND HIS COLONY—THE FUSION OF THE TWO NATIONS—MOSIAH MADE KING—HIS HAPPY REIGN.

(BOOK OF OMNI.)

MOSIAH resided in the land of Nephi, and lived there as near as we can discover during the latter half of the third century before Christ. Whether he was originally a prophet, priest, or king, the historian (Amaleki) does not inform us. Most certainly he was a righteous man, for the Lord made choice of him to guide the obedient Nephites from their native country to a land that he would show them.

The causes that led the Lord to make this call upon the Nephites are not stated, but some of them can be easily surmised. Amongst such we suggest that:

The aggressive Lamanites were constantly crowding upon them, ravaging their more remote districts, entrapping and enslaving the inhabitants of the out-lying settlements, driving off their flocks and herds, and keeping them in a constant state of anxiety and dread, which hindered their progress and stayed the growth of the work of God. The Lord therefore led them to a land of peace.

Again, this course of events, continued for so long a period, had caused much hard-heartedness and stiff-neckedness in the midst of the Nephites. Some of the people had remained righteous, some had grown very wicked. To separate these classes the Lord called the faithful and obedient to follow Mosiah to another land.

For a third reason: there was a portion of the house of

Israel, a few hundred miles to the north, entirely unknown to their Nephite brethren. These people had sunk very low in true civilization; they were so degraded that they denied the being of their Creator, they had had many wars and contentions among themselves; they had corrupted their language, had no records nor scriptures, and were altogether in a deplorable condition. To save and regenerate this branch of God's covenant people, Mosiah and his people were led to the place where they dwelt.

Few are the words and brief is the statement made by Amaleki regarding this great migration under Mosiah. We are altogether left to our imagination to picture the scenes that occurred at this division of a nation.

Imagine the conflict that perplexed many a heart between the appeals of love and faith, between duty and affection, when the old homes had to be deserted, when families had to be parted, and the one stern, uncompromising feeling of duty to the right and devotion to God had to be the all-controlling sentiment. Nor can we tell how many, preferring home, kindred and friends, and the endearments and associations of their native land, faltered and tarried behind, whilst the faithful started on their journey northward into the untrodden wilderness. Nor are we told what afterwards became of those who allowed the allurements of the world to prevail. It is most probable that they united with the Lamanites, were absorbed into that race, and, like them, became darkened, blood-thirsty and savage. Neither do we know the proportion to the whole population of those who left with Mosiah and those who stayed behind.

The Nephite evacuation of the cities built in the land of Nephi no doubt had a beneficial effect on those portions of the Lamanite race that took possession of them. They thereby became acquainted with some of the comforts and excellencies of civilization, and, though very slow to learn, their experience at this time laid the foundation for a slight advance of the arts of peace in their midst, and from this time we read of two classes of this people, the one living in cities, the other roaming in the wilderness.

Mosiah gathered up the willing and obedient and, as directed by the Lord, started on the journey.

Whither they were going they understood not, only they knew that the Lord was leading them. Like their forefathers under Moses, when in the wilderness of Sinai, they were taught continually by the word of Jehovah and were led by his arm. With preachings and prophesyings they crossed the wilderness and passed down into the land of Zarahemla.

On the west bank of the river Sidon the people of Mosiah found a populous city of whose existence they had never before heard. Its people were a semi-civilized and irreligious race, speaking a strange language, and with many habits and customs different from those of the new comers.

The meeting must have been a perplexing one to both people. Heretofore both had considered themselves the owners of the whole continent. Now they were brought face to face, but unable to understand each other by reason of their different modes of speech. We often read in history of the irruption of an inferior or more barbarous race into the domains of one more highly civilized, but it is seldom, as in this case, that the superior race moves in a body, occupies the country, and unites with the less enlightened people. It is probable that the first feelings of the old settlers were akin to awe and dismay as they learned of the hosts of the invaders that were marching upon them; but these feelings were soon soothed and an understanding arrived at by which the two people became one nation. Though the Book of Mormon gives us no details on this point, we are forced to the conclusion that this arrangement could not have been effected without the direct interposition of heaven, by and through which both people were brought to a united purpose and common understanding.

When the Nephites began to comprehend the language of their new fellow citizens, they found that they were the descendants of a colony which had been led from Jerusalem by the hand of the Lord in the year that that city was destroyed by the king of Babylon (say B. C. 589). In that little colony was a child named Mulek: he was the only son of king Zedekiah who had escaped the fury of the Babylonish monarch. After wandering in the wilderness, they were brought across the great waters and landed in the southern portion of

THE JEWS LED AWAY TO CAPTIVITY.

the North American continent, and in after years moved southward to the place where they were discovered by Mosiah and his people. At this time their king or ruler was named Zarahemla (about B. C. 200). He was a descendant of Mulek, and consequently of the tribe of Judah and of the house of David. The reason assigned for their departure from the worship of the true God, their degradation and the corruption of their language, was that their forefathers brought from their ancient home in Palestine no records or copies of the holy scriptures to guide and preserve them from error in their isolated land of adoption.

When the two races joined, it was decided that Mosiah should be the king of the united people, though the Nephites were then the less numerous. This arrangement probably grew out of the fact that though less in numbers they were the most civilized, and being worshipers of the God of Israel they would not willingly submit to be ruled by those who had no knowledge of his laws.

The education of the people of Zarahemla to the standard of the Nephites, and the work of harmonizing the two races, were not the task of an hour. It required much wisdom, patience and faith. Mosiah gave stability to the new kingdom by his own virtues and wise example, by the just laws he established, and by placing the service of the Lord before all earthly considerations. It is evident that he built a temple in the new land, as its existence is particularly mentioned in the days of his son, king Benjamin, and as the people observed the law of Moses in the matter of sacrifices and offerings, a temple would be one of the very first necessities to enable them to carry out the requirements of their religion. But to the forms, types, shadows and ceremonies of the Mosaic law were added gospel principles, with a clear and definite understanding of the coming and divine work of the Messiah, all of which is very evident in the instructions given to their subjects by Mosiah's two successors.

Mosiah was not only a divinely inspired leader and king, but he was also a seer. Whilst reigning in Zarahemla a large engraved stone was brought to him, and by the gift and power of God he translated the engravings thereon. They gave an account of the rise, fall and destruction of the great Jaredite nation, from the days of its founders, who came out from the Tower of Babel, to the time of their last king, Coriantumr, who himself was discovered by the people of Zarahemla and lived with them nine moons.

When Mosiah died he was succeeded by his son Benjamin.

CHAPTER X.

THE REIGN OF KING BENJAMIN—THE PROGRESS OF HIS PEOPLE—HIS LAST GREAT SPEECH—HE ESTABLISHES THE CHURCH OF CHRIST—ALL THE PEOPLE COVENANT WITH GOD—MOSIAH II. ANOINTED KING.

(MOSIAH CHAP. 1 TO 6.)

A MIGHTY man in the midst of Israel was Benjamin, the son of Mosiah. Blessed were the people over whom he reigned, for he governed them in righteousness, and for their welfare he labored with all the might of his body and every faculty of his soul. Holy and pure in his individual life, he was ministered to by angels, and was the frequent recipient of revelations from on high.

The reign of Benjamin was a long one; he died at a very advanced age. Some time during this period, the aggressive Lamanites, not content with occupying the land of Nephi, actually followed the Nephites into the land of Zarahemla and invaded that also. The war was a bloody one. King Benjamin led his forces, armed with the historic sword of Laban, (which appears to have been handed down from monarch to monarch from the days that Nephi first wielded it,) and with his own strong arm slew many of the enemy. Benjamin was ultimately successful in driving the invading hosts out of all the regions occupied by his people, with a loss to the Lamanites of many thousand warriors slain.

The reign of Benjamin was also troubled with various religious impostors, false Christs, pretended prophets, etc., who caused apostasy and dissensions among the people, much to the sorrow of the good king. However, by the aid of some of the many righteous men who dwelt in his dominions, he exposed the heresies, made manifest the falsity of the claims of the self-styled Messiahs and prophets, and restored unity of faith and worship among his subjects; and where these innovators had broken the civil law, they were arraigned, tried, and punished by that law. It must not be forgotten that freedom of conscience was absolutely protected among the Nephites, and even the civil law was administered with great mercy in the days of these kings. In his last great speech to his people, Benjamin reminded them of the justice and clemency with which he had caused the law to be administered, how none of them had been arbitrarily cast into prison or otherwise punished, but only for actual proven violations of the law. He also reminded them how he, their king, had labored with his own hands to defray the expenses of royalty, in order that they might not be ground down by excessive taxation. No wonder that he was so greatly loved and his name held in such high reverence by his people. Recorded history scarcely affords such another instance of kingly humility and regard for the welfare of his people.

We may presume that the original inhabitants of Zarahemla, just awakening to a newness of religious life, were particularly subject to the influences brought to bear by impostors. They had but lately learned the mysteries of the plan of salvation and of the coming of the Messiah to dwell among men. The glory and beauty of this Divine advent filled their new-born souls with joyous hope. Looking forward for the arrival of that happy day, with their first love undiminished and their zeal unslackened, they were especially open to the deception of those who cried, Lo, the Christ is come! or, Behold, a great prophet hath arisen! To this peculiar phase of spiritual condition in the midst of the lately consolidated races in the land of Zarahemla, we may attribute the frequency with which false prophets troubled the reign of Benjamin.

There was another class who, moved by the spirit of

unrest, were a source of perplexity to the king. They were those who, having left the land of Nephi with the righteous, still permitted their thoughts and affections to be drawn toward their former homes and old associations. Like Lot's wife, these Nephites were ever longing for that which they had left behind. The natural consequence was that they were constantly agitating the idea of organizing expeditions to visit their old homes. The first of these that actually started, of which we have an account, was led by an austere and bloodthirsty man. When they approached the land of Nephi, a great dissension arose in the company. The leader and some others desired to attack, and if possible, destroy the Lamanite inhabitants, but others, seeing that there was good amongst them, desired to make a treaty with them. This division of feeling led to a disastrous battle, in which the members of the expedition fought against each other with such fury that they ceased not to contend until all were slain except fifty men, who, in shame and sorrow, returned to Zarahemla to recount the miserable end of their venture. Yet some remained unsatisfied, they were still over-zealous to inherit the land of their forefathers, and, under the leadership of a man named Zeniff, another company started on the ill-advised journey. Nothing was heard from them while Benjamin reigned.

When king Benjamin was well stricken with years, the Lord directed him to consecrate his son Mosiah as his successor on the Nephite throne. Feeling that age was impairing his energies he directed his son to gather the people together at the temple that had been erected in Zarahemla, and he would then give them his parting instructions. (B. C. 125.) Agreeable to this call the people gathered at the temple, but so numerous had they grown that it was too small to hold them. They also brought with them the firstlings of their flocks that they might offer sacrifice and burnt offerings according to the Mosaic law. As the assembled thousands could not get inside the temple they pitched their tents by families, every one with its door towards the building, and the king had a tower erected near the temple from which he spake.

The teachings of king Benjamin at these meetings were some of the most divine and glorious ever uttered by man. He preached to them the pure principles of the gospel—the duties which men owe to their God and to their fellows. He also told them how he had been visited by an angel, and what wondrous things that angel had shown him concerning the coming of the God of Israel to dwell with men in the flesh. So great were the things that this angel revealed and king Benjamin repeated to the people that we think it best to give his own words. They are:

"For behold the time cometh, and is not far distant, that with power, the Lord Omnipotent, who reigneth, who was, and is from all eternity to all eternity, shall come down from heaven, among the children of men, and shall dwell in a tabernacle of clay, and shall go forth amongst men, working mighty miracles, such as healing the sick, raising the dead, causing the lame to walk, the blind to receive their sight and the deaf to hear, and curing all manner of diseases. And he shall cast out devils, or the evil spirits which dwell in the hearts of the children of men. And lo, he shall suffer temptations, and pain of body, hunger, thirst and fatigue, even more than men can suffer, except it be unto death; for behold, blood cometh from every pore, so great shall be his anguish for the wickedness and the abominations of his people.

"And he shall be called Jesus Christ, the Son of God, the Father of heaven and earth, the Creator of all things, from the beginning; and his mother shall be called Mary. And lo, he cometh unto his own, that salvation might come unto the children of men, even through faith on his name; and even after all this they shall consider him a man, and say that he hath a devil and shall scourge him and shall crucify him. And he shall rise the third day from the dead; and behold he standeth to judge the world; and behold all these things are done, that a righteous judgment might come upon the children of men."

When Benjamin had made an end of speaking the words which had been delivered to him by the angel, he observed that the power of his testimony had so worked upon the Nephites that they, in the deep sense of their own unworthiness, had fallen to the ground. And they cried out confessing their faith in the coming Messiah, and pleading that through his atoning blood they might receive the forgiveness of their sins, and that their hearts might be purified. After they had lifted their deep-felt cry to heaven, the Spirit of the Lord came down upon them, and because of their exceeding faith they received a remission of their sins.

Their inspired ruler then continued his discourse. He enlarged therein on the truths of the atonement and other soul-saving doctrines. Having finished his address he sent amongst his hearers to know if they believed and accepted the heavenly truths he had been teaching. Great was his joy when he found that they not only believed, but, because of the workings of the Spirit of the Lord in their hearts, they knew of their truth. Still more, the Holy Spirit had wrought such a change within them that they had no more disposition to do evil, but to do good continually. The visions of eternity were opened to their minds, their souls were filled with the spirit of prophecy, they longed to serve the Lord with undivided hearts, and declared themselves willing to make a covenant with him to keep his commandments and do his will the remainder of their days.

The king then gave them a new name, because of the covenant they desired to make, which thing he had greatly desired. The name they were to bear for ever after was the name of Christ, which should never be blotted out except through transgression. Thus was established the first Christian church in Zarahemla (B. C. 125), for every soul who heard these teachings (except the very little children who could not understand) entered into this sacred covenant with God, which most of them faithfully observed.

King Benjamin's truly royal work was now done. He had lived to bring his people into communion with their Creator, his spirit was full of heavenly joy, but his body trembled under the weight of many years. So before he dismissed the multitude he consecrated his son Mosiah to be their king, appointed priests to instruct the people in the ways of the Lord, and, with his patriarchal blessing, dismissed his subjects. Then according to their respective families they all departed for their own homes.

Mosiah now reigned in his father's stead, whilst Benjamin, beloved and honored, remained yet another three years on the earth before he returned to the presence of his Father in heaven.

CHAPTER XI.

ZENIFF RETURNS TO THE LAND OF NEPHI—HIS TREATY WITH THE LAMANITES—THE PROSPERITY OF THE PEOPLE OF ZENIFF—THE TREATY BROKEN—WAR—PEACE AND WARS AGAIN—THE DEATH OF ZENIFF—NOAH'S WICKED REIGN—HIS WARS WITH THE LAMANITES—THE PROPHET ABINADI—HIS TERRIBLE MESSAGE OF GOD'S WRATH—HE IS MARTYRED—ALMA—HE PLEADS FOR ABINADI—IS CAST OUT—FLEES TO THE PLACE OF MORMON.

(MOSIAH CHAP. 7 TO 18.)

BEFORE proceeding with the story of king Mosiah's reign, we will return to the land of Nephi, and learn how matters are progressing there. It will be recollected that during the reign of king Benjamin a company started from Zarahemla to return to the old home of the Nephites. Their leader's name was Zeniff. What became of him and them was a question that was never answered during Benjamin's lifetime.

Zeniff and his people, having left Zarahemla, traveled southward towards the land of Nephi. The blessings of the Lord were not greatly with them, for they did not seek him nor strive to do his will. In the wilderness they lost their way, and suffered from famine and many afflictions; but after many days they reached the neighborhood of the city of Lehi-Nephi, the former home of their race. Here Zeniff chose four of his company, and accompanied by them went to the king of the Lamanites. This monarch received them with the appearance of kindness. He made a treaty with them, and gave them the lands of Lehi-Nephi and Shilom to dwell in. He also caused his own people to remove out of these cities and the surrounding country that Zeniff's people might have full possession. The king of the Lamanites was in reality not as friendly as he pretended to be. His object was to get the industrious Nephites to settle in the midst of his people, then by his superior numbers to make them his slaves; for his own subjects were a lazy, unprogressive race.

As soon as Zeniff and his followers occupied their new possessions they went to work to build houses and to repair the walls of the city; for the idle Lamanites had suffered them to fall into decay. They also commenced to till the ground, and to plant all manner of seeds of grain, vegetables and fruit therein. Soon, through their thrift and industry, they began to prosper and multiply. This caused king Laman to grow uneasy. He desired to bring them into bondage that his people might reap the benefits of the labors of the Nephites. But they were growing so rapidly that he feared that if he did not soon put a stop to their increase they would be the stronger of the two people. To prevent this he began to stir up the hearts of his people in anger against the Nephites. He succeeded so well that in the thirteenth year of Zeniff's reign in the land of Lehi-Nephi a numerous host of Lamanites suddenly fell upon his people, while they were feeding and watering their flocks, and began to slay them. They also carried off some of their flocks, and the corn from their fields.

Those of the Nephites who were not slain or overtaken fled to Zeniff. As quickly as he could he armed his people with bows and arrows, swords and cimeters, clubs and slings, and with such other weapons as they could invent. Thus armed they went forth in the strength of the Lord to meet the enemy, for in their hour of peril they had cried mightily unto him, and he heard their cries and answered their prayers.

Thus strengthened they met their foes. The battle was an obstinate and a bloody one. It lasted all day and all night. At last the Lamanites were driven back with a loss of 3043 warriors, while the people of Zeniff had to mourn the death of 279 of their brethren. After this there was peace in the land for many years.

During this time of peace Zeniff taught his people to be very industrious. He caused his men to till the ground and raise all kinds of fruit and grain. The women he had spin and make cloth for clothing, fine linen, etc. In this way for twenty-two years they prospered and had uninterrupted peace; but at the end of that period the Lamanites again came up to war against them.

At this time the old king Laman died, and his son succeeded him upon the throne. Like many young men, he desired to distinguish himself in war. So he gathered a numerous host of the Lamanites and having armed them in the same manner as the Nephites, he led them to the north of the land of Shemlon, which lay by the side of the land of Nephi-Lehi.

The warriors of the Lamanites were at this era a strange sight to look upon. Their heads were shaven, the only covering of their bodies was a leathern girdle around their loins, otherwise they were naked. Their arms were bows, arrows, slings, swords, etc.

When Zeniff learned of the approach of young king Laman's armies, he caused the women and children of his people to hide in the wilderness; but every man, young or old, who was able to bear arms was placed in the ranks to go out against the foe. Zeniff himself was then an aged man, but he still continued to command his forces and to lead them in person to battle. But before doing so he recounted to his soldiery the history of the two peoples, stimulated them to valor by showing them that in this contest they were in the right; then calling upon them to put their trust in God, he led them to the onset. Strengthened by the faith Zeniff had renewed in their hearts, the Nephites gained a great victory; and so numerous were the slain of the Lamanites that they were not counted. After this there was peace again in the land, which continued all the remaining days of Zeniff. Shortly after this he died, and, unfortunately for his kingdom, chose for his successor an unworthy son, named Noah, who drew the people into many sins and ruled with such folly and weakness that they fell an easy prey to the ever-watchful foe that everywhere surrounded them.

King Noah did not walk in the ways of his father, for he was a very wicked man. He was filled with lust and cruelty, and ruled his people with a tyrant's hand. He removed the good priests who had been consecrated by his father, and placed corrupt men, of his own stamp, in their stead. Then he lay heavy taxes upon the people, even one-fifth of all they possessed, whether it was gold or silver, grain or fruit, flocks or herds. These taxes he wasted upon himself and his priests, upon his wives and concubines, and the harlots with whom the priests consorted. Noah also built a very grand palace in Lehi-Nephi for his own comfort, and spent much in lavishly ornamenting the temple in that city. Near the temple he erected a very high tower, so high that any one standing on its top could see all over the surrounding country. He also did much building in the land of Shilom, and there erected another high tower. Furthermore, he planted many vineyards and made his people a drunken race. All this he did with the riches which he ground out of his tax-burdened subjects.

How different was his course to that of the righteous Benjamin, who was at that time reigning in Zarahemla! We can scarcely conceive of two men more different in habits and character. The great care of the one was to serve God and benefit his people, the other had no other thought than to gratify his own desires and live for his own pleasure, no matter how much pain or suffering it caused his fellow-men.

Again the Lamanites attacked the Nephites while engaged in their labors, killed many and drove off their flocks. King Noah then set guards around the land, but in such small numbers that they were destroyed. He finally sent his armies and drove the Lamanites away. This victory made him and his people conceited and boastful, and developed in them a delight in shedding the blood of the Lamanites.

At this time a prophet, named Abinadi, appeared among them, and predicted that they would be brought into bondage unless they repented of their wickedness. The king and the people were very angry with Abinadi, and sought to take his life. Two years after he came among them in disguise. This time he uttered, in the name of the Lord, very terrible prophecies against Noah and his people. He told them that they should go into bondage to their enemies, that they should be smitten like dumb beasts and be slain. That vultures and dogs should devour their carcasses. That famine and pestilence should come upon them, and hail and insects should destroy their crops. And in the end, if they did not repent, they should be utterly destroyed. All of which was fulfilled in a very few years.

Abinadi was one of the greatest of prophets; he was filled with the Holy Ghost, but the people would not heed him, and the more he exposed their iniquities the more furious raged their anger against him. Neither did they believe his words; in their own opinion they were everything that was good. They were mighty in their own strength, and unapproachably wise in their own conceit. Never, if you could believe them, had a better, more valiant, more innocent people lived. Filled with this spirit of self-conceit they took Abinadi, bound him, and hurried him, with railing accusations, before the king. There the priests began to cross-question him, that they might confuse him and cause him to say something that would give them a pretext for slaying him. This conduct was providentially turned to the glory of God and to the good of many souls. It gave Abinadi the chance in turn to question his accusers, by which he showed their deceit and iniquity; and it also enabled him to explain many of the principles of the gospel of life and salvation. His teachings pricked the hearts of a few, while they more greatly enraged the greater number. Particularly did he impress upon their minds the great truth that Christ should come, and quoted the words of Isaiah and other Hebrew prophets to sustain his words. His teachings are among the strongest and plainest that any of the scriptures record, and should be read by all who desire to become fully acquainted with the truths of Divine love and mercy for fallen humanity.

These doctrines were, however, exactly what Noah's infidel priests did not want. They charged Abinadi with having reviled the king, and on this charge obtained Noah's consent for his execution. So Abinadi was cruelly tortured and burned to death by his fellow-citizens in the sin-stained city of Lehi-Nephi. How strange that a people could so quickly grow wicked! In Zeniff's reign they kept God's laws, if only after a fashion, but in Noah's days, led by his bad example, they sank to the depth of shedding innocent blood, and taking the life of one who had done them no wrong, but whose only fault lay in reproving them for their sins, and in striving to teach them repentance and the road to heaven.

Abinadi's last words were very terrible in their prophetic denunciations. When the flames began to scorch him he cried out:

Behold even as ye have done unto me, so shall it come to pass that thy seed shall cause that many shall suffer, even the pains of death by fire; and this because they believe in the salvation of the Lord their God. And it will come to pass that ye shall be afflicted with all manner of diseases because of your iniquities. Yea, and ye shall be smitten on every hand, and shall be driven and scattered to and fro, even as a wild flock is driven by wild and ferocious beasts. And in that day ye shall be hunted, and ye shall be taken by the hands of your enemies, and then ye shall suffer, as I suffer, the pains of death by fire. Thus God executeth vengeance upon those that destroy his people. O God, receive my soul.

But all the people did not in their hearts consent to this great crime. One among them especially, whose name was Alma, confessed to the truth of Abinadi's words. He knew that the grave charges the prophet made were true. He was a young man, one of Noah's priests, and when the clamor was highest for Abinadi's death, he went to the king and plead in Abinadi's behalf. This so angered Noah that he had Alma cast out of his presence, and then sent his servants after the young priest to slay him. Alma, however, hid from his pursuers, and, during his concealment, wrote the words he had heard Abinadi speak, which teachings now form one of the most important of the doctrinal portions of the Book of Mormon.

The power and importance of Abinadi's teachings had

sunk deep in the heart of Alma; he not only realized their truth, but he comprehended their saving value. The first lesson they impressed upon his mind was the necessity of his own repentance. This he did sincerely; and then began to teach the same lesson to others. For fear of the king he did not do this openly, but secretly as opportunity permitted.

Alma's preaching of God's holy word was not without fruit. Many received the truth with joy. These gathered to a convenient spot on the borders of the wilderness, but not far off their city. This place was called Mormon. It was admirably suited for a hiding-place, having been formerly infested by ravenous beasts, and as such was dreaded and avoided by the people. Near by was a thicket or forest of small trees, in which the gospel believers could hide should they be pursued by the king's servants; here also was a fountain of pure water, most excellently adapted for the purposes of baptism. Here was this holy rite first administered, and here was the church of Christ organized. How different the circumstances of its organization to those which attended the same event in the land of Zarahemla, under king Benjamin, of which we have already spoken.

CHAPTER XII.

THE WATERS OF MORMON—ALMA, HELAM AND OTHERS BAPTIZED THEREIN—THE CHURCH ORGANIZED—THE KING WARNED—HE SENDS TROOPS—ALMA AND HIS PEOPLE FLEE TO THE LAND OF HELAM—THEY BUILD A CITY.

(MOSIAH CHAP. 18 AND 23.)

THE FIRST to go down into the waters of Mormon for baptism were Alma and a fellow-believer named Helam. When they entered the water Alma lifted his voice in prayer, and besought the Lord for his Holy Spirit. This blessing having been bestowed, he proceeded with the sacred ordinance. Addressing his companion, he said, Helam, I baptize thee, having authority from the Almighty God, as a testimony that ye have entered into a covenant to serve him until you are dead as to the mortal body; and may the Spirit of the Lord be poured out upon you; and may he grant unto you eternal life, through the redemption of Christ, whom he has prepared from the foundation of the world. Having said these words, both Alma and Helam were buried in the water, from which they came forth rejoicing, being filled with the Holy Spirit.

Others, to the number of two hundred and four souls, followed Helam into the waters of baptism, but in none of these cases did Alma again bury himself beneath the wave, but only the repentant believer. From this time we may date the organization of the Church of Jesus Christ in that land, and henceforth its members assembled for worship and testimony once a week.

Notwithstanding the care and secrecy with which the members of the church acted, Noah soon discovered that there was some hidden movement among his subjects, and by the help of his spies he discovered what was taking place at Mormon. Making the tyrant's usual excuse, that the Christians were in rebellion against him, he sent his armies to capture and destroy them. But a greater than he stretched forth his arm to preserve his people. The Lord warned Alma of the king's intentions, and by divine direction he assembled his people, (some 450 souls,) and they gathered their flocks and herds, loaded up their grain, provisions and other supplies, and departed into the wilderness.

Being strengthened by the Lord, notwithstanding that they were impeded by their flocks and families, the pilgrims traveled with sufficient rapidity to escape the pursuing forces of king Noah, who were reluctantly compelled to return to the land of Nephi without having accomplished the object of the expedition. At the end of eight days Alma's company ceased their flight, and settled in a very beautiful and pleasant land where there was an abundant supply of pure water. We have no direct information with regard to the course taken by this colony, but it is evident from the details of their later history that the new settlement lay somewhere between the lands of Nephi and Zarahemla, though possibly somewhat aside from the most direct route. We think it far from improbable that it was situated at the head waters of some one of the numerous tributaries to the Amazon that take their rise on the eastern slope of the Andes.

The colonists, whose industry is especially referred to by the inspired historian, immediately set to work to till the soil and build a city. The city, with the surrounding territory, they named the city and land of Helam. Now that they were established as a separate people, independent of both Lamanite and Nephite princes, they desired a form of government and requested Alma to be their king. This honor he declined. He rehearsed to them the history of their fathers; he pictured to them the infamies of king Noah's reign; he showed them how a wicked ruler could lead his subjects into all manner of evil, and how such things led to bondage; and, on the other hand, how much better it was to have the Lord as their king and ruler, and to be guided by his servants under his inspiration. This counsel the people wisely accepted. Alma, though not bearing the title of king, acted as their leader, as their high priest and prophet, and as the mouthpiece of Heaven whenever God's holy word was graciously given them. In this happy state the people of

THE LAND OF HELAM.

Helam continued for some years, the Lord greatly prospering them and crowning their labors with abundant increase. Nevertheless, the Lord saw fit to chasten this devoted people, and to try their patience and their faith, of which trial and its results we shall have more to say as we proceed with our story.

We must leave Alma and his people for a time and return to king Noah.

CHAPTER XIII.

KING NOAH'S SUBJECTS REBEL—GIDEON—THE LAMANITES INVADE LEHI-NEPHI—THE NEPHITES RETREAT—A PART SURRENDER—THE NEW TERMS OF PEACE—NOAH IS BURNED TO DEATH—LIMHI MADE KING—NOAH'S PRIESTS ESCAPE—THEY SEIZE SOME LAMANITE MAIDENS—ANOTHER WAR—THE NEPHITES VICTORIOUS—THE KING OF THE LAMANITES WOUNDED—MUTUAL EXPLANATIONS.

(MOSIAH CHAP. 19 AND 20.)

SOON AFTER the return of Noah's army from their unsuccessful attempt to capture Alma and his people, a great division grew up amongst that monarch's subjects. They were heartily tired of his tyranny and his debaucheries. One of those most dissatisfied was an officer of the king's army named Gideon. We have no reason to believe that he was at that time a wicked man though he did rebel against the king, but rather that he was a good, pure and wise man, for in after life he proved that he possessed all these virtues. In the disturbances that now arose between Noah and his people Gideon sought to slay the king. But Noah fled to the tower near the temple in the city of Lehi-Nephi. Thither Gideon, sword in hand, quickly followed. The king mounted to the top, and there his eye accidentally caught sight of an army of Lamanites in the land of Shemlon. In the terror caused by this unexpected sight, he appealed to Gideon's patriotism and besought him to spare him. Not that the king cared for his people, but he made this excuse for pleading for his own life. Gideon consented, and Noah in mortal terror ordered his people to flee into the wilderness from before the advancing hosts of the Lamanites.

The people obeyed their king's command, and with their wives and children fled into the wilderness. But the forces of the Lamanites, unencumbered by women and children, soon overtook them. Then the coward king commanded the men to continue their flight and leave their wives and children to the mercy of the enemy. Some obeyed and fled, others would not, but preferred to stay and perish with those to whom they were the natural protectors. Those who stayed, in the agony of their terror when the Lamanites drew near, sent their fair daughters to plead with their enemies for their lives. This act saved them. For the dark-skinned warriors of Laman were so charmed with the beauty of the women that they spared all their lives. Yet they took them captives, carried them back to Lehi-Nephi, and gave them permission to retain that land, but under some very hard conditions. These conditions were that they should surrender king Noah into the hands of the Lamanites, and deliver up one-half of everything they possessed, and continue this tribute of one-half of their property year by year.

Gideon now sent men to search for Noah that he might be delivered up to the Lamanites. They found that the men who were with Noah, being ashamed of their cowardly flight, swore that they would return; and, if their wives and children had been killed, they would have revenge. The king commanded that they should not return, at which they grew angry with him, and burned him to death as he had done Abinadi. His priests saved themselves from a like terrible fate by flight. When the men who put Noah to death were about to return to the land of Nephi, they met Gideon and his party, and informed them of the end of Noah and the escape of the priests; then, when they heard the news that Gideon brought, they rejoiced much that their wives and children had been spared by the Lamanites.

Noah being dead, one of his sons, Limhi by name, was made king. It was almost an empty honor, for his people were in bondage to the Lamanites. Still he made a treaty of peace with the king of the Lamanites, and because he could do no better he agreed to pay a yearly tribute of one-half of the increase of the products of his subjects. The Lamanites set guards all around the land, for they were now most anxious that the Nephites should not escape. The latter were to all intents and purposes bond-servants, and the Lamanites obtained all the advantages of their labor without any of the responsibilities that generally fall upon the slave owner. Out of the tribute the guards that held them in bondage were paid. This state of things continued without an outbreak for two years.

In these times there was a romantic spot in the Land of Shemlon, on the Nephite borders, where the Lamanite maidens were in the habit of gathering on pleasure bent. Here they sang, danced and made merry with all the gaiety of youthful innocence and overflowing spirits. One day when a few were thus gathered they were suddenly surprised, and twenty-four of their number were carried off by strange men, who, from their appearance, were unmistakably Nephites.

On learning of this act of treachery the Lamanites were stirred to uncontrollable anger, and without seeking an explanation they made a sudden incursion into the territory held by king Limhi. This attack, however, was not successful, for their movements, though not understood, had been discovered, and their intended victims poured forth to meet them.

With Limhi and his people it was a war for existence; to be defeated was to be annihilated; his warriors therefore fought with superhuman energy and desperation, and eventually they succeeded in driving the Lamanites back. So speedy did their flight become, that in their confusion the Lamanites left their wounded king lying amongst the heaps of slain. There he was discovered by his victors. In the interview between him and Limhi that followed, mutual explanations ensued. The Lamanite king complained bitterly of the outrage committed on the daughters of his people, while Limhi protested that he and his subjects were innocent of the base act. Further investigation developed the fact that some of the iniquitous priests of king Noah, who had fled into the wilderness from the dreaded vengeance of their abused countrymen, were the guilty parties. Being without wives, and fearing to return home, they had adopted this plan to obtain them.

On hearing this explanation, king Laman consented to make an effort to pacify his angry hosts. At the head of an unarmed body of Nephites he went forth and met his armies who were returning to the attack. He explained what he had learned, and the Lamanites, possibly somewhat ashamed of their rashness, renewed the covenant of peace.

This peace, unfortunately, was of short duration. The Lamanites grew arrogant and grievously oppressive, and under their exactions and cruelty the condition of Limhi's subjects grew continually worse, until they were little better off than were their ancestors in Egypt before Moses, their deliverer, arose. Three times they broke out in ineffectual rebellion, and just as often their task-masters grew more cruel and exacting, until their spirits were entirely broken; they cowered before their oppressors, and bowed "to the yoke of bondage, submitting themselves to be smitten, and to be driven to and fro, and burdened according to the desires of their enemies."

CHAPTER XIV.

THE BONDAGE OF THE PEOPLE OF LIMHI—AN EXPEDITION NORTH—FINDING OF THE JAREDITE RECORDS—THE ARRIVAL OF AMMON—THE PEOPLE OF LIMHI ESCAPE—THE PURSUIT—THE AMULONITES—THE PEOPLE OF ALMA—THEY ARE BROUGHT INTO BONDAGE—THEIR DELIVERANCE.

(MOSIAH CHAP. 21 TO 24.)

AFTER A TIME the Lord softened the hearts of the Lamanites so that they began to ease the burdens of their slaves, but he did not at once deliver the Nephites out of bondage. They, however, gradually prospered, and raised more grain, flocks and herds, so that they did not suffer with hunger.

The people of Limhi kept together as much as possible for protection. Even the king did not trust himself outside the walls of the city without his guards, lest he might fall into the hands of the Lamanites.

In this sad condition of bondage and serfdom the people of Limhi had one hope. It was to communicate with their Nephite friends in the land of Zarahemla. To this end Limhi secretly fitted out an expedition consisting of a small number of men. This company became lost in the wilderness, and traveled a long distance northward until they found a land covered with the dry bones of men who appeared to have fallen in battle. Limhi's people thought this must be the land of Zarahemla and that their Nephite brethren who dwelt there had been destroyed. But in this they were wrong, for they found with the dead some records engraved on plates of ore, which, when afterwards translated by the

DISCOVERY OF THE RECORDS OF THE JAREDITES.

power of God, showed that these bones were those of some of the Jaredites who had been slain in war.

They missed the land of Zarahemla, having probably traveled to the west of it and passed northward through the Isthmus of Panama.

Shortly after this a small company numbering sixteen men reached them from Zarahemla. Their leader's name was Ammon. He had been sent by king Mosiah to the land of Nephi to find out what had become of the people, or their descendants, who left with Zeniff. When Ammon and those that were with him reached Lehi-Nephi, king Limhi happened to be without the walls of the city, and his guards fancying that Ammon and his friends were some of the priests of Noah took them and put them in prison. The next day the mistake was discovered, and Limhi and his people were overjoyed to hear from their friends. Soon plans were laid to effect the escape of the enslaved Nephites, which, under the guidance of Limhi, Ammon and Gideon, was successfully accomplished. The Lamanite guards were made drowsy with a large present of wine, and while they were in this drunken stupor, the people of Limhi escaped through an unfrequented pass, taking with them such things as they could safely carry away. They were then led by Ammon to Zarahemla.

When the Lamanites found, to their great surprise, that their bond servants had escaped, they sent an army after them. It so happened that these troops lost themselves in the wilderness. Whilst traveling hither and thither, not knowing which way to go, they came across the priests of king Noah. These priests, at the instigation of Amulon, their leader, joined the Lamanite troops, and they unitedly endeavored to get back to the land of Nephi. While thus engaged, they wandered near the city of Helam.

When the people of Alma first perceived the approach of this body of men, they were engaged in tilling the soil around their city, into which they immediately fled in great fear. In this perilous hour the faith and courage of Alma were conspicuous. He gathered his people around him, called upon them to cast aside their unsaintly fears, and to remember the God who had ever delivered those who trusted in him. The words of their leader had the desired effect; the people silenced their fears and called mightily upon the Lord to soften the hearts of the Lamanites that they might spare their lives and those of their wives and little ones. Then, with the assurance in their hearts that God would hearken unto their prayers, Alma and his brethren went forth out of their city and delivered themselves up to their former foes.

The Lamanites were in a dilemma, therefore they were profuse in promises. They were willing to grant the people of Helam their lives and liberty if they would show them the way to the land of Nephi. Having obtained this information and reached home in safety, they broke their promises and made Amulon the king over a wide district of country, including the land of Helam.

Alma and Amulon had known each other in the days when they both belonged to king Noah's priesthood, and with the venom so often conspicuous in apostates, the latter soon commenced to persecute those who were faithful to the Lord. He placed task-masters over them, imposed inhuman burdens upon them, and otherwise afflicted them grievously.

In their agony they called continually upon the Lord for deliverance. Their prayers annoyed their cruel masters and they were forbidden to pray aloud; but no tyrants, however powerful or cruel, could prevent them praying in their hearts. This the people of Alma continued to do most fervently, and in due time, though not immediately, deliverance came. In the meanwhile the Lord comforted and strengthened them in their afflictions, so that their burdens were easily borne.

The time for their deliverance finally came, for on a certain day the Lord promised them that he would deliver them on the morrow. The night was occupied in getting their flocks and provisions together, and preparing for their journey. In the morning, when their Lamanite guards and taskmasters were in a deep sleep, they set out on their journey into the wilderness. After traveling all day they pitched their tents in a valley which they named Alma. The Lord warned Alma to hasten out of this country, for the Lamanites were in pursuit, but he said he would stop them in the valley where Alma was then camped. Alma and his company traveled yet twelve days, at the end of which time they arrived in Zarahemla. This, with the eight days occupied in traveling from the waters of Mormon to the land of Helam, makes twenty-one days' travel from Lehi-Nephi* to Zarahemla.

Amulon and the priests of Noah, possibly because of their Lamanitish wives, soon gained great favor with king Laman and were made teachers to his people. Educated in the language of the Nephites, they began to instruct the Lamanites therein. They, however, taught the people nothing of the religion of their fathers, or of the law of Moses, but instructed them how to keep their records, and to write one to another. All this time king Laman ruled over a numerous people, inhabiting distant regions, governed by tributary kings and rulers. Having no written standard, the language of the Lamanites had become greatly corrupted. The coming of the priests of Noah among them gave rise to the introduction of a higher civilization. As a result, they increased in wealth; and trade and commerce extended among them. They became cunning and wise, and therefore powerful, but were still addicted to robbery and plunder, except among themselves.

---

*To prevent confusion in the minds of our readers, we desire to draw attention to the fact that the city of Lehi-Nephi and the city of Nephi are not two separate cities, but one and the same city with two names.

CHAPTER XV.

MOSIAH'S GOOD REIGN—THE CIRCUMSTANCES OF HIS ADVENT—HE ASSEMBLES THE PEOPLE—THE BAPTISM OF LIMHI—CHURCHES ORGANIZED THROUGHOUT THE LAND.

(MOSIAH CHAP. 25.)

WE MUST now leave the Lamanites in the land of Nephi, and return to king Mosiah in Zarahemla. It will be remembered that we left the people of Zarahemla at the time of the death of king Benjamin, three years after the ascent of his son Mosiah to the throne.

Mosiah was born in the land of Zarahemla, 154 or 155 years before the coming of Christ. He was instructed in all the wisdom of the Nephites, and trained in youth in the fear of the Lord. By the direction of the Almighty he was consecrated by his father to succeed him on the throne, which ceremony was attended to at the time the whole nation had gathered at the temple to listen to the words of their aged and beloved ruler; at the same time, they all covenanted with God to be his servants ever after. There, in the presence of his future subjects, under the shadow of the holy house, he was set apart to rule a people whose sins were all forgiven through their abiding faith in the unborn Savior. Could a king come to a throne under more auspicious circumstances? Profound peace with all outside his dominions, and within its borders reigned union, contentment, prosperity, happiness, and what is more, righteousness.

Mosiah was thirty years old when he began to reign, which event happened 476 years after Lehi left Jerusalem.

Mosiah followed in the footsteps of his father, taught his people to be industrious, and set them the example by tilling a portion of the earth to maintain himself and his dependents.

It was in the fourth year of his reign that Mosiah sent out the expedition under Ammon to find the people of Zeniff. Of its success, and the happy arrival of Limhi and his subjects, and of Alma and his people, we have already spoken.

Soon after the coming of Limhi and Alma, Mosiah gathered all the Nephites at one place that they might hear how God had dealt with both. First he had the records of Zeniff and Alma read in their hearing, at which they were greatly amazed; but when they beheld the new comers they were filled with exceeding great joy, mingled with sadness for the loss of their kindred slain by the inhuman Lamanites, and many tears were shed for those departed ones. Again, when they listened to the marvelous deliverances wrought by heaven in behalf of Alma and his faithful few, the assembled thousands raised their voices on high and gave thanks to God. Still another shade of feeling came across their sympathetic hearts, that of pain and anguish when they learned of the sinful and polluted state of their Lamanite brethren.

Taking advantage of the presence of so many of his subjects, Mosiah addressed them on such matters as he deemed necessary and desirable. At his request Alma also taught them. When assembled in large bodies Alma went from one multitude to another, preaching repentance and faith in the Lord. After hearing his teaching Limhi requested to be baptized, and so did all his people. Then Alma baptized them in the same manner as he had their brethren He afterwards, by Mosiah's direction, went through the land, organizing and establishing churches and ordaining priests and teachers over every church. Thus were seven churches established at this time in the land of Zarahemla.

BAPTISM OF LIMHI.

CHAPTER XVI.

THE UNBELIEF OF THE YOUTH OF ZARAHEMLA—THE YOUNGER ALMA AND THE SONS OF MOSIAH—THEY ENCOURAGE THE PERSECUTIONS AGAINST THE CHURCH—THEY ARE MET BY AN ANGEL—HIS MESSAGE—ALMA'S AWFUL CONDITION—HIS VISION AND TESTIMONY—THE CHANGED LIFE OF THE YOUNG MEN.

(MOSIAH CHAP. 26 AND 27.)

IN THE course of the years many of the rising generation gave no heed to the word of God. These were mostly such as were too young to enter into covenant with the Lord at the time that king Benjamin anointed Mosiah to be his successor. Not only did they themselves reject the doctrines of the atonement, the resurrection and other gospel principles, but they led away many of the members of the church into darkness and iniquity, and abused, reviled and persecuted those who remained faithful to the cause of Christ. Neither the fear of the civil nor of the divine law restrained them. Their course, and that of those in the church who gave way to evil doing, gave much trouble, and caused deep anxiety to Mosiah and Alma, the latter now the high priest of the whole church. When sought in prayer, the Lord directed what action should be taken with transgressors in the church, and after due consultation with his priests, with Alma and others, Mosiah issued a proclamation of equality to his people, forbidding all his subjects to persecute, vex or abuse their fellows because of their faith or religion, and announcing that in matters of conscience all men were equal before the law, and all were the subjects of his protection. Still it required a greater than an earthly king to bring to naught the evil intents of the disbelievers, who were greatly encouraged in their misdeeds by the fact that the king's four sons and one of the sons of Alma were their leaders.

Frequent and fervent were the prayers offered by Mosiah and the elder Alma in behalf of their rebellious sons, and those prayers prevailed with Him who sits on heaven's eternal throne.

One day, as the younger Alma and his company were going about persecuting the members of the church, an angel descended in a cloud and stopped them in the way. When he spoke his voice was as thunder, that caused the whole earth to tremble beneath their feet. Naturally this manifestation of the power of God spread terror and dismay in the hearts of those who witnessed it. They fell to the ground, and so confused and terrified were they that they failed to understand the words of the holy messenger. Arise, Alma, and stand forth, he cried; and when Alma arose, his eyes were opened to see who stood before him. Why persecutest thou the Church of God? he was asked, for the Lord hath said, This is my Church, and I will establish it; and nothing shall overthrow it, save it is the transgression of my people. If thou wilt of thyself be destroyed, seek no more to destroy the Church of God. Besides this, the angel spoke to him of his father's prayers in his behalf, and told him that because of those prayers, he had been sent to convince him of the power of God. The messenger also recounted to Alma the captivity of his fathers in the lands of Helam and Nephi, and of their miraculous deliverance therefrom. But Alma heard none of these latter sayings, for the terrors of the first salutation had overpowered him.

When the angel departed Alma was overcome, and dismayed and soul-stricken, he sank to the ground. When his companions gathered around him, they found he could not move, neither could he speak. Outwardly he was dead to the world; but the torments of the damned had taken hold of his soul, and in the most bitter pain and mental anguish he lay racked with the remembrance of all his past sins. The thought of standing before the bar of God to be judged for his iniquities overwhelmed him with horror. He desired to become extinct both body and soul without being brought before his Creator. Thus he continued for three days and three nights to suffer the pains of hell, which, to his racked conscience, must have seemed an eternity.

When his companions found that he could neither speak nor move, they carried him to his father, and related all that had happened. Strange as it must have seemed to them, the elder Alma's heart was filled with joy and praise when he looked upon the body of his much-loved son, for he realized it was God's power that had wrought all this, and that his long-continued prayers had been answered. In his joy he gathered the people to witness the mighty manifestation of the goodness and power of Jehovah. He assembled the priests, sought their co-operation, and unitedly, in God's own way, they prayed and fasted for the stricken youth. For two days they continued their cries to heaven, at the end of which time Alma stood upon his feet and spoke. He comforted them by declaring, I have repented of my sins, and have been redeemed of the Lord, behold I am born of the Spirit.

In later years, Alma, in relating to his son Helaman the details of his conversion, thus decribes the causes that led him to bear this testimony. He says: Behold, I remembered also to have heard my father prophesy unto the people concerning the coming of one Jesus Christ, a Son of God, to atone for the sins of the world. Now as my mind caught hold upon this thought, I cried within my heart, O Jesus, thou Son of God, have mercy on me, who art in the gall of bitterness and art encircled about by the everlasting chains of death. And now, behold, when I thought this, I could remember my pains no more; yea, I was harrowed up by the memory of my sins no more. And oh, what joy, and what marvelous light I did behold; yea, my soul was filled with joy as exceeding as was my pain; yea, I say unto you my son, there could be nothing so exquisite and so bitter as my pain. Yea, and again I say unto you, my son, that on the other hand, there can be nothing so exquisite and sweet as was my joy; yea, methought I saw, even as our father Lehi saw, God sitting upon his throne, surrounded with numberless concourses of angels, in the attitude of singing and praising their God; yea, my soul did long to be there.

From that time to the end of his mortal career, Alma labored without ceasing to bring souls to Christ, and to guide his fellow-man in the paths of salvation.

What effect had this heavenly visit upon the sons of Mosiah? A very great one. From that moment they were changed men. As the voice of the angel reached their astonished ears, the essence of divinity entered their souls, they knew, they felt, they realized there was a God, and that they had been fighting against him. The sense of their own utter unworthiness filled their hearts; remorse and anguish reigned supreme therein, and they condemned themselves as the vilest of sinners. By and by the bitterness of their remorse was swallowed up in their faith in the coming of Christ, and they determined by God's help, to their utmost strength, to undo the evil that their previous course had wrought. These resolutions they faithfully carried out. If they had been energetic in their wrong-doing they were yet more active in their works of restitution. They journeyed from city to city, from land to land, and everywhere bore triumphant testimony of the incidents of their miraculous conversion, and in no equivocal tones proclaimed the glorious gospel message of love to God, salvation to mankind.

CHAPTER XVII.

THE GROWTH OF THE PEOPLE IN ZARAHEMLA—THEY BUILD MANY CITIES—MOSIAH'S SONS DESIRE TO TAKE A MISSION TO THE LAMANITES—MOSIAH INQUIRES OF THE LORD—THE DIVINE ANSWER.

(MOSIAH CHAP. 28.)

THE INHABITANTS of Zarahemla at this time were all considered Nephites, though the descendants of Mulek and his companions were the most numerous. But the Nephites, though the last comers to Zarahemla, were the governing race, and the kingdom had been conferred upon none but those who were the descendants of Nephi. The Nephites ruled by the right of their higher civilization, the possession of the records and the authority of the holy priesthood. There is another strange fact with regard to the inhabitants of South America at this time, it is that the Lamanites were twice as numerous as the combined people of Nephi and Zarahemla. This may have been owing to the fact that when any defection occurred among the Nephites, the dissatisfied portions of the community generally went over to the Lamanites and became absorbed in that race.

In these days there was much peace in the land of Zarahemla. The Lord blessed the people and they became very numerous, contented and wealthy. When Benjamin was king his people appear to have all resided in and immediately around the city of Zarahemla, as the king directed his son to gather them at the temple on the morrow, and on the morrow they were all there, which would have been impossible had they lived at any great distance from headquarters. We judge that at that time the majority inhabited the city and farmed the land around. Up to this time no other city than Zarahemla is mentioned in that land, but now the people began to spread abroad, building, as the historian states, large cities and villages in all quarters of the land. We may reasonably suppose that at this epoch were founded the cities of Aaron, Ammonihah, Gideon, Manti, Melek and others mentioned in the annals of the succeeding twenty years.

Notwithstanding the great good they had done, the sons of king Mosiah were not content to confine their labors to the land of Zarahemla. They longed to carry the glad tidings of salvation to the benighted Lamanites. Ignoring the dangers and despising the pains of such a mission, they plead with their father many days for his consent for them to go to the land of Nephi. The bloodthirsty, revengeful character of the Lamanites was too well known to the king for him to think of his sons going into their midst without causing him feelings of dread and apprehension, but he had no desire to quench their holy zeal towards God and their love towards their unfortunate fellows, lest he should sin by so doing, and rob thousands of the opportunity of hearing the everlasting truths through obedience to which mankind is saved. He therefore inquired of the Lord. The answer came, Let them go up, for many shall believe on their words, and they shall have eternal life, and I will deliver thy sons out of the hands of the Lamanites. With this divine assurance Mosiah consented, and shortly after, with some other missionaries, whom they had chosen, these four valiant, God-fearing youths started on their perilous mission.

CHAPTER XVIII.

MOSIAH'S SONS REFUSE THE KINGDOM—HE GRANTS THE PEOPLE A CONSTITUTION—THE PEOPLE TO ELECT THEIR RULERS—ALMA, THE YOUNGER, FIRST CHIEF JUDGE.

(MOSIAH CHAP. 29.)

MOSIAH now felt that it was time that the question of the succession to the throne should be settled. In his magnanimity he sent among the people to learn whom they would have for their king. The people chose his son Aaron, but Aaron would not accept the royal power; his heart was set upon the conversion of his fellow-men to the truths of the gospel. This refusal troubled the mind of Mosiah; he apprehended difficulties if Aaron at some future time should change his mind and demand his rights. Mosiah therefore issued another address to his much-loved subjects, as usual full of the spirit of divine wisdom and love. In it, after recounting the peculiarities of the situation, he says: Let us be wise and consider these things, for we have no right to destroy my son, neither should we have a right to destroy another, if he should be appointed in his stead. And if my son should turn again to his pride and vain things, he would recall the things which he had said and claim his right to the kingdom, which would cause him and also his people to commit much sin. * * * Therefore, I will be your king the remainder of my days; nevertheless, let us appoint judges, to judge this people according to our law, and we will newly arrange the affairs of this people; for we will appoint wise men to be judges that will judge this people according to the commandments of God.

Inspired and directed by the Lord, the king further advised many changes of the law, so that all things might be done by the voice of the whole people. These changes were gladly accepted by the people, as they gave them greater liberty and a voice in all important national affairs. As a law-maker Mosiah may be ranked among the most eminent this world has produced. We regard him in some respects as the Moses, in others as the Alfred the Great, of his age and nation. But besides being a king he was also a seer. The gift of interpreting strange tongues and languages was his. By this gift he translated from the twenty-four plates of gold, found by the people of king Limhi, the records of the Jaredites. No wonder that a man possessed of such gifts, so just and merciful in the administration of the law, so perfect in his private life, should be esteemed more than any man by his subjects, and that they waxed strong in their love towards him. As a king, he was a father to them, but as a prophet, seer and revelator he was the source whence divine wisdom flowed unto them. We must go back to the days of the antediluvian patriarchs to find the peers of these three kings (the two Mosiahs and Benjamin), when monarchs ruled by right divine, and men were prophets, priests and kings by virtue of heaven's gifts and God's will.

His sons having started on their mission to the Lamanites, Mosiah chose Alma, the younger, and gave the sacred plates and the associate holy things into his care. The elder Alma made this same son the presiding high priest of the church, and the people chose him for their first chief judge. The church, the records, the nation, all things being thus provided for, Mosiah passed away to the joys of eternity, B. C. 91. He was sixty-three years old, and he had ruled his people in righteousness thirty-three years. When he passed away no fierce convulsions wrecked the ship of state, the political atmosphere was calm, the people joyfully assumed their new responsibilities, and the first of the judges succeeded the last of the kings without causing one disturbing wave on the placid waters of the national life.

CHAPTER XIX.

THE MISSION OF THE SONS OF MOSIAH TO THE LAMANITES—THEIR JOURNEY IN THE WILDERNESS—AMMON BROUGHT BEFORE KING LAMONI—THE CONFLICT AT THE WATERS OF SEBUS—THE MIRACULOUS CONVERSION OF LAMONI AND HIS FAMILY—ABISH THE WAITING WOMAN.

(ALMA CHAP. 17 TO 19.)

BEFORE we take up the history of the Nephites, during the reigns of their judges, we will follow the sons of Mosiah and their brethren to the land of Nephi, on the perilous mission that they had undertaken, to convert the Lamanites. The names of the four sons of Mosiah were Aaron, Ammon, Omner and Himni; amongst their companions were Muloki and Ammah.

These all took their journey into the southern wilderness during the last year of Mosiah's reign, or B. C. 91. They carried with them their bows and arrows and other weapons, not to wage war but to kill game for their food in the wilderness. Their journey was a tedious one; they lost their way and almost lost heart, and indeed were on the point of returning when they received divine assurance of their ultimate success. Nerved by this assurance, and with much fasting and prayer, they continued their wanderings, and before long reached the borders of the Lamanites. Commending themselves to God they here separated, each one trusting to the Lord to guide him to the place where he could best accomplish the purposes of heaven.

Ammon entered the Lamanite territory at a land called Ishmael. Here Lamoni was the chief ruler, under his father, who was king of all the Lamanites. Ammon was no sooner discovered than he was taken, bound with cords and conducted into the presence of Lamoni. It was the custom of the Lamanites to so use every Nephite they captured, and it rested with the whim of the king whether the captive be slain, imprisoned or sent out of the country. The king's will and pleasure were the only law on such matters.

Through God's grace, Ammon found favor in the eyes of Lamoni, and, learning that it was his desire to reside amongst the Lamanites, the king offered him one of his daughters to wife. Ammon courteously declined this intended honor and begged to be accepted as one of the king's servants, which arrangement pleased Lamoni, and Ammon was placed in that part of the royal household that had charge of the monarch's flocks and herds.

A glance at Lamanite society may not here be out of place. It would appear that in Lamoni's days the will of the sovereign was the law of the land. The king's power over the lives and property of his subjects was unlimited. We read of no constitution that prescribed or limited his authority. The more degraded portions of the race wandered in the vast wilderness, dwelling in tents, and subsisting on what they killed in the chase or stole. The more civilized Lamanites resided in cities, were wealthy in cattle, and followed the occupations general among semi-civilized races.

Lamoni was rich in flocks and herds, probably the results of the taxation of the people, but even the king's property was not secure from theft. Marauding bands would watch for his numerous cattle as they approached their watering places. Then with yell and prolonged shout they would stampede the herds and drive away all they could beyond the reach of the king's servants. These would gather up what few animals, if any, they found, and return to the king in the full expectancy of being made to pay for the loss by the forfeit of their lives. They were seldom disappointed, for Lamoni or some of his predecessors had established a somewhat unique criminal code with regard to stealing the royal cattle. They had adopted the idea that it was easier and cheaper to make the herdsmen responsible for the losses and punish them therefor, than to hunt out and capture the thieves. It had at least one virtue, it prevented collusion between the robbers and the servants; but it produced much dissatisfaction among Lamoni's subjects.

On the third day of Ammon's service, one of these raids was made on the king's cattle as they were being taken to the waters of Sebus, the common watering place. The cattle fled in all directions, and the dispirited servants, with the fear of death before their eyes, sat down and wept instead of attempting to stop them. Ammon perceived that this was his opportunity. He first reasoned with the servants, then encouraged them, and having sufficiently aroused their feelings, he led them in the attempt to head off the flying herds. With much exertion they succeeded. The cattle were all gathered, but the robbers still waited at the watering place to renew the attack when they drew near enough. Ammon perceiving this, placed the servants at various points on the outside of the flock and himself went forward to contend with the robbers. Though they were many, he knew that he was more powerful than them all, for God was with him. The idea of one man withstanding so many was supremely ridiculous to the robbers. But as one after another fell before his unerring aim, they were astonished, and dreaded him as something more than human. Enraged at the loss of six of their number they rushed upon him in a body, determined to crush him with their clubs. Ammon, undaunted, drew his sword and awaited the onslaught. Their leader fell dead at his feet, and as one after another raised their clubs, Ammon struck off their arms until none dared to approach him, but instead retreated afar off.

It was a strange procession that returned to the palace. The fears of the herdsmen had been turned to joy, and they marched in triumph into the presence of the king, with the arms of the robbers as testimonies of the truth of the story of Ammon's prowess. Doubtless they did not diminish the telling points in the narrative; the numbers of the band, the courage and strength of the Nephite, were each dilated upon with the vividness of superstitious imagination. When the king had heard their marvelous story his heart was troubled, and he came to the conclusion that Ammon must be the Great Spirit, of whose existence he had an indistinct idea. He trembled at the thought that perhaps this Spirit had come to punish him because of the number of his servants whom he had slain for permitting his cattle to be stolen.

Notwithstanding his misgivings, Lamoni desired to see Ammon, who, acting as though nothing particular had happened, was preparing the king's horses and chariots, as the servants had been directed. When he entered the royal presence, the king was too much filled with emotion to speak to him. More than once Ammon drew to the king's attention that he stood before him, as he had been requested, and wished to know what were his commands. But Ammon's inquiries elicited no response. At last, perceiving the monarch's thoughts, he began to question Lamoni regarding sacred things, and afterwards to expound to him the principles of life and salvation. Lamoni listened and believed. He was conscience-stricken, and with all the strength of his newborn faith, he humbly begged that the Lord would show that same mercy to him and to his people that he had shown to the Nephites. Overcome with the intensity of his feelings he sank to the earth as in a trance. In this state he was carried to his wife, who with her children anxiously watched over him for two days and two nights, awaiting his return to consciousness. There was great diversity of opinion among his retainers as to what troubled the king. Some said the power of the Great Spirit was upon him, others that an evil power possessed him, yet others asserted that he was dead, and with remarkable acuteness of smell affirmed, He stinketh. At the end of this time they had resolved to lay him away in the sepulchre, when the queen sent for Ammon and plead with him in her husband's behalf. Ammon gave her the joyful assurance, He is not dead, but sleepeth in God, and tomorrow he shall rise again. Then he added, Believest thou this? She answered, I have no witness, save thy word and the word of our servants, nevertheless I believe it shall be according as thou hast said. Then Ammon blessed her, and told her there had not been such great faith among all the people of the Nephites.

So the queen lovingly continued her watch by the bed of her husband until the appointed hour. Lamoni then arose, as Ammon had foretold. His soul was filled with heavenly joy. His first words were of praise to God, his next were blessings on his faithful wife whose faith he felt or knew. He testified to the coming of the Redeemer, of whose greatness, glory, power and mercy he had learned while in the spirit. His body was too weak for the realities of eternity that filled his heart. Again he sank overpowered to the earth, and the same spirit overcame his wife also. Ammon's rejoicing heart swelled within him as he heard and witnessed these things. He fell on his knees and poured out his soul in praise and thanksgiving until he also could not contain the brightness of the glory, the completeness of the joy that overwhelmed him. Unconscious of all earthly things he sank beside the royal pair. The same spirit of unmeasured joy then fell upon all present and with the same results. There was but one exception, a Lamanitish waiting woman named Abish, who many years before had been converted to the Lord, but kept the secret in her own bosom. She comprehended the why and wherefore of this strange scene. She saw the workings of the Almighty through which the untutored minds of the Lamanites could be brought to an understanding of the plan of salvation. From house to house she went, calling the people to witness what had occurred in the palace. They gathered at her call, but as might naturally be expected their impressions were very conflicting. Some said one thing, some another; some argued for good, some for evil; to some, Ammon was a god, to others, a demon. One man, who had his brother slain at the waters of Sebus, drew his sword and attempted to slay Ammon, but was struck dead by an unseen power before he could carry his rash intent into action. So fierce was the contention, so angry grew the controversy, that Abish, fearing greater trouble, by an inspiration took hold of the hand of the queen, who thereupon rose to her feet. The queen's first thought was of her husband. She took his hand and raised him up, and ere long all who had been reposing in the spirit stood upon their feet. The king, the queen, the servants, all rejoiced with joy unspeakable. They all bore testimony to God's abundant love and goodness, and some declared that holy angels had visited them. Still the contention was not entirely appeased until Lamoni stood forth and explained to them the divine mysteries of which they were so ignorant. Many believed, others did not, but Ammon had the indescribable happiness of shortly after establishing a church to the Lord in the midst of the people of the land of Ishmael. Ammon's humility, faith and patience were bringing forth their fruit; while his soul gathered faith and strength in the fulfillment of the promises of the great Jehovah in answer to the pleadings of his faithful, loving father.

CHAPTER XX.

AMMON AND LAMONI START FOR THE LAND OF MIDDONI—THEY MEET THE OLD KING—HIS RAGE AT SEEING AMMON—HE ENDEAVORS TO KILL HIS SON—AARON AND HIS BRETHREN LIBERATED—A SKETCH OF THEIR LABORS AND SUFFERINGS—THE CONVERSION OF LAMONI'S FATHER AND HIS HOUSEHOLD.

(ALMA CHAP. 20 TO 22.)

WHEN the church was satisfactorily established in the land of Ishmael, Lamoni arranged to pay a visit to his father, the great king in the land of Nephi, to whom he was desirous of introducing Ammon. However, the voice of the Lord warned his servant not to go, but instead thereof to proceed to the land of Middoni, where his brother Aaron and other missionaries were suffering in prison. When Lamoni heard of Ammon's intention, and the cause thereof, he decided to accompany him. He felt that he could be of service in delivering the prisoners, as Antiomno, the king of Middoni, was one of his special friends, and likely to grant any favor he might ask. They accordingly started on their errand of mercy, but on their way were surprised to meet Lamoni's father, who grew exceedingly angry when he found Ammon in the company of his son. All the hatred born and nurtured of false tradition boiled up in his breast. He listened impatiently to Lamoni's story of Ammon's visit and its fruits, and when it was finished he broke out in a torrent of abuse toward the Nephite "son of a liar," as he ungraciously styled him, and ordered Lamoni to slay him. Lamoni without hesitation refused to become the murderer of his most loved friend, whereupon the old monarch, in the blind fury of his anger, turned upon his own son, and would have killed him if Ammon had not interposed. Little used to controversy, much less to direct opposition, the king was not softened by Ammon's interference. Savagely he turned upon him; but youth, strength, dexterity, and above all the protecting care of the Lord were with Ammon, and he struck the king's sword arm so heavy a blow that it fell useless at his side. Realizing he was now in the power of the man he had so foully abused, he made abundant promises, even to half his kingdom, if his life was spared. This boon Ammon immediately granted, asking only favors for Lamoni and his own imprisoned brethren. The king, unused to such generosity and manly love, granted all his requests, and when he proceeded on his journey his mind was filled with reflections regarding Ammon's courage and great love for his son. He was also troubled in his heart concerning certain expressions of Ammon on doctrinal points, which opened up ideas that were entirely new to his mind.

Lamoni and Ammon continued their journey to Middoni, where by God's grace, they found favor in the eyes of king Antiomno, and by his commands the prisoners were released from the horrors and inhumanities practiced upon them. When Ammon met these faithful brethren, he was greatly grieved because of their naked, wounded, starved and wretched condition, but when they were delivered they enjoyed a season of grateful joy, thanksgiving and mutual congratulation. After this Ammon returned to the land of Ishmael to continue his labors.

It appears that when Ammon and his brethren separated on the borders of the Lamanites, Aaron took his journey towards a land called Jerusalem, which was situated near the waters of Mormon. Here the Lamanites, the people of Amulon and others, had built a great city to which they gave the name of Jerusalem. In this great city the people, many of whom were Nephite apostates, were very wicked. They would not listen to his teachings, so he left them and went to a village called Ani-Anti. There he found Muloki, Ammah and others preaching the word. But their efforts were fruitless; the people of this place would not receive the truth, therefore they left them and went over into the land Middoni. There they preached unto many though but few believed in their words. Before long the wicked raised a persecution, and some of the brethren were cast into prison, whilst others fled into the regions round about. In prison they were treated with great cruelty; they were bound with strong cords, which cut into their flesh; they were deprived of proper food, drink and clothing, and otherwise suffered nameless afflictions. There they remained until they were released through the intercession of Ammon and Lamoni.

Some time after Aaron and his fellow-prisoners were released, he, with some others, went to the land of Nephi, or Lehi-Nephi, as it is sometimes called. They there presented themselves before the old king who was the father of Lamoni. When this monarch saw them he was greatly pleased, for his heart had been touched by the words and conduct of Ammon. At his request Aaron explained to him many things relating to the nature of God; for, though he recognized the power and might of the Great Spirit, he was altogether ignorant of things concerning the Deity.

Aaron by degrees explained to him the principles of the everlasting gospel. He commenced with the creation of man, showed how Adam fell that man might be, and how the plan of redemption through a Savior's sufferings was devised before the world was, and how man, by obedience to the gospel, would triumph over death, hell, and the grave.

His words were gratefully received by the king, who besought Aaron to teach him how he might obtain this eternal life of which he spoke. Aaron instructed him to bow down before the Lord in prayer, and then in faith ask for the blessings he desired.

The aged king did so. He prostrated himself on the ground and cried mightily, saying, O God, Aaron hath told me there is a God, and if there is a God, and if thou art God, wilt thou make thyself known unto me, and I will give away all my sins to know thee, and that I may be raised from the dead, and be saved at the last day. So great was his emotion, that when he had said these words, he was struck as if he were dead.

When the king thus fell his servants ran and told the queen what had happened. She at once came into the room where he lay, and seeing Aaron and his brethren standing by she became very angry, as she supposed that they were the cause of the evil that had, in her estimation, befallen her husband. She, without hesitation, ordered the king's servants to take the brethren and slay them; but the servants dared not, for they feared the power which was in Aaron. The queen was also afraid, but she seemed to think that the best way to get rid of the trouble was to destroy those who she fancied brought it. As the king's servants refused to obey her command, she ordered them to go out into the streets and call upon the people to come in and kill Aaron and his companions.

When Aaron saw the temper of the queen, he feared lest the multitude, in the hardness of their hearts, would raise a great commotion, and be a cause of hindering the work of God, which had so auspiciously commenced with the king. Therefore he put forth his hand and raised the monarch from the earth, and at the same time said unto him, Stand. The king at once received his strength and arose, at the sight of which the queen and the servants wondered greatly and were filled with fear.

Then the king began to explain to them what he had learned with regard to God and the Gospel, and he spoke with such great power that his whole household was converted. The multitude also that had gathered at the call of the queen were pacified by his words, and when he saw that their hearts were softened he caused that Aaron and his brethren should teach them the word of God.

CHAPTER XXI.

THE KING ISSUES A PROCLAMATION—THE RESULTS OF THE LABORS OF THE SONS OF MOSIAH—THE PEOPLE OF ANTI-NEPHI-LEHI—THEY BURY THEIR WEAPONS OF WAR—ARE MASSACRED BY THE THOUSAND—THEY REMOVE TO THE TERRITORY OF THE NEPHITES, WHO GIVE THEM THE LAND OF JERSHON.

(ALMA CHAP. 23 TO 27.)

AFTER the king was converted he sent a proclamation throughout the land forbidding any and all from persecuting Ammon and his fellow-missionaries, giving them liberty to preach anywhere and everywhere that they desired. Our readers may be sure that this privilege was not neglected. To use Ammon's own words, the missionaries entered into the houses of the people and taught them; they taught them in their temples and synagogues, in the open streets and on the lofty hills. But often they were cast out, spit upon, smitten, stoned, bound, cast into prison and made to suffer all manner of afflictions, from which the Lord, in his mercy, delivered them and from which the king's proclamation afterward protected them. Nor was the result of their labors trifling, but glorious in the saving of many thousand souls; for unto the Lord were converted the people of the Lamanites who dwelt in the lands of Ishmael, Middoni, Shilom and

Shemlon, and in the cities of Nephi, Lemuel and Shimnilon; and they became a righteous, peaceful, God-serving people; and from faithful obedience to his law they never fell away. But the various bodies of Nephite apostates who dwelt among the Lamanites universally rejected the gospel message, with the exception of one single Amalekite, and of what ultimately became of him we have no record.

History often repeats itself, but we have no recollection of any parallel to the events that followed this marvelous conversion. The Lamanite people now became two as distinct and separate bodies as they and the Nephites had beforetimes been. But with this strange complication, the apostate Nephites now occupied the place and did the work of the natural Lamanites, while the true descendants of Laman and Lemuel took the ground previously held by the righteous Nephites. So clearly defined did the division become that the supreme ruler (Lamoni's father), having turned from the tradition, habits and customs of the Lamanites, was determined to also cast aside the old name. If they were Lamanites in name only they would cut that weak cord which alone held them to the past, and be as new in name as they were in feelings, hopes, loyalty and religion. So, after advising with Ammon and his fellow-missionaries, he gave to his people the name of Anti-Nephi-Lehies, and to his són, to whom he transferred the royal power, that of Anti-Nephi-Lehi.

The renegade Amalekites, Amulonites and others were not willing to be ruled by a Christian monarch. They had rejected Christianity altogether, and would not have it as the ruling power, either in Nephi or Zarahemla. With the old sophistries and falsehoods they raised a mutiny in the hearts of their associate Lamanites and urged them on to rebellion against the rightful king and his believing subjects. But the converted Lamanites made no preparations to resist them; **they felt that in times past with unholy hands they had spilt** blood as water on the land; blood that they could never atone for, but they would do it no more. Passive non-resistance should for the future be their policy, but the blood of a fellow-being they would never again shed, no matter how great the peril, how intense the aggravation. As a witness of the completeness of this resolve, they took their weapons of war and buried them deep in the earth with an oath and covenant that they would never dig them up again. When the maddened hosts of their embittered brethren rushed upon them, they came forth unarmed, bowed down before their assailants, and submitted to their fate. With them to live was Christ, to die was salvation. The vengeful Nephite apostates led the inglorious charge and shed most of the blood that flowed that day, when one thousand and five unresisting martyrs glorified the Lamanite race by the tribute of their lives to God and the truth. A thousand ransomed souls, washed white in the blood of the Lamb, that day entered the gates of heaven to stand amongst the saviors on Mount Zion in the great day of the redeemed. Nor was there joy alone in that bright world beyond, but on earth the church was gladdened by fresh accessions to the cause. When many of the actual Lamanites witnessed the great change that had taken place in their brethren, that they would quietly, peacefully joyously lay down their lives, their consciences smote them; they stayed their hands, and rose in tumult against their Amalekite leaders, and would no longer be the murderers of their kin. The blood of the martyrs was indeed the seed of the church, for there were more added to the fold of Christ on that memorable day than those who passed away to the presence of their God.

Foiled in their attempt to destroy the Anti-Nephi-Lehies (or Ammonites as we shall hereafter call them), the blood-thirsty Lamanites, led as usual by Nephite apostates, made a sudden incursion into the land of Zarahemla, and, in fulfillment of Alma's prophecies, destroyed the great city of Ammonihah, of which we shall say more hereafter, but met with most disastrous defeat later on in the campaign. Still vowing vengeance they returned to their own lands, and feeling that the Ammonites were in sympathy with the Nephites, they satisfied their hatred by again slaughtering many of these unresisting people, who, as before, permitted themselves to be slain, without making the first effort at defense. But Ammon and his brethren were not willing to have the disciples continually harassed and eventually exterminated; they judged that the Lord having so thoroughly tried the faith of this devoted people, would provide some way of escape.

Ammon counseled with the king and it was thought it would be better to forsake their all so far as wordly possessions were concerned, than to sacrifice their lives. But first let them inquire of the Lord. Ammon did so and the Lord said, Get this people out of this land, that they perish not, for Satan has great hold upon the hearts of the Amalekites who do stir up the Lamanites to anger against their brethren to slay them; therefore get thee out of this land; and blessed are the people of this generation for I will preserve them.

The word of the Lord thus received was joyfully obeyed. The Ammonites gathered up their flocks and their herds and departed into the wilderness that lay between the lands of Nephi and Zarahemla. There they rested whilst Ammon and his brethren went forward and treated with the Nephites in behalf of the persecuted hosts they had left behind. The people, by united voice, gladly welcomed their co-religionists and set apart the land of Jershon as their inheritance. Thither the Ammonites with happy feet repaired, and there they dwelt until the breaking out of war made it desirable that they should remove to the land of Melek, and many thousands in after years emigrated to the land north. Of their future history we shall speak, from time to time, when it connects with that of the Nephites.

CHAPTER XXII.

REVIEW OF THE MISSION OF THE SONS OF MOSIAH—ITS IMPORTANCE AND GREAT LENGTH—ITS RESULTS TO BOTH RACES—THE DATES OF ITS LEADING OCCURRENCES.

(ALMA CHAP. 17 TO 27.)

SO FAR as we can gather from the records, the great mission of Ammon and his brethren to the Lamanites was productive of results new to the history of the Nephites. On many previous occasions dissenters from the latter had gone over to the Lamanites, until that nation consisted of a mixed race. But the Nephite people appear to have been, almost without exception, the literal descendants of the first founders of the monarchy, Nephi, Sam, Jacob, Joseph and Zoram, and of the people of Zarahemla. But·now a large body of Lamanites was incorporated in the Nephite nation and became partakers of the liberties accorded to all other citizens. As the history of the two nations proceeds, the original distinctions of descent become less and less observable, as defections from both people were constantly occurring, so that in process of time a Nephite was not so much a literal descendant of Lehi's greatest son, as one who recognized the Nephite government, was an observer of the law of Moses and a believer in the gospel; while the Lamanite was he who dwelt in the dominions of that people, rejected the law and the gospel, and adopted the false traditions of that race.

The mission of Ammon and his brethren was not only important but it was of great length. They left Zarahemla in the first year of the Judges (B. C. 91) and returned in the fourteenth (B. C. 78). It seems altogether probable that the conversion of king Lamoni took place in the first year of their ministry, unless Ammon was detained in prison a lengthened period before he was brought before the king (for which suggestion we find no warrant), as it was only the third day of Ammon's service when his conflict occurred with the cattle thieves at the waters of Sebus. The conversion of Lamoni was the immediate result. Yet we judge that the establishment and organization of the church in the land of Ishmael was a work of considerable time. We are strengthened in this opinion by the account of the labors performed by Aaron and others during this same period.

In the fifth year of the Nephite Judges (B. C. 87) the Lamanites invaded Zarahemla and were disastrously defeated, about which time we suggest Aaron and his fellows were confined in prison in the land of Middoni, and the results of the war would measurably account for the great cruelty with which they were treated by the exasperated Lamanites, as well as for the ferocity of the old king when he found his son in the company of the hated Nephite. After the incidents of that eventful meeting the king was not in a frame of mind to go to war with the Nephites; the generous words and magnanimous conduct of Ammon had produced such a deep influence, that though not yet converted, his heart had experienced a great change. Probably a year or two passed before Aaron and his fellow-laborers brought him to a full knowledge of the true plan of redemption. For these reasons we consider the meeting of Lamoni and his father did not take place earlier than B. C. 87. The old king's conversion was followed by the issuance of his proclamation of protection and unqualified religious liberty to the Nephite missionaries and to all his subjects; of which proclamation Aaron and his co-laborers took the fullest benefit by preaching from city to city throughout the wide Lamanite territory, establishing churches and ordaining officers therein. This labor occupied some years. As the church grew the spirit of rebellion developed amongst the unconverted, until they declared open war against the king, and massacred their gospel-believing brethren.

Immediately after the massacre of the 1005 Anti-Nephi-Lehies the angry Lamanites broke out in war with the Nephites, under the idea that the latter were the cause of their internal troubles. They made a sudden incursion into the land of Zarahemla and destroyed the city of Ammonihah, which event took place in the eleventh year of the Judges (B. C. 81), and after that they had many battles with the Nephites, in which they were driven and slain. After their return from this inglorious campaign they wreaked their vengeance on their unoffending brethren, and again commenced to massacre them, which murders, we suggest, took place during the thirteenth year of the reign of the Judges (B. C. 79), as in the year following the whole of the believing Lamanites migrated to the land of Jershon, as before narrated (B. C. 78). These dates are simply suggestive as far as the history of the mission is concerned, but those that relate to the Nephites are distinctly stated in the annals of that people.

CHAPTER XXIII.

THE DAYS OF THE JUDGES—THEIR NAMES AND REIGNS—THE HERESY OF NEHOR—HE SLAYS GIDEON AND IS EXECUTED—AMLICI'S REBELLION—THE BATTLE OF AMNIHU—THE CONFLICT AT THE CROSSING OF THE SIDON—A THIRD BATTLE.

(ALMA CHAP. 1 TO 3.)

FOR a period of about one hundred and twenty years succeeding the death of king Mosiah, the Nephite commonwealth was governed by judges. These were chosen by the united voice of the people, as provided in the constitution framed under Divine inspiration by the last king, and acknowledged as the supreme law of the nation, through its unanimous acceptance as such, by the entire people. At the end of this period the republic was overthrown through the great wickedness of all classes of the community, and the people divided themselves into numerous independent tribes.

It is not actually certain that the Book of Mormon gives us the names of all the Nephite chief judges. In the earlier portion of the annals of these times the order of succession is plainly stated, but in the record of later years the name of the judge is sometimes only mentioned incidentally in the historic narrative. It is therefore beyond our power to determine if there were, or were not, others whose names have been omitted by the sacred historians. The judges mentioned by name or description are twelve in number. Of these, five, Pahoran II., Cezoram, Cezoram's son (whose name is not given), Seezoram and Lachoneus II., were assassinated; one, Pacumeni, was slain in battle with the Lamanites; two, Alma and Nephi, were translated or taken by the Lord;

three, Nephihah, Pahoran I., and Helaman, died a natural death, whilst of the manner of the decease of one, Lachoneus I., we have no record. They judged the Nephites in the following order: 1 Alma (the younger), from B. C. 91 to B. C. 83; 2 Nephihah, from B. C. 83 to B. C. 68; 3 Pahoran I., from B. C. 68 to B. C. 53; 4 Pahoran II., from B. C. 52 to B. C. 52; 5 Pacumeni, from B. C. 52 to B. C. 51; 6 Helaman (the younger), from B. C. 50 to B. C. 39; 7 Nephi, from B. C. 39 to B. C. 30; 8 Cecoram, from B. C. 30 to B. C. 26; 9 Cezoram's son, from B. C. 26 to B. C. 26; 10 Seezoram, B. C. — to B. C. 23, 11 Lachoneus I., from — to —; 12 Lachoneus II., from — to A. C. 30.

It is possible that some unnamed judge may have ruled the Nephites for a short time after the murder of Cezoram's son, and before Seezoram was chosen, and still more probable that one or more rulers presided over the destinies of the nation between the death of Seezoram and the election of Lachoneus I., as there was a space of fifty-three years between the murder of Seezoram and that of Lachoneus II., who succeeded his father. Alma, the son of Alma, was the first chief judge of the Nephite republic, having been called to that high position before the death of king Mosiah.

It was the first year of Alma's reign. Could our readers have taken a glimpse at the fair capital of the Nephites at that time (B. C. 91), already rich in the awards of human industry, combined with the lavish productions of nature in that much favored land, they might have noticed in the principal street, a portly, handsome man, manifesting in his carriage the evidence of great bodily strength, combined with vanity, self-sufficiency and subtlety. They might have observed that his raiment was made of the finest fabrics that the looms of Zarahemla could produce, lavishly embroidered and ornamented with labors of the cunning workman in silk, in feathers and the precious metals, whilst at his side hung a richly decorated sword. This man was no king, no governor, no general of the armies of Israel; he was simply Nehor, the successful religious charlatan of the hour, to whom the unstable listened and the weak-minded flocked. His teachings had at any rate the interest of novelty to the Nephites, yet some of his theories were older than Idumea. They had been rejected in the counsels of heaven before Lucifer, the son of the morning, fell. He would save all men in their sins and with their sins; he abolished hell, established a paid order of priests, and taught doctrines so liberal that every man could be a member of his church and yet continue to gratify every vice his nature inclined to. For this liberality of doctrine, Nehor expected in return liberality of support for himself and assistants, in which anticipation he was not disappointed. Many adopted his heresies; his success fired his zeal and developed his vanity. He was so used to the sycophancy of his converts that he was restive under contradiction, and when Gideon, the aged patriot, and teacher in the true church, one day met him in the streets of Zarahemla and upbraided him for his wicked course, neither respecting his great age nor his many virtues, Nehor drew his sword and smote him till he died. For this wilful and unprovoked crime, the murderer was tried, convicted, and afterward executed. His execution took place on the hill Manti, and, from the way in which his death is spoken of, we imagine that he was hanged.

Though Nehor's shameful life was thus ended, unfortunately his doctrine did not die with him. It was too pleasant to those who desired to gain heaven without a life of righteousness. Consequently it spread widely through the teachings of his followers. In later years the traitorous Amlicites, the apostate Amalekites, the blood-thirsty Amulonites and Ammonihahites, were all believers in his soul-destroying doctrines. The bloodshed, the misery produced, the treasure expended through the wickedness and folly of these base creatures, cannot be computed.

The increase of these false teachers among the Nephites rapidly developed class distinctions and social divisions; their adherents being generally gathered from amongst those who loved the vain things of the world. Naturally they became proud and overbearing, and bitter in their feelings towards the members of the true church of Christ. Many of the latter received severe persecution at the hands of the dissenters and bore it without retaliation, while others returned insult for insult and gave blow for blow.

The example of these self-appointed teachers produced a like spirit throughout their churches, and their members became idle and full of devices to enable them to live without honest toil. They gave way to sorcery and idolatry, to robbery and murder, and to all manner of wickedness, for which offenses they were duly punished according to the law, whenever conviction could be obtained, and when the intent of the law was not thwarted by their unholy combinations. This development of priestcraft also gave rise to another evil. Many belonging to the apostate churches, though not willing to openly plunder or murder for gain, were anxious for a monarchy to be established, that thereby they might be appointed office holders, etc., and fatten at the public crib. Their hope and intention was to destroy the church of God, and undoubtedly to despoil its members.

In the fifth year of the Judges, a willing instrument arose to effect their purpose. His name was Amlici, a follower of Nehor, corrupt and ambitious, but cunning in the wisdom of the world. He was chosen by the enemies of the commonwealth to be the king of the Nephites. The whole question was brought before the people at a general election, as provided by the code of Mosiah. The monarchists were outvoted; the republic and the church were saved.

This should have ended the matter, but it did not; the turbulent minority, incited by Amlici, would not accept this constitutional decision. They assembled and crowned their favorite as king of the Nephites, and he at once began to prepare for war, that he might force the rest of the people to accept his government. Nor was Alma idle; he also made ready for the impending contest. He gathered his people and armed them with all the weapons known to Nephite warfare. The two armies of those who so short a time before were brethren, met near a hill called Amnihu, on the east bank of the river Sidon. There a bloody battle followed, in which Amlici's forces were disastrously defeated with a loss of 12,532 men, whilst the victors had to mourn the loss of 6,562 warriors slain.

After pursuing the defeated monarchists as far as he was able, Alma rested his troops in the valley of Gideon (named after the martyr slain by Nehor). He there took the precaution to send out four officers with their companies to watch the movements and learn the intentions of the retreating foe. These officers were named Zeram, Amnor, Manti and Limher. On the morrow these scouts returned in great haste, and reported that the Amlicites had joined a vast host of Lamanites in the land Minon, where unitedly they were slaying the Nephite population and ravaging their possessions; at the same time they were pushing rapidly towards the Nephite capital with the intent of capturing it before Alma's army could return. Alma at once headed his troops for Zarahemla, and with all haste marched toward it. He reached the crossing of the Sidon without meeting the enemy, but while attempting to pass to the western bank he was confronted by the allied armies.

A terrible battle ensued; the Nephites were taken somewhat at a disadvantage, but being men of faith, they fervently sought Heaven's aid, and in the increased fervor this faith inspired, they hastened to the combat. With Alma at their

WILDERNESS OF HERMOUNTS.

head, the advanced guard forded the river and broke upon the enemy who stood awaiting them. By the impetuosity of their charge they drove in the ranks of the enemy, and as they pushed onward they cleared the ground by throwing the bodies of their fallen foes into the Sidon, thus making an opening for the main body to obtain a foothold. In this charge Alma met Amlici face to face, and they fought desperately. In the midst of this hand to hand combat, Alma lifted his heart on high, and prayed for renewed strength that he might not be overpowered, but live to do more good to his people. His prayers were answered, and thereby he gained new vigor to battle with and eventually slay Amlici. Amlici slain, Alma led the attack to where the king of the Lamanites fought. But that monarch retired before the impetuous valor of the high priest and commanded his guards to close in upon his assailant. The order was promptly obeyed, but it did not succeed. Alma and his guards bore down upon them with such fury that the few of the monarch's warriors who escaped made a hasty retreat. Pushing steadily on, Alma kept driving the allies before him, until his whole army had crossed the Sidon. There the enemy, no longer able to meet his well ordered advance, broke in all directions, and retreated into the wilderness that lay to the north and west. They were hotly pursued by the Nephites as long as the latter's strength permitted, and were met on all quarters by patriots rallying to the call of the commonwealth who slew them by thousands. A remnant eventually reached that part of the wilderness known as Hermounts. There many died and were devoured by the wild beasts and vultures with which that region abounded.

A few days after this decisive battle, another invading Lamanite army appeared. This one advanced along the east bank of the Sidon. Alma, having been wounded, sent one of his officers, who met the hosts of the Lamanites, and drove them back to their own lands.

CHAPTER XXIV.

ALMA RESIGNS THE CHIEF JUDGESHIP—NEPHIHAH CHOSEN—ALMA MINISTERS IN ZARAHEMLA, GIDEON, MELEK AND AMMONIHAH—CONDITION OF THE LAST NAMED CITY—IT REJECTS THE MESSAGE ALMA BEARS—AN ANGEL MEETS HIM—AMULEK—THE LAWYER ZEEZROM—THE GREAT CONTROVERSY—ZEEZROM CONVERTED AND CAST OUT—THE MARTYRDOM OF THE BELIEVERS—ALMA AND AMULEK IN PRISON—THEIR DELIVERANCE.

(ALMA CHAP. 4 TO 14.)

THE great losses sustained by the Nephites in this war, not of warriors alone, but of women and children, together with the vast amount of their property destroyed, had the effect of humbling them and softening their wayward hearts, so that many thousands, during the next few years, were added to the church by baptism. But the recollection of their former disasters was gradually worn away by time and prosperity. Three years later we find great inequality in the church—some poor and some rich, the more powerful abusing and oppressing their weaker brethren. This course proved a great stumbling-block to those who were not numbered with the church, as well as being the cause of much sorrow and ill-feeling amongst its members. Finding that no man could properly attend to the duties of his many offices, Alma determined to resign the chief judgeship, and devote his entire time to his duties as the earthly head of the church. Preparatory to this resignation, he selected one of the leading elders, named Nephihah, to be his successor as chief judge. This choice was confirmed by the people. (B. C. 83.)

Alma now gave his entire attention to the duties of his calling as a preacher of righteousness. He commenced his labors in Zarahemla. Thence he went to the city of Gideon. After ministering there for some time, he returned for rest to his home in the capital city.

The next year (B. C. 82), Alma turned his face westward. He visited the land of Melek, where his labors were crowned with abundant blessings. Having satisfied himself with the good that he had accomplished, he traveled three days' journey on the north of the land of Melek, to a great and corrupt city called Ammonihah. There he found a godless people, filled with the falsehoods of Nehor, who were committing all manner of abominations without repentance, because they cherished the flattering lie, as the foundation of their creed, that all men would be saved. This city was in the hands of a corrupt clique of judges and lawyers, who stirred up sedition, tumult and rioting, that they might make money out of the suits that followed such disturbances. Further than this, they were secretly plotting to overthrow the government, and rob the people of their highly prized liberties. Among such a people Alma labored in vain; none would listen, none would obey, none offered him rest and food. Scorn and mockery were his reward; and he was spat upon, maltreated and cast out of the city.

Weary in body and sick at heart because of the iniquity of the people, after many fruitless efforts, fervent prayers and long fastings, Alma sought some other people more worthy of salvation's priceless gifts. He bent his way toward the city of Aaron; but as he journeyed, an angel of the Lord (that same angel that beforetime had been the agent in his conversion to God) stood before him and blessed him. He told him to lift up his heart and rejoice, for because of his faithfulness he had great cause to do so. The angel then directed Alma to return to the sin-cursed city he had just left, and proclaim unto its citizens the awful message that except they repented the Lord would destroy them.

Without delay the prophet obeyed the angel's words. By another road he drew near the doomed city, which he entered by its south gate. As he passed in he hungered, and asked a man whom he met, Will ye give to an humble servant of God something to eat? With joy the man (and, strange though it appear, he was a rich man) took him to his home and fed, clothed and lodged him. Furthermore, Amulek, for such was his name, told Alma that he also had received a visit from a holy angel who had informed him of the high priest's coming, and directed him to receive him into his house. Then Alma blessed Amulek and all his household, and tarried with them and recruited his strength under the generous hospitality which their home afforded. But his rest was not to be a lengthened one; the people waxed stronger in sin; the cup of their iniquity was nearly full. Go, came the word of the Lord, Go forth, and take with thee my servant Amulek, and prophesy unto his people, saying, Repent ye, for thus saith the Lord, Except ye repent, I will visit this people in mine anger; yea, I will not turn my fierce anger away. Filled with the Holy Ghost, these servants of God went forth and valiantly delivered their terrible message. One of those who most bitterly opposed Alma and Amulek was a lawyer named Zeezrom. We find recorded at great length, in the Book of Mormon, the details of the controversy that occurred between him and the two servants of the Lord. As a result we have handed down to us some of the plainest teachings regarding the atonement, the resurrection, the powers of the priesthood, etc., that are had among mankind. No matter what Alma and his companion said, Zeezrom could twist it from its proper meaning; find blasphemy and heresy in the sublime truths of the gospel, and extract treason from the simplest of God's laws. He questioned and cross-questioned, he promised and threatened, he twisted and turned, he abused and vilified, but all to no purpose, he was caught in his own trap. His heaven-inspired opponents made manifest his thoughts and intentions, they exposed his lying, they overthrew his sophistries and, with a power more than human, they exhibited the blackness of his heart. As they proceeded the power of God increased upon them, their words grew yet more forcible until Zeezrom himself felt their power. As his corruptions were laid bare he began to tremble, first with rage, then with fear. Bad as he was, he was not the worst among his people, and when once he realized the power he was combating, his heart began to acknowledge its guilt.

With this feeling he commenced to inquire of Alma, not now in mockery, but in solemn earnestness, with regard to the kingdom of God. The answers he received were like a two-edged sword, piercing to his inmost soul, bringing to him a terrible sense of his awful position before God, and encompassing him about with the pains of hell. He realized that he had been a leader in iniquity, that his lyings and deceivings had greatly contributed to drag the people down to their existing corruption, and that he was among those most responsible for their hardness of heart.

In this frame of mind he made an effort to plead with the people; he acknowledged his guilt, testified to the virtue and integrity of Alma and Amulek and interceded in their behalf. But in vain. The degraded populace reviled him, they mocked at him, they said he also was possessed of a devil, and further, they spat on him; then they cast stones at him, and ultimately, with some others, drove him out of their city; while the two prophets, with many who believed in their holy message, were thrown into prison, there to suffer all the indignities, persecutions and annoyances that apostate hate could inflict. Nor was this the worst; these reprobates took the wives and babes of those believers whom they had driven away, with such as had accepted the truth who still remained in the city, and, gathering them in a body they mercilessly burned them to death in one great martyrs' fire. Into the torturing flames they also cast the records that contained the holy scriptures, as though they imagined, in their blind fury, that they could thereby destroy the truths that were so odious to them.

In their devilish glee and savage exultation they carried the two enchained prophets to the place of sacrifice, that they might harrow up their souls with a view of the sufferings of the perishing women and children. Amulek's brave and impetuous spirit could ill bear the fearful scene. The groans, the cries and supplications of the tortured innocents carried untold agony to his soul. He begged Alma to exercise the power of God that was in them to save the martyrs. But the Holy Spirit revealed to Alma that this sacrifice was by heaven's consent, and he replied, The Spirit constraineth me that I must not stretch forth mine hand, for behold the Lord receiveth them up unto himself in glory; and he doth suffer that the people may do this thing, according to the hardness of their hearts, that the judgments which he shall exercise upon them in his wrath may be just; and the blood of the innocent shall stand as a witness against them, yea, and cry mightily against them at the last day. Then Amulek said, Perhaps they will burn us also. To which Alma responded, Be it according to the will of the Lord. But, behold, our work is not finished; therefore they burn us not.

When the fire had burned low, and the precious fuel of human bodies and sacred records was consumed, the chief judge of the city came to the two prisoners as they stood bound, and mocked them. He smote them on the cheek, and jeeringly asked them if they would preach again that his people should be cast into a lake of fire and brimstone, seeing that they had no power to save those who had been burned, neither had God exercised his power in their behalf.

But neither answered him a word. Then he smote them again and remanded them to prison.

After they had been confined three days, they were visited by many judges and lawyers, priests and teachers, after the order of Nehor, who came to exult in the misery of their prisoners. They questioned and badgered them, but neither would reply. They came again the next day, and went through the same performance. They mocked at, smote and spat upon the two disciples. They tantalized them with blasphemous questions, such as the nature of their peculiar faith inspired. How shall we look when we are damned? sneeringly asked these unbelievers in damnation.

Patiently and silently all this was borne. Day after day was it repeated. Harder and harder grew the hearts of the Ammonihahites towards their prisoners. Fiercer and stronger grew their hatred. They stripped Alma and Amulek, and, when naked, bound them with strong ropes. They withheld food and drink from them, and in various ways they tortured their bodies, and sought to aggravate and tantalize them and harrow up their minds. On the 12th day of the tenth month of the tenth year of the Judges (B. C. 82), the chief judge with his followers again went to the prison. According to his usual custom he smote the brethren, saying as he did so, If ye have the power of God, deliver yourselves from these bonds, and then we will believe that the Lord will destroy this people according to your words. This impious challenge the crowd one by one repeated as they passed by the prophets, and smote them in imitation of their leader. Thus each individual assumed the responsibility of the defiance cast at the Almighty, and virtually said, Our blood be upon our own heads.

The hour of God's power had now come—the challenge had been accepted. The prophets, in the majesty of their calling, rose to their feet. They were endowed with the strength of Jehovah. Like burnt thread the cords that bound them were snapped asunder and they stood free and unshackled before the terror-stricken crowd. To rush from the prison was the first impulse of the God-defying followers of Nehor. In their fear some fell to the earth, others, impelled by the crowd behind stumbled and fell over the prostrate bodies, until they became one confused mass, blocking each other's way; struggling, yelling, cursing, pleading, fighting; frantically, but vainly, endeavoring to reach the outer gate.

At this moment of supreme horror an earthquake rent the prison walls. They trembled, then tottered, then fell on the struggling mass of humanity below, burying in one vast, unconsecrated grave, rulers and judges, lawyers and officers, priests and teachers. Not one was left alive of all the impious mob who a few moments before defied heaven and challenged Jehovah's might. But Alma and Amulek stood in the midst of the ruins unhurt. Straightway they left this scene of desolation and went into the city. When the citizens saw the two servants of God, great fear fell upon them, and they fled, as a goat fleeth with her young from two lions.

Alma and Amulek were then ordered to leave the city. This they did, and went to the neighboring town of Sidom. There they found those who had been cast out of Ammonihah, and in grief and sorrow they related the story of the burning of the wives and children of the fugitives, and also the history of their own miraculous deliverance.

CHAPTER XXV.

ZEEZROM SICK WITH FEVER—HIS MIRACULOUS RECOVERY—THE DESTRUCTION OF AMMONIHAH—THE INVASION OF THE LAND OF NOAH—ZORAM, THE NEPHITE COMMANDER, SEEKS THE MIND OF THE LORD—IT IS GIVEN—ITS RESULTS—THE WAR ENDED—ALMA'S MINISTRATIONS.

(ALMA CHAP. 15 AND 16.)

WHILE the fearful tragedy that we have just related was being enacted in Ammonihah, Zeezrom—trembling, heart-sick and faint—wandered with the others to Sidom. The horrors of the damned took hold of him, until his body succumbed to the agony of his mind. He was scorched with a burning fever, which continually increased until the glad tidings reached his ears that Alma and Amulek were safe; for he had feared that through his iniquities they had been slain. No sooner did they reach Sidom than he sent for them, as his heart then began to take courage. They did not hesitate, but at once proceeded to where he lay. When they entered his presence, he stretched forth his hands and besought them to heal him. Alma questioned him regarding his faith in Christ, and finding that the good seed planted in his bosom had brought forth fruit, this mighty high priest cried unto the Lord, O Lord our God, have mercy on this man, and heal him according to his faith which is in Christ. When Alma had said these words, Zeezrom leaped upon his feet and walked, to the great astonishment of all who witnessed it. Alma then baptized the repentant lawyer, who began from that time forth to preach the glorious message of eternal salvation. His energy, wisdom, learning and talents were now used towards the upbuilding of the kingdom of God, with as much zeal as he had before labored for corruptible riches and worldly fame; for Zeezrom was a whole-souled, courageous man, he did nothing by halves—when he served the devil, he was a profitable servant; when he turned to God, he did it with all his heart. From this time Zeezrom became a preacher of righteousness, laboring under the direction of Alma, and we next hear of him ministering with Amulek to the people in the land of Melek.

Next year Ammonihah was destroyed. Less than four months had elapsed since the two inspired followers of the Lamb had left it to its fate, when the Lamanites fell upon it like a whirlwind in its suddenness, and as an avalanche in its utter desolation. The dark skinned warriors of Laman swept over these murderers of the saints like a tempest of fire, leaving neither young nor old, babe nor grandsire, to repeat the story of their woes. Not one of Ammonihah's boasting children was left to defy heaven.

Nor was the city spared; it, also, was given to the destroyer, and its palaces and temples, its homes and its workshops, were consumed by the devouring fire. For one day the fierce flames consumed the walls and towers of Ammonihah. Their light illumined the lurid sky, shone on the distant mountain tops, and lit the neighboring valleys. Then an uninhabitable desolation, stinking with the rotting carcasses of man and beast, only remained to mark the place where Ammonihah once stood. As the Desolation of Nehors, it was known and avoided by the Nephites for many succeeding years.

Emboldened by this signal triumph, the Lamanites entered the borders of the neighboring land of Noah. There they continued their depredations, carrying off many Nephite captives into the wilderness. At this juncture the Nephite general Zoram, with his two sons (Lehi and Aha), rallied his forces, in the hope of intercepting the Lamanite armies in their return to the land of Nephi, and of delivering the captives.

Before starting on their march Zoram determined to inquire of the Lord. He and his sons knew that Alma was a prophet and revelator to the nation. Wisely they went first to him and inquired if it was the Lord's will that they should advance into the wilderness in search of their captive brethren.

Alma laid the matter before the Lord. The Divine answer came: Behold the Lamanites will cross the river Sidon in the south wilderness, away up beyond the borders of the land of Manti. And behold there shall ye meet them, on the east of the river Sidon, and there the Lord will deliver unto thee thy brethren who have been taken captive by the Lamanites.

Obedient to these plain instructions, Zoram and his sons crossed over the river Sidon with their armies, and marched southward beyond the borders of the land of Manti, into that portion of the great southern wilderness which lay east of the river Sidon. There they came upon the enemy, as the word of the Lord had declared, and there they joined in battle. The Lamanites were defeated, scattered and driven into the wilderness, and the Nephite captives were delivered. Great was the joy in the land of Zarahemla when it was found that not one Nephite had been lost of all those taken prisoners; but every one, great and small, had escaped the horrors of slavery in the hands of the Lamanites, and they all returned in peace to possess their own lands. Here we have a most happy result of seeking the word of the Lord and then faithfully carrying out his instructions.

Again there was peace throughout the land, and the name of Zoram is no more mentioned in the sacred record.

During this period of peace, Alma and his fellow-priesthood preached God's holy word in the power and demonstration of the Spirit, and with much success. Great prosperity came to the church throughout all the lands of the Nephites. At this happy time there was no inequality among them; the Lord poured out his Spirit on all the face of the land, as Alma supposed to prepare the hearts of his people for the coming of Christ. Like many others of the ancient prophets, he antedated that glorious appearing. He little knew of the wars and contentions, the apostasies and dissensions, the spiritual tribulation and material commotion that would precede that blessed day. But with this prospect full in view, he labored and rejoiced, preached, blessed and prophesied, never tiring in his energies, and feeling sorrowful only because of the hard-heartedness and spiritual blindness of some of the people.

In one most glorious event, Alma had unspeakable joy. His youthful companions, the sons of king Mosiah, returned from their fourteen years' mission amongst the Lamanites, during which time, after sore trials and great tribulation, they, by the grace of the Father, had brought many thousands of that benighted race to a knowledge of the principles of the everlasting gospel.

Alma was traveling south on one of his missionary journeys from the land of Zarahemla to the land of Manti, when he met Ammon and his brethren coming from the land of Nephi. On hearing the story of the mission, he at once returned with them to Zarahemla. There the condition of affairs amongst the Lamanites was rehearsed to the chief judge, who laid the whole subject before the people, so that whatever was done in relation to the Christian Lamanites might be done by common consent. The Nephites decided to give the land of Jershon to these people for an inheritance. With this cheering news Ammon, accompanied by Alma, returned into the southern wilderness, to the place where his people were awaiting the decision of the Nephites. There the Ammonites were ministered to and comforted by Alma and others, after which they resumed their march to the land set apart for their future abode. There, however, we shall find, as we proceed with our story, they remained but a few years.

CHAPTER XXVI.

KORIHOR THE ANTI-CHRIST—HIS FALSE TEACHINGS AND BLASPHEMY—HE IS TAKEN BEFORE ALMA—IS STRUCK DUMB—HIS MISERABLE END—THE HERESY ROOTED OUT.

(ALMA CHAP. 30.)

THE NEXT notable event in the history of the Nephites was the appearance of Korihor, the anti-Christ. (B. C. 75.)

The doctrines advocated by Korihor were of a kind that would gain ready adhesion from those who did not fervently love purity, truth and righteousness, as they flattered their vanity and gave them liberty to follow the lead of their passions without fear of the judgment or condemnation of a Divine Being. Spiritually he was a Nihilist. He denied the coming of the Messiah, he ridiculed prophecy and revelation, and asserted that it was impossible for men to know the future. He inveighed against the atonement of the Redeemer as a foolish superstition, and taught, instead of the unchanging truths of the everlasting gospel, the theory that every man fared in this life according to the management of the creature, prospered according to his genius, and conquered according to his strength. Further, he announced that whatsoever a man did was no crime, for that when a man was dead, there was an end thereof.

It is almost needless to say that those who accepted such

dogmas gave way to all manner of evil doing. They became overbearing to others, exceedingly keen in business transactions, were full of covetousness, duplicity, and lasciviousness, and indulged in various wanton pleasures. Their motto might be said to have been, Let us eat, drink and be merry, for tomorrow we die; and what we do here will not be brought against us hereafter.

Korihor also gained a strong hold among the discontented, for such are ever found where universal perfection does not dwell. He railed at the holy priesthood with fierce words of falsehood. He charged that they sought to keep the people down, that they encouraged ignorance in the masses, that they bound their minds with foolish traditions; all this, and much more, that they might usurp power and authority, and glut themselves with the results of their victims' daily toil.

In Alma's answer to this charge we have a pleasing insight into his private life. He said: Thou knowest that we do not glut ourselves upon the labors of this people, for behold, I have labored even from the commencement of the reign of the Judges until now, with mine own hands, for my support, notwithstanding my many travels round about the land to declare the word of God unto my people; and notwithstanding the many labors I have performed in the church, I have not so much as received even one senine for my labor; neither has any of my brethren, save it were in the judgment seat, and then we have received only according to law for our time.

As a propagandist, Korihor, for a short time, was a success. We first hear of him preaching his satanic doctrines in the land of Zarahemla, and as he claimed to fully believe all he taught, the law could not touch him, as full religious liberty was guaranteed under the constitution and laws of the Nephite commonwealth. From Zarahemla he went to the land of Jershon to inoculate the Ammonites with his soul-destroying vagaries. But they were a wiser and more zealous people for the gospel than were many of the Nephites. They took him, bound him, and carried him before Ammon (son of king Mosiah), their high priest. He directed that Korihor should be removed beyond the border of their land, which command having been obeyed, we next find the unabashed impostor laboring amongst the people of the land of Gideon. There he also met with rebuffs. He was arrested by the people and taken before the chief officers in that land. They found they could do nothing that would be satisfactory with him, so they remanded him into the custody of the proper officers, with instructions to carry him before Alma and Nephihah, in Zarahemla.

When brought before these worthies—the highest dignitaries of the church and state—Korihor continued in his course of loud-mouthed blasphemy, defiant assumption, and wilful falsehood.

He argued against the existence of the Father and the coming of his Only Begotten. Alma accused him of arguing against his convictions, but this he stoutly denied, and clamored for a sign to be given, as he pretended, that he might be convinced. Alma at length, wearied by his impious importunities, told him that God, as a sign, would smite him dumb. This terrible warning, though it caused the pretender some uneasiness, only resulted in an attempt at prevarication on his part. He said: I do not deny the existence of a God, but I do not believe there is a God; and I say also, that ye do not know that there is a God; and except ye show me a sign I will not believe. Then Alma answered: This will I give unto thee for a sign, that thou shalt be struck dumb according to my words; and I say that, in the name of God, ye shall be struck dumb, that ye shall no more have utterance.

Korihor received his sign; Alma's words were fulfilled; the sign-seeker never more spoke on earth. When the hand of the Lord fell upon him he recanted. By writing, as he could not speak, he confessed the power of God, and acknowledged that he had been led astray by Satan, who had come to him in the form of an angel of light. He begged that the curse might be removed, but Alma, well knowing the baseness of his heart, refused to intercede before heaven in his behalf lest when restored to speech he would again strive to deceive the people.

And it came to pass that the curse was not taken off Korihor; but he was cast out and went about from house to house begging for his food.

A proclamation was next sent throughout all the land. In it the chief judge recited what had happened to Korihor, and called upon those who had believed in his words to speedily repent, lest the same judgments should come upon them.

This proclamation put an end to the iniquity of Korihor, for his followers were all brought back again to the truth. But Korihor, deserted by the devil, a vagabond and a beggar, still continued to beg his way from town to town, from house to house; until, one day, in a city of the Zoramites, he was run over and trodden down. The injuries that he received at this time were so great that he soon after died.

CHAPTER XXVII.

ZORAM AND THE ZORAMITES—THEIR PECULIAR HERESY—THE LAND OF ANTIONUM—THE RAMEUMPTOM—ALMA'S MISSION TO THESE PEOPLE—THOSE WHO RECEIVE HIS TEACHINGS PERSECUTED—THEY FLEE TO JERSHON.

(ALMA CHAP. 31 TO 35.)

IN OUR last chapter we stated that Korihor, the anti-Christ was killed in a city of the Zoramites. Who was Zoram? and who were the Zoramites? are the questions that now present themselves.

There are two distinct classes of people called Zoramites in the Book of Mormon. The first, the descendants of Zoram, the servant of Laban, who accompanied Nephi from Jerusalem. The second were the followers of the apostate Zoram, whose defection and treason caused so much trouble and bloodshed in the Nephite republic.

Of the last named Zoram and his individual life we have no history. We only know him through his pernicious teachings, and the sad results thereof. But it is altogether probable that before he started out as a religious reformer on his own account, he was a follower of Nehor, as the majority of his adherents appear to have been gathered from that sect and to have belonged to that order.

Zoram assembled his people in a region of the South American continent, at that time but very thinly settled by the Nephites. It was called the land of Antionum, and lay to the east of the river Sidon, while it stretched from the land of Jershon in the north, to the great wilderness south, which was infested with the more savage, wandering Lamanites. To this broad land the Zoramites gathered, and there built their cities, erected their synagogues, and grew in material wealth; until, in the year B. C. 75, they had become an important, though undesirable portion of the Nephite commonwealth. As friends they were unreliable, as enemies formidable.

In the various apostasies, partial or total, that from time to time disgraced the Nephites, there is one characteristic feature that seems universal to them all, however much they may have differed on minor points. It was the denial of the coming of the Savior in the flesh, and of the necessity of His atonement for the sins of the world. This was the evil one's strong point in his efforts to mislead the ancient Nephites. Let him but persuade any people to reject this, the foundation of the gospel scheme, and little he cares what else they believe or disbelieve; for when this fundamental truth is rejected their spiritual enslavement is secured.

This was the case with the Zoramites. They claimed to be a chosen and a holy people, separate from their fellow-men, and elected of God to eternal salvation, while all around were predestined to be cast down to hell. This atrocious creed naturally resulted in its adherents and advocates being puffed up in vanity and consumed with pride. They became haughty, uncharitable and tyrannical, and oppressors of their poorer neighbors. They covered their bodies with the finest apparel, and profusely adorned their persons with costly ornaments of gold and jewels. In their arrogance and self-righteousness they became the Pharisees of their age and country; but in other phases of iniquity they far exceeded their counterparts in the Holy Land. They bowed down to idols, denied the coming of Christ, declared the doctrine of the atonement to be a foolish tradition, and, like many of the sects of modern Christendom, they misinterpreted the teachings of holy scripture with regard to the being of God. Their declaration of faith was: Holy, holy God; we believe that thou art God, and we believe that thou art holy, and that thou wast a spirit, and that thou art a spirit, and that thou wilt be a spirit forever.

This strange medley of ideas gave birth to corresponding vagaries of worship. They left off praying. Being chosen and elected to be God's holy children, they had no need of prayer. Once a week they assembled in their synagogues and went through an empty form, which was a little prayer, a little praise and considerable self-glorification. Having done this, they never mentioned God or holy things again throughout the week; indeed, it was a portion of their creed that their synagogues were the only places in which it was lawful to talk or think of religious matters.

Their ceremonies were as absurd as their creed. In the centre of each of their synagogues was erected a holy stand, or pulpit, called rameumptom, which stood high above the congregation. From the slight description given of it in the book of Alma we judge it may have been somewhat pyramidical in form, the top being only large enough for one person to stand upon. Each worshiper mounted to the top, stretched out his hands toward heaven, and, in a loud voice, repeated their set form of worship. Having done this, he descended and another took his place, and so on, until all who desired to go through the mummery had satisfied their conscience or gratified their pride.

The tidings of this defection having reached Alma, he selected several of the leading members of the priesthood, and, as soon as possible, proceeded to the land of Antionum. Those who accompanied him were his two younger sons, three of the sons of king Mosiah, Amulek and Zeezrom. To his anxiety to bring these dissenters back from the error of their ways and to avert heaven's righteous wrath from falling upon them, was added the fear that if they remained in their wickedness they would join the Lamanites and bring trouble upon the more faithful Nephites by urging the renewal of war.

On the arrival of Alma and his fellow-laborers at the seat of this apostasy, they at once commenced their ministrations. They taught in the synagogues and preached in the streets. They visited the people from house to house, using every possible effort to bring these misguided dissenters to an understanding of their perilous condition. To these labors we are indebted for some of the plainest and most powerful gospel teachings contained in the Book of Mormon, all of which will well repay our perusal. Suffice it to say, that many of the poor and humble, those who were oppressed, abused and trodden down by their false priests and unrighteous rulers, as well as by the wealthier portion of the community, received the words of salvation, while the majority rejected them with contemptuous scorn. Some of the missionaries were maltreated. Shiblon, the son of Alma, was imprisoned and stoned for the truth's sake, while others fared but little better. Unfortunately the work of God was retarded by the misconduct of Corianton, the brother of Shiblon, who, for a time, deserted his ministerial duties for the company of a harlot. This folly caused Alma great sorrow, as it gave the ungodly a pretext for rejecting the gospel, of which they were not slow to avail themselves.

When Alma and his associates had done all the good they deemed possible, they withdrew to the neighboring land of Jershon. No sooner had they left than the more crafty of the Zoramites devised a plan to discover the feelings of the community. They gathered the people together throughout the land and consulted with them concerning that which they had heard. In this way they discovered who favored the truth and who rejected it. Finding that the poor and uninfluential were those who had received it, they resorted to persecution and plunder. They drove the believers from their homes and out of the land. Most of these fled to the land of Jershon, whither the priesthood had preceded them.

The land of Jershon was inhabited by the people of

Ammon. They also had left home and country for the truth's sake, and now that others were suffering from the same cause, they received them with open arms. They fed and clothed those who needed such help, and gave them lands whereon they might build up new homes.

When the wicked Zoramites heard of the kind reception their injured fellow-citizens had received in Jershon they were greatly angered. They were not content to spoil them themselves, but they wanted to make them fugitives and vagabonds on the face of the whole earth. Their leader, a very wicked man, sent messages to the Ammonites, desiring them to expel the refugees, adding many threats of what would follow, should his cruel demand not be complied with. But the Ammonites were a brave people; they had already suffered unto death for the cause of God; and they were not of the stamp to desert their afflicted brethren. Rather than do so, they would again forsake their homes and find in some other region a land of peace: for we must remind our readers that the Ammonites had entered into covenant with God never again to bend the bow or draw the sword to take human life. They, therefore, withdrew to the land of Melek, and the armies of the Nephites occupied the land of Jershon.

CHAPTER XXVIII.

ANOTHER WAR—MORONI, THE LEADER OF THE NEPHITES—THE TACTICS OF THE LAMANITES—ZERAHEMNAH—THE BATTLE AT RIPLAH—DEFEAT OF THE LAMANITES.

(ALMA CHAP. 43 AND 44.)

THE cause which led the Nephite armies to occupy Jershon was that the Zoramites, finding that their haughty and unjust demands would not be complied with, had excited the Lamanites to invade the territory of the Nephites. The Lamanite forces which were commanded almost entirely by Nephite apostates, on account of their fierce hatred to their former associates, marched first into the land of Antionum, where they were joined by the Zoramites. Then the whole of the invading hosts, under the command of a dissenter named Zerahemnah, advanced northward towards the land of Jershon.

This was a day of peril for the Nephites. Their enemies were much more numerous than they, and were filled with a savage thirst for blood, which was especially felt against those who were of their own race and kindred who had bowed in obedience to Heaven's commands. At this juncture the Lord raised up one of the greatest heroes ever born on American soil. He was not only a military leader, but a priest and prophet, and by his inspiration and devoted courage the Nephites were for many years led to uninterrupted victory. Such was Moroni, who now, though but twenty-five years old, took the chief command of the armies of his nation.

Though the forces of the Lamanites were much more numerous, all other advantages were on the side of their foes.

The discipline of the Nephites was better by far; the bodies of their soldiers were protected by armor, breastplates, helmets, shields, etc., and they were fighting for the sacred cause of their religion and their country, their altars and their firesides, their wives and their little ones. Inspired by the justness of their cause and the extremity of their circumstances, they fought with a courage and a desperation never exceeded in their annals.

The Lamanites, on the other hand, had no such holy impulses to nerve their arms for the combat. They were the aggressors, and were hasting to shed the blood of their brethren. Insane and infernal hatred alone inspired them for the warfare. Besides, they were ill-prepared to meet the Nephites, who had such a tactician as Moroni for their commander-in-chief. The descendants of Laman were simply armed with swords and cimeters, bows and arrows, slings and stones. Their bodies were naked with the exception of a skin wrapped about their loins. The Zoramites and other dissenters from the Nephites were better clothed; in dress they followed the fashion of the people from whom they sprang.

The Lamanites, finding that Moroni was too well prepared for their attack on the land of Jershon, retired through Antionum into the wilderness, where they changed direction and marched towards the headwaters of the river Sidon, with the intention of taking possession of the land of Manti. But Moroni was too vigilant to allow his enemies to slip away without knowing what had become of them. He had his spies watch the movements of Zerahemnah's forces, and in the meanwhile sent to Alma to inquire the mind and will of the Lord with regard to his future course. The word of the Lord was given to Alma, and he informed Moroni's messengers of the movements of the Lamanites. The young general, with becoming prudence, then divided his army. One corps he left to protect Jershon, and with the remainder he advanced by rapid marches toward Manti, by the most direct route. On his arrival he at once mustered all the men who could bear arms into his forces, to help in the defense of their rights and their liberties against the advancing foe. So rapid had been his movements and so prompt had been the response to his calls that when the Lamanites reached the neighborhood of the Sidon he was prepared for their coming.

The battle that was fought when the opposing armies met was one of the most stubborn and bloody in Nephite history. Never from the beginning had the Lamanites been known to fight with such exceeding great strength and courage. Time after time their hosts rushed upon the well-ordered ranks of the Nephites, and notwithstanding the latter's armor they crushed in their heads and cut off their arms. But the cost of these charges to their own numbers was terrible. The battle began at a hill called Riplah, and afterwards extended to both banks of the Sidon. At one time a lull took place in the carnage, and Moroni, who had no pleasure in the shedding of blood, made an offer of such terms of surrender as he considered the circumstances warranted. But Zerahemnah and other captains of the Lamanite hosts rejected the offer and urged their troops to renewed resistance. So the battle recommenced with unabated ferocity. At last the faith and valor of the Nephites prevailed; many of the Lamanites surrendered and agreed to a covenant of peace. Even Zerahemnah himself, wounded and scalped by one of Moroni's body guard, to prevent the total annihilation of his armies, at last consented to the proposed terms and entered into the required covenant of peace. So great were the losses on both sides, especially of the Lamanites, that the dead were not numbered.

Thus ended the war, but not the Zoramite heresy, for we read, in the history of later wars between the two nations, of certain Lamanite captains being of the Zoramites. Foiled in their attempts to destroy their former brethren and to overthrow the church of God, they still adhered to their false faith, and on every possible occasion made manifest their undying hatred to those whose only offense was that they would not join them in their crimes nor consent to the destruction of the liberties of the people.

CHAPTER XXIX.

ALMA'S CHARGE TO HIS SONS—HE TRANSFERS THE RECORDS TO HELAMAN—HE LEAVES THIS WORLD—ZEEZROM'S LATTER DAYS—HELAMAN'S MINISTRATIONS.

(ALMA CHAP. 36 TO 42, 45.)

ALMA was now growing old. Notwithstanding his unceasing efforts and fervent prayers, the Nephites were again backsliding into inquity. To every Nephite city, and to every Nephite land he went or sent, to revive the gospel fires in the souls of the inhabitants. But many became offended because of the strictness of the gospel's laws, which forbade not only sin itself, but the very appearance of sin. As this feeling grew, Alma's heart became exceedingly sorrowful and he mourned the depravity of his people.

Like many of the ancient patriarchs, when they felt that their mortal career was drawing to its close, he called his sons to him, and gave them his last charge and blessing, speaking to each as the spirit of instruction and prophecy inspired. To Helaman, his eldest, he transferred the custody of the sacred plates, with many words of warning and caution regarding them. With hearts strengthened and renewed by the inspiration of his fervent admonitions, his sons went forth among the people; nor could Alma himself rest while there was a soul to save or a wrong to make right. He also went forth once again in the spirit of his holy calling, and raised his voice in advocacy of the principles of the everlasting gospel.

It was in the nineteenth year of the Judges (B. C. 73), that Alma took his beloved son, Helaman, and after having discovered, through divers questions, the strength and integrity of his faith, he prophesied to him of many important events in the distant future, especially with regard to the destruction of the Nephites. This prophecy he commanded him to record on the plates, but not to reveal to anyone. Alma then blessed Helaman, also his other sons; indeed he blessed all who should stand firm in the truth of Christ from that time forth. Shortly after this he departed out of the land of Zarahemla, as if to go to the land of Melek, and was never heard of more. Of his death and burial no men were witnesses. Then the saying went abroad throughout the church that the Lord had taken him, as he beforetime had taken Moses. This event occurred exactly one hundred years from the time of the elder Alma's birth.

After the departure of Alma we learn no more of the life of his associate Zeezrom, though his name and teachings are more than once referred to by later servants of God. We also read of a city of Zeezrom, and, as it was the custom of the Nephites to name their cities, towns and villages after whoever founded them, it is highly probable that, in the colonization of the country so vigorously carried on in the age that these men lived, he commenced the building of this place, and it would not be unreasonable to believe that he dwelt in the midst of its citizens as their high priest or chief judge.

Alma's son Helaman appears to have succeeded him as the presiding High Priest. After Alma's departure from this earth Helaman and others went through the cities of the Nephites and regulated the affairs of the church. Owing to the pride of many who would not give heed to the instructions given them, nor walk uprightly, dissensions arose, which in after years led to numerous evils, among the greatest of which was a long continued war, or series of wars, between the faithful Nephites on one side, and the apostates, and afterwards the Lamanites on the other. Still, for four years, Helaman and his associate priesthood were enabled to maintain order in the church. Many died in full faith of the gospel and in joyous hope of its never-ending rewards; indeed, during that period there was much peace and great prosperity enjoyed by those who remained faithful.

CHAPTER XXX.

AMALICKIAH—HIS APOSTASY AND TREASON—MORONI'S TITLE OF LIBERTY—THE NEPHITES RESPOND TO HIS CALL—LEHONTI—HE IS POISONED BY AMALICKIAH—THE KING OF THE LAMANITES TREACHEROUSLY SLAIN—AMALICKIAH MARRIES THE QUEEN AND IS PROCLAIMED KING—A DISASTROUS LAMANITE RAID.

(ALMA CHAP. 46 AND 50.)

PEACE, however, was but short lived. Internal dissensions created by the intrigues of apostates and royalists convulsed the Nephite community. The rebels were led by a descendant of Zoram, the servant of Laban, named Amalickiah, one of the most ambitious, cunning and unscrupulous characters that ever disgraced the history of ancient America. It was a perilous day for the Nephite nation when this subtle creature bent all his brilliant energies to the fulfillment of his ambitious dreams. True, he had been a member of Christ's holy church, but now the love of God had given place to the hatred of his servants; he was the citizen of a republic, but he aspired to overthrow its liberties, and reign as king over his fellow-citizens. Indeed he had cherished thoughts of still greater power, even to be monarch of the entire continent; both Nephite and Lamanite should bow to his undisputed sway. Such were his nightly dreams, and the continual thoughts of his waking hours, and to this end he bent all the energies of his mind, all the craft of his soul, all the cunning of his tongue, all the weight of his influence. With promises rich as the gold of Ophir and numerous as the snowflakes in a winter's hurricane, he beguiled his weaker fellows; men who, like him, loved power, hated the truth, delighted in iniquity, but who had not the lofty ambition, the unhallowed valor, and the deep designing cunning that distinguished their leader. To his call the dissatisfied, the corrupt and the apostate rallied.

Opposed to him stood Moroni, the dauntless leader of the armies of the Nephites. Inspired by an unquenchable love for truth and liberty, he sensed with every heart's pulsation that no man could fight for a holier, more glorious cause than virtue and liberty. Thus inspired, he tore a portion of his robe from it surrounding parts, and inscribing thereon his battle cry, he lifted it high upon a pole. Then girding on his armor, incasing his head with its fit covering, shielding his body with its breastplates, placing the proper pieces round his thighs and loins, he kneeled in humble, heartfelt prayer before Jehovah, presented his "Title of Liberty" before him and asked his blessing, protection, guidance and victorious aid in the coming struggle. Then he gathered the hosts of the Nephites; from place to place he sped, waving in the air the ensign on which all could read the burning words he had inscribed: In memory of our God, our religion and freedom, and our peace, our wives and our children.

MORONI RAISES THE "TITLE OF LIBERTY."

Nor did he cry in vain; the patriot Nephites, the members of the church of Christ, hastened with ready feet to the response. The streets of Zarahemla were alive with the gathering hosts. Each warrior, to show his devotion to the liberties with which God had endowed them, and his fealty to the Great Giver, rent his robe, as the young general had done, and thereby made covenant with God and his brethren to be faithful and true, in life and in death, in the council chamber and on the battle field, while an enemy remained to menace their liberties, national or religious.

Nor was Zarahemla alone in the manifestation of her patriotic love. Moroni's stirring appeal was spread far and wide throughout the lands of the Nephites. Swift-footed, banner-bearing messengers hastened down the Sidon's banks to the dwellers in the north, arousing the patriots of each peaceful city to the peril of the hour. Onward they hurried until Desolation echoed back to Bountiful the battle cry of liberty. Others gave no rest to the soles of their feet until Mulek, and her sister cities that lined the Caribbean Sea had flung from their tower tops the hallowed banner. Through the narrow defiles and rocky canyons that lay between the Andes' lofty peaks, other couriers pushed their unwearied way into the western wilderness and hence to the Pacific's strand, until every city held by Nephites had gathered her sons to the defense of their rights and their liberties, their altars and their firesides. Nor were Manti and the other cities of the south forgotten; the faithful and the brave who lined the borders of the great southern wilderness heard the rallying cry. From every city, every vale, the converging hosts poured forth with sword and spear, with bow and arrow, with slings and stones; while from the top of every tower and citadel throughout the Nephites' land, the sacred standard fluttered in the breeze. Men of strong arms and stout hearts were they, of faith unfaltering, and courage undiminished.

No wonder, then, that when Amalickiah's emissaries brought the evil-boding news of this great awakening to his unwilling ears that he faltered in his purpose, that his followers lost heart, that retreat was deemed the fittest show of wisdom, and discretion the better part of valor. No wonder that when, by Moroni's vigilance, that retreat was cut off, that the rebels succumbed and surrendered, that Amalickiah fled for safety to the Lamanites, and that the "Title of Liberty" continued to float uninterruptedly from the Atlantic to the Pacific coast, as far as Nephi's children ruled or Nephite homes were found, and that Moroni and his people rejoiced with intensified joy in their liberties, now more than ever dear to them through the valorous efforts they had put forth for their preservation.

When Amalickiah fled to the court of the king of the Lamanites he evolved a plot worthy of a demon, which only ceased with life. He was a Napoleon in ambition and diplomacy, and possibly also in military skill. On the first favorable opportunity after reaching the Lamanite court, he commenced to rekindle the fires of hatred toward his former friends. At first he was unsuccessful, the recollection of their late defeats was too fresh in the memory of the multitude. The king issued a war proclamation, but it was disregarded. Much as his subjects feared the imperial power, they dreaded a renewal of war more. Many gathered to resist the royal mandate. The king, unused to such objections, raised an army to quell the advocates of peace, and placed it under the command of the now zealous Amalickiah.

The peace-men had chosen an officer named Lehonti for their king and leader, and he had assembled his followers at a mountain called Antipas. Thither Amalickiah marched, but with no intention of provoking a conflict; he was working for the good feelings of the entire Lamanite people. On his arrival he entered into a secret correspondence with Lehonti, in which he agreed to surrender his forces on condition that he should be appointed second in command of the united armies. The plan succeeded. Amalickiah surrendered to Lehonti and assumed the second position. Lehonti now stood in the way of his ambition; it was but a little thing to remove him: he died by slow poison administered by Amalickiah's command.

Amalickiah now assumed supreme command, and at the head of his forces he marched towards the Lamanite capital. The king, supposing that the approaching hosts had been raised to carry the war into Zarahemla, came out of the royal city to greet and congratulate him. As the monarch drew near he was traitorously slain by some of the creatures of the subtle general, who at the same time raised the hue and cry that the king's own servants were the authors of the vile deed. Amalickiah assumed all the airs of grief, affection and righteous indignation that he thought would best suit his purpose. He next made apparently desperate, but purposely ineffectual, efforts to capture those who were charged with the crime, and so adroitly did he carry out his schemes, that before long he wheedled himself into the affections of the queen, whom he married, and he was recognised by the Lamanites as their king. Thus far his ambition was realized, but it was far from satisfied; ambition seldom is.

Amalickiah now cherished the stupendous design of subjugating the Nephites and ruling singly and alone from ocean to ocean (B. C. 73). To accomplish this iniquitous purpose, he dispatched emissaries in all directions whose mission was to stir up the angry passions of the populace against the Nephites. When this vile object was sufficiently accomplished, and the deluded people had become clamorous for war, he raised an immense army, armed and equipped with an excellence never before known among the Lamanites. This force he placed under the command of Zoramite officers, and ordered its advance into the western possessions of the

Nephites, where, amongst others, stood the cities of Ammonihah, now rebuilt, and Noah.

The Nephites, during this time, had been watching Amalickiah's movements and energetically preparing for war. When the Lamanites reached Ammonihah they found it too strongly fortified to be taken by assault; they therefore retired to Noah, originally a very weak place, but now, through Moroni's foresight and energy, made stronger than Ammonihah. The Zoramite officers well knew that to return home without having attempted something would be most disastrous, and therefore, though with little hope, made an assault upon Noah. This step resulted in throwing away a thousand lives outside its walls, while its well-protected defenders had but fifty men wounded. After this disastrous attempt the Lamanites marched home. Great was the anger of Amalickiah at the miscarriage of his scheme; he cursed God and swore he would yet drink the blood of Moroni.

During the next year the Lamanites were driven out of the great eastern wilderness, which was occupied by numerous Nephite colonies, who laid the foundations of several new cities along the Atlantic coast. Moroni also established a line of fortifications along the Nephites' southern border, which stretched from one side of the continent to the other.

CHAPTER XXXI.

A FEW YEARS OF PEACE—TEANCUM—THE CONTENTION BETWEEN LEHI AND MORIANTON—AMALICKIAH'S TERRIBLE INVASION—HIS SUCCESS—HE IS STOPPED AT BOUNTIFUL BY TEANCUM—TEANCUM SLAYS AMALICKIAH—AMMORON MADE KING OF THE LAMANITES.

(ALMA CHAP. 50 AND 52.)

A FEW YEARS of peace and prosperity now followed. The Nephites multiplied exceedingly and grew very rich. They were also greatly blessed of the Lord; and the sacred historian informs us there never was a happier time among the people of Nephi than at this time. Sad to say, this blessed era lasted but a few years. A local quarrel between two cities on the Atlantic sea-board regarding their respective boundaries was the cause of the first fresh outbreak. At this point we are introduced to another great general of the Nephites, named Teancum.

Teancum appears to have had command of the Nephite army of the north (under the direction of Moroni, the commander-in-chief of all the forces of the republic), and to have had committed to him the defense of the land Bountiful and the Isthmus of Panama. His first exploit to which our attention is drawn is the defeat of the dissatisfied people of Morianton, who, having unjustly quarreled with their neighbors, the people of the city of Lehi, and being apparently aware of the unrighteousness of their cause, determined to migrate to the land northward, and there establish an independent government.

Such a movement being evidently dangerous to the peace and stability of the republic, Moroni determined to prevent the accomplishment of their schemes. He dispatched Teancum with a body of troops to head them off. This the gallant officer succeeded in doing, but not until they had reached the Isthmus, when a stubbornly fought battle ensued, in which Teancum slew Morianton with his own hand, and compelled the surrender of his followers. (B. C. 68.) The prisoners were brought back, the grievances of the two people were investigated, a union between them brought about, and both were restored to their own lands.*

In the following year (B. C. 67), Amalickiah commenced his devastating invasion of the Atlantic provinces of the Nephites. Commencing at Moroni, on the extreme southeast, he gradually advanced northward, capturing and garrisoning all the Nephite cities along the coast, until toward the close of the year he reached the borders of the land Bountiful, driving the forces of the republic before him. At this point he was met by Teancum and a corps of veterans renowned for their courage, skill and discipline. The Lamanite leader endeavored to force his way to the Isthmus, with the intention of occupying the northern continent. In this he was foiled, for the trained valor of Teancum's warriors was too much for that of Amalickiah's half-savage hordes. All day the fight lasted, and at night the worn out soldiers of the two armies camped close together, the Lamanites on the sea-beach, and the Nephites on the borders of the land Bountiful.

It was the last night of the old year, according to Nephite reckoning. The great heat and the terrible efforts of the day had overcome both officers and men. The murmur of the Atlantic's waves sounded a soft lullaby in the ears of Amalickiah and his hosts, who, for the first time during the campaign, had suffered a check in their triumphal march. Even Amalickiah slept; but not so with Teancum. He was

---

*During this year Nephihah the second Chief Judge died, and his son Pahoran, succeeded him on the judgment seat.

brooding over the wrongs and perils of his beloved country, as well as his own sufferings, both the deadly fruit of one man's unholy ambition. As he pondered he grew more angry, and at last he determined by one desperate stroke to put an end to the war; or, if not that, at least to slay the cause of it. Taking one servant with him, he secretly stole out of his own camp into that of the enemy. A death-like silence reigned in both. Cautiously and unobserved he searched out the royal tent. There lay the foe, there lay his guards, all overcome with resistless fatigue. To draw his javelin, thrust it into the king's heart and then flee, was but the work of a moment, and so adroitly did he fulfill his purpose that Amalickiah died without a struggle or a cry, and it was not until the morning that his guards discovered that the hosts of Laman were without a head.

When Teancum returned to his own warriors he awoke them from their slumbers and rehearsed to them all that he had done. It is not difficult to imagine their enthusiasm, which, for fear they should arouse the enemy, they were compelled to restrain. They, however, kept a strong guard on the alert, lest when the Lamanites awoke and discovered that their king was dead, they should, in their anger make a sudden onslaught on the Nephite lines. This thought, however, was not realized. When the Lamanites found that Amalickiah was slain, they hastily retreated to the fortified city of Mulek.

Amalickiah was succeeded on the Lamanitish throne by his brother Ammoron, who continued the war with unrelenting vindictiveness.

CHAPTER XXXII.

JACOB THE ZORAMITE—HIS CHARACTERISTICS—THE STRATEGY BY WHICH MULEK WAS TAKEN—THE FIERCE BATTLE BETWEEN JACOB AND THE NEPHITE FORCES—JACOB'S DEATH.

(ALMA CHAP. 52.)

THE general who commanded the Lamanite forces at Mulek was named Jacob. He was a Nephite apostate, who had accepted the errors of the Zoramites. His appointment was one characteristic of the prevailing policy of Amalickiah and of his successor, Ammoron. It was to give the command of the Lamanite armies to men who, like themselves, were traitors to their own government; for, in such cases, to military knowledge was almost invariably added intense religious hate, which neither asked nor gave quarter on the battlefield, but fought to the last extremity with unconquerable fury.

Such a one was Jacob. He had entrenched himself in the strongly fortified city of Mulek, the most northern of the Nephite cities that had fallen into the enemy's hands. It was a key to the surrounding country. While it remained in Lamanite possession it was very little use for Moroni to attempt to recover the cities that lay yet farther south along the shores of the east sea. The Nephite generals did not consider themselves justified in making an attempt to carry the place by assault. Such an effort would have cost too many noble lives, and probably have proven unsuccessful. Moroni had with him at this time two of his most trusted lieutenants, Lehi and Teancum, both of whom were little inferior to the chief captain in wisdom and valor. At a council of war it was determined to attempt the capture of Mulek by strategy. They had already sent embassies to Jacob desiring him to bring his armies into the open plain to meet the Nephites in battle, but the Lamanite commanders were too well acquainted with the discipline and courage of the Nephite forces to take such a risk. There was, therefore, but one plan left, other than to patiently sit down before the city and reduce it by a regular siege, and that was to decoy a portion of its defenders beyond the protection of its walls, and when it was thus weakened to carry it by storm. Moroni determined on this course.

By command of Moroni, the gallant Teancum, with a small force, marched along the sea shore to the neighborhood of Mulek, while Moroni, with the main body of the army, unperceived by the enemy, made a forced march by night into the wilderness which lay on the west of the city. There he rested. Lehi, with a third corps, remained in the city of Bountiful.

On the morrow Teancum's detachment was discovered by the Lamanite outposts, and from the smallness of its numbers they judged it would fall an easy prey. Jacob at once sallied forth at the head of his warriors to attack the presumptuous Nephites. On their approach Teancum cautiously retreated along the sea shore towards the city of Bountiful. Jacob followed in vigorous pursuit. Moroni, in the meanwhile, divided his army into two corps, one of which he dispatched to capture the city, and with the other he closed in between Jacob's army and Mulek. The first corps accomplished its work without difficulty, for Jacob had left but a small force behind him, and all who would not surrender were slain.

The Lamanites crowded after Teancum in hot pursuit until they came nigh unto Bountiful, when they were met by Lehi and the small force under his command. At his appearance the Lamanite captains fled in confusion, lest they should be out-generaled and cut off from their fortifications. Jacob's warriors were weary by reason of their long and hasty advance, while Lehi's soldiers were fresh and unfatigued. But Lehi refrained from pressing too vigorously on his retreating foes, as his object was not to exhaust his men before the hour of battle came, and he was anxious to avoid a conflict till he and Moroni could at the same moment attack the Lamanites in front and rear.

When Jacob drew near the city he found himself confronted by the soldiers of Moroni, who closed in around his warriors and barred their further progress southward; while Lehi, putting forth his pent-up energies, fell with fury on their rear. Weary and worn though his troops were, Jacob would not surrender. Whatever his faults may have been, and they were doubtless numerous, he had a resolute, unconquerable spirit that would fight to the last. He determined, if possible, to cut his way through to Mulek. With this intent he made a desperate, though ineffectual, charge on Moroni's lines. The Nephites being fresh and unwearied, never wavered, but received the shock firm as a rock upon which the waves of the ocean break in vain. The battle here raged with indescribable fierceness, and with heavy losses to both sides. The wild Lamanites, in the frenzy of desperation, dashed with all their strength and prowess against the well-ordered ranks of the Nephites, in the one absorbing endeavor to force their way through; while the Nephites, in the heroic courage which religion and patriotism inspire, stood cool and undismayed, breaking the force of the shock of each charge, then

> On the wounded and the slain
> Closed their diminished files again.

to receive the next onslaught. In this desperate encounter Moroni was wounded and Jacob slain.

While Jacob was thus impetuously charging on Moroni's corps, Lehi with his "strong men" was as furiously driving in the Lamanite rear. At last the soldiers of Jacob in that part of the field surrendered. Their leader being slain, the remainder of the troops hesitated between throwing down their arms and continuing the hopeless strife. Moroni, with his intense hatred of unnecessary bloodshed, when he noticed that they wavered, cried out that if they would lay down their weapons and deliver themselves up he would spare their lives. His offer was accepted. The chief captains, who remained, came forward and placed their weapons at his feet and commanded their men to do the same. Most of the warriors obeyed, yet numbers would not. They preferred death to surrender, and force had to be used to wrest their weapons from them. The Lamanite prisoners were then sent under an escort to the city of Bountiful, and when counted were found to exceed in numbers the slain on both sides in the late battle. Thus fell Mulek, and thus died its defender, Jacob the Zoramite.

CHAPTER XXXIII.

THE WAR IN THE SOUTH-WEST—ANTIPUS—HELAMAN AND HIS TWO THOUSAND SONS—THEIR VALOR AND FAITH—THE REPULSE OF THE LAMANITES.

(ALMA CHAP. 56 AND 57.)

THE war had been raging about a couple of years, and was working disastrously to the Nephites, when the people of Ammon, feeling that they were a burden rather than a help to their benefactors, though indeed they were not, desired to be released from their oath and covenant never again to take up deadly weapons against their fellows. They desired in this hour of extreme peril to take up arms in defense of the liberties of their adopted country. From this rash step Helaman and his brethren dissuaded them, lest by so doing they should imperil their eternal salvation. But they had sons who had grown far towards manhood who had not entered into this covenant, and consequently were not shut off from participating in the dangers and glories of the war. So with their fathers' and mothers' consent, faith, prayers and words of encouragement, two thousand of these youths were mustered into the Nephite army (B. C. 66). These striplings were all men of truth, faith, soberness and integrity, and were conspicuous for their courage, strength and activity. Being organized they desired that Helaman, for whom they had great love and respect, should be their leader. He consented, and at their head marched to the relief of the forces of the republic that were struggling against considerable odds on the southern borders of the Nephite dominions, from the shores of the Pacific Ocean eastward.

Helaman found the Nephite forces, numbering about six thousand warriors, in a somewhat deplorable condition. The Lamanites, in the strength of greatly superior numbers, had captured the cities of Manti, Cumeni, Zeezrom and Antiparah, and held possession of the country round about. These cities had not been taken without much bloodshed on both sides. The Nephites especially had lost large numbers in prisoners, who were generally put to death by their captors, except the superior officers, who were sent to the land of Nephi. Antipus, the Nephite commander, was locked up in the city of Judea, where, dispirited and weakened by excessive toil and fighting, his troops were making a desperate and painful effort to fortify the city. The arrival of Helaman and his corps brought hope and joy again to their hearts, and renewed vigor to their endeavors.

King Ammoron, learning that reinforcements had

reached the defenders of Judea, ordered all active operations to be suspended for a season. This suspension was most providential for the soldiers of Antipus, as it gave them time to finish the work of fortifying the beleaguered city, and also to recruit their health and energies. By the commencement of the following year the works of defense were completed, and the Nephites became anxious for the onslaught they had so greatly dreaded a few months previous. But they were disappointed. The Lamanites did not feel sufficiently strong to renew aggressive movements. They contented themselves with occupying the Nephite cities they had already captured. In the second month of this year (B. C. 65) a convoy of provisions and two thousand additional warriors arrived from the land of Zarahemla. The Nephites in the city of Judea were now ten thousand strong, with abundant provisions, and they were anxious for a forward movement in order, if possible, to retake some of their cities in the hands of the enemy.

Antipus and Helaman resolved on a ruse to entice the Lamanites from behind their fortifications. It was decided that Helaman and his command should march out of Judea with the apparent intention of carrying supplies to one of the cities in the hands of the Nephites, that was built near the seashore. In executing this manœuvre, they purposely passed at no great distance from the city of Antiparah, in which was stationed the most numerous of the Lamanite armies, in the hope that the Lamanites would notice that their numbers were few, and thus be led to attack them. The stratagem proved successful. The garrison of Antiparah issued forth in pursuit of Helaman, who, with all haste, retreated into the wilderness northward, his intent being to draw his pursuers as far as possible from Antiparah. When the Lamanites had started in pursuit of Helaman, Antipus, with a considerable portion of his army, marched out of the city of Judea and fell in the Lamanites' rear. The retreat soon became a race. The Lamanites crowded forward with all possible expedition in the endeavor to reach Helaman before Antipus caught them. Helaman, on the other hand, used his utmost energy to keep out of their clutches. Neither of the three bodies turned to the right or to the left, but kept straight on in the effort to out-march their foes. Night came and went, and on the morrow the double pursuit was still kept up. Another night fell, but neither dare turn from its course.

On the third morning the race for life and victory was again renewed, but before long the Lamanites, concluding they could not overtake Helaman, suddenly stopped, and awaited the coming of Antipus and his weary soldiers, whom they unexpectedly attacked with great fury, slew Antipus and several of his captains, threw the Nephite troops into great confusion and forced them to commence a retreat.

In the meantime, Helaman discovered that he was no longer pursued, and not knowing the reason, was in doubt what course to take. He called a hasty council of war, at which it was determined to return at once, and risk the chances of being caught in a trap by the crafty Lamanites.

The statement which Helaman makes regarding the conduct of his young soldiers at this council is very interesting. After he had explained the situation to them, he inquired, What say ye, my sons, will ye go against them in battle? Without hesitancy they answered in the affirmative, saying: Father, behold our God is with us, and he will not suffer that we shall fall; then let us go forth; we would not slay our brethren if they would let us alone; therefore let us go lest they should overpower the army of Antipus. Here Helaman remarks: Now they never had fought, yet they did not fear death; and they did think more of the liberty of their fathers than they did upon their lives; yea, they had been taught by their mothers that if they did not doubt that God would deliver them. And they rehearsed unto me the words of their mothers, saying, We do not doubt our mothers knew it.

Helaman and his sons arrived none too soon on the field of battle. The soldiers of Antipus were already fleeing before their more numerous foes, but the valor and impetuosity of the youthful Ammonites was irresistible. They fell on the Lamanite rear with a daring and miraculous strength possessed only by men who put their whole trust in God. Thus attacked in the rear, the Lamanites immediately halted, changed front, and threw their whole force against the Ammonites. The surviving officers of Antipus' army, finding that Helaman had come to their rescue, stopped the retreat, reorganized their scattered bands, and renewed the attack. The Lamanites were compelled to succumb; they could not resist the desperate courage of the Nephites that was driving them in at both front and rear. Their legions all surrendered, and, by Helaman's orders, were sent as prisoners of war to Zarahemla.

And what about the young warriors of Ammon? So great was their faith, so potent its workings, that when, after the battle, Helaman called the roll of his youthful heroes, not one was missing. The faith sown by their mothers' words had borne fruit—they were all preserved. To their undaunted prowess, for they fought as if with the strength of God, the Nephites unhesitatingly accorded the glory of the day.

Still the hardly contested war continued. Six thousand men, with provisions, reached Helaman from Zarahemla and the regions round about (B. C. 63), besides sixty more young Ammonites who had grown sufficiently vigorous to assume the hardships of military life. The city of Cumeni shortly afterwards surrendered through the want of provisions, their supplies having been continuously cut off by Helaman's troops. This surrender threw so many prisoners on the hands of the Nephites that they were unable to guard or feed them. An officer named Gid, with a sufficient force, was detailed to convey them to Zarahemla, but on their way, passing near to an invading body of Lamanites, the prisoners made a desperate attempt to escape. A few succeeded in getting away, but the greater number were slain by their guard. Gid and his command returned to headquarters, as it proved, just in time, for the Lamanites had made a sudden and unexpected attack at Cumeni, and but for Gid's timely arrival the Nephite forces would probably have received a severe defeat. As it was, defeat was turned to victory by their coming.

In this desperate battle every one of the young Ammonites was wounded, but not one was slain. According to the promise made to them they were preserved by the marvelous power of God.

CHAPTER XXXIV.

THE RELIEF OF MANTI—THE OVERTHROW OF THE KING MEN—PACHUS SLAIN—THE STRUGGLE AT MORONI—TEANCUM SLAYS AMMORON, BUT AT THE COST OF HIS OWN LIFE—TEANCUM'S NOBLE CHARACTER.

(ALMA CHAP. 58 TO 62.)

AFTER the battle at Cumeni, the Lamanites retreated eastward to Manti, which was situated on the upper waters of the Sidon. Nor was it for several months that this city could be taken, as owing to internal dissensions at the Nephite capital, and the attempts on the part of some of the people to overthrow the republic and establish a monarchy, Pahoran, the chief judge, was unable to supply the necessary provisions and reinforcements.

In this strait Helaman and his fellow officers called on the Lord in fervent prayer, which was not unanswered. They received assurances of deliverance and victory. These blessed assurances inspired fresh faith and infused renewed courage in the war-weary hearts of those not given to the love of carnage. Fired with the determination, by God's grace, to conquer, they entered on a campaign against the city of Manti, which, by strategy, they captured before the end of the year (B. C. 63). The moral effect of this victory was so great that the Lamanites retreated into the wilderness, evacuating the whole of the territory on the west, but unfortunately taking with them, as prisoners, many women and children.

For more than a year Moroni could not send the needed help to Helaman. The rebels in Zarahemla had driven the chief judge out of the city, and he had taken refuge in Gideon. From there he wrote to Moroni to come to his assistance, which that officer did at the earliest possible moment, leaving the armies in the northeast under the command of Lehi and Teancum. As he advanced he rallied the people on his line of march to the defense of the liberties of the republic, and was so successful that, after having joined the chief judge, Pahoran, he succeeded in overthrowing the "king men," killing their leader, Pachus, and completely crushing the rebellion. This being accomplished, he sent 6,000 men with the necessary provisions to reinforce Helaman (B. C. 61).

The campaign during this year, along the Atlantic coast, was a decisive one. At last the soldiers of Ammoron were driven out of Omner, Morianton, Gid, Lehi, Nephihah, and every other Nephite city on that sea-board, except the outlying one, called Moroni, where the whole of the invading host was massed for a final desperate stand, and around which Moroni, by hurried and lengthened marches, had concentrated his warriors.

It was the night before an expected decisive battle, and the Nephite officers and soldiers were too fatigued to either devise stratagems or execute them. Teancum alone was in a condition of unrest. He remembered with intense bitterness all the bloodshed, woes, hardships, famine, etc., that had been brought about in this great and lasting war between the two races, which he rightly attributed to the infamous ambition of Amalickiah and Ammoron. He reflected how he had slain the former, and determined that as he had slain Amalickiah, so should Ammoron fall. In his anger he stole forth into the enemy's camp, let himself over the walls of the city, sought out the king's tent, and when he had found the object of his search, he cast a javelin at him, which pierced him near the heart. But, unlike Amalickiah, Ammoron's death was not instantaneous. He had time to awaken his servant before he passed away. The alarm was given, the guards started in pursuit; Teancum was overtaken, caught and slain. On the morrow Moroni attacked the Lamanites, defeated them with great slaughter, captured the city, and drove them entirely out of Nephite territory. (B. C. 61).

The writer of the Book of Alma records: When Lehi and Moroni knew that Teancum was dead, they were exceedingly sorrowful; for behold, he had been a man who had fought valiantly for his country; yea, a true friend to liberty, and he had suffered very many exceeding sore afflictions. But behold, he was dead, and had gone the way of all the earth.

In that glorious galaxy of patriot-priests, or warrior-prophets, call them which we may, to whose stern integrity, inspired valor, and unflinching virtue the Nephite republic, in the days of which we write, owed so much of its stability and was so greatly indebted for its perpetuity, Teancum shines among the brightest. View him from whatever point we please, there is no mistaking the man. His ardent disposition, his fiery impetuosity, his zealous patriotism, his undaunted courage, his love of liberty, his entire disinterestedness, shine forth in every action. Indeed, we might almost call him rash, so little did he consider his personal safety when he thought the good of his country required the sacrifice.

In picturing the heroes of those days, Teancum looms up before us almost as a Hotspur or Murat. In our mind's eye we can see him charging the solid phalanxes of the Lamanites, rushing at full speed towards the enemy several lengths ahead of his line of battle; his commanding presence inspiring confidence, his unwavering voice ringing out the word of command, his bright armor shining in the sun, and his hair streaming from beneath his helmet, as, regardless of all save the liberties of his country, he falls upon the thickest of the foe, seeking out their chief captains, that by their death an end may possibly be put to the horrors of war. Thus we find him slaying with his own hand, at different times, Morianton, Amalickiah and Ammoron. In fact, it is quite noticeable that in nearly all the great battles of this age, the Nephites appear to have made it a conspicuous part of their policy to slay the commander of the opposing hosts. So fell Amlici, Morianton, Jacob, Coriantumr and others.

CHAPTER XXXV.

PEACE ONCE MORE—THE RESULTS OF THE WAR—THE LABORS OF HELAMAN—SHIBLON RECEIVES THE RECORDS—HAGOTH, THE SHIP-BUILDER—ANOTHER WAR—MORONIHAH—PAHORAN'S DEATH — CONTENTION REGARDING THE CHIEF JUDGESHIP—PAANCHI'S REBELLION—THE GADIANTON BANDS—ASSASSINATION OF PAHORAN II.—ANOTHER LAMANITE INVASION.

(ALMA CHAP. 62 TO HELAMAN CHAP. 1.)

IN THE next year after the capture of the city of Moroni peace was established in all the land; not a Lamanite warrior remained on Nephite soil. Then Pahoran returned to his judgment seat, and Helaman recommenced his labors in the ministry.

The long-continued and savage war just closed had brought various evils to the church. In many parts of the land it may be said to have been disorganized. The occupancy of so many of the Nephite cities by the unbelieving Lamanites had produced numerous demoralizing effects. Murders, contentions, dissensions and all manner of iniquity had become rife, and the hearts of the people had grown hardened. Yet not altogether so, for there were some who acknowledged the hand of the Lord in all their afflictions. These humbled themselves in the depths of humility; and because of the prayers of the righteous the people were spared.

Such was the state of affairs when Helaman went forth to call the people to repentance and set the church in order. In this blessed work he had much success, and with the help of his brethren he again established the Church of God throughout all the land. These labors he continued until the time of his death, and his joy therein was greatly increased by the continued faithfulness of the people. They, notwithstanding their abundant prosperity, which, as ever, followed their repentance, remained humble, fervent in prayer and diligent in well-doing. Such was the happy condition of the people of Nephi when Helaman died (B. C. 57), he having survived his illustrious father sixteen years. Shiblon, at the death of his brother, took possession of the sacred things that had been delivered unto Helaman by Alma, and held them for four years.

The next year (B. C. 56) the valiant Moroni, one of the greatest and most virtuous of God's sons, passed away from this state of mortality to the glories of eternity, at the early age of forty-three years. Some time before his death he had given the chief command of the armies of the Nephites to his son, Moronihah, who, from the history of later years, we judge to have been a worthy son of so illustrious a sire.

The four years that Shiblon held the plates are principally noteworthy for the commencement of Nephite emigration to the northern continent. It was during this period that Hagoth established his ship-building yards on the Pacific, near the land Bountiful. It is probable that ships were built by the Nephites before Hagoth's time, but he being an exceedingly expert mechanic, constructed much larger ones than had hitherto been built, and thus inaugurated a new feature in Nephite colonization.*

---

*These ships of Hagoth carried many colonies to the land northward; as it was their custom to take one load of emigrants and when they had disembarked, to return for another. Some of these vessels were eventually lost; that is, the ships and their passengers never reached their destination. It is supposed by many that a part of them were carried out to mid-ocean by storms and probably wrecked; and that the survivors found safety and shelter on some of the islands of the Pacific Ocean. In this way, it is suggested, the Hawaiian, Samoan and other islands were first peopled.

When Shiblon died he committed the records to the care of Helaman, the son of his brother Helaman. The history of the Nephites and Lamanites still continued a history of wars. In the same year that Shiblon died, the Lamanites again raised a numerous army and went down against their traditional foes. The campaign was a short one. Moronihah, the son of Moroni, inflicted a signal blow upon their advancing legions, and drove them back to their own lands. Their loss in this deservedly ill-fated expedition was great.

Still this blood-thirsty race never seemed to gain experience by the things it suffered. This, no doubt, arose to a great extent from the continued irritation kept up by the wily apostates, who had much private spleen to gratify in the sufferings of the Nephites, and who held no particular love or respect for their credulous dupes and cat's-paws, the Lamanites.

It was in the year B. C. 53 that Helaman took charge of the sacred plates, etc. In the next year Pahoran, the chief judge, died, which event gave rise to serious contention amongst the Nephite people. Three of his sons, named Pahoran, Pacumeni and Paanchi, were ambitious to fill the exalted position left vacant by their father's death. Each had his adherents and following, but, according to the national law, the matter was decided by the voice of the people, and Pahoran was chosen.

Pacumeni assented to the decision of the citizens, but Paanchi attempted to raise a rebellion, for which crime he was arrested, tried by the law, and condemned to death. Still the more wicked part of the community supported his unlawful claims. These determined to slay Pahoran, which resolve they carried into effect, and the chief judge was slain by an assassin named Kishkumen.* This foul murder was committed while the chief magistrate was sitting in the judgment

---

*Pacumeni was chosen to succeed Pahoran as Chief Judge.

seat administering the law, but through the connivance of the murderer's associates in iniquity he escaped.

These lawless men bound themselves together by a secret oath and covenant, that they would never divulge who was the murderer of Pahoran, and they swore, by the most horrible oaths, one to another, to conceal each other's crimes, to aid and sustain each other in their villainies, and to carry out the designs and directions of their leaders. Over this band of conspirators, assassins and robbers, Gadianton stood as the head.

The next year after Pahoran's assassination, the Lamanites invaded the lands of the Nephites. The Lamanite armies were commanded by a Nephite dissenter named Coriantumr. He was a descendant of Zarahemla, therefore, presumedly, of the tribe of Judah. He determined on new and venturesome tactics, and caused his forces to make an unexpected dash through the Nephite territory. The Nephites everywhere gave way before them. They marched through the center of the country, ravaging its most populous and richest districts. Before the astonished Nephites could collect their armies the enemy had assaulted and captured their beautiful and strongly fortified capital, and for the first time the savage soldiery of Laman held possession of the towers, temples and palaces of Zarahemla. On this occasion the chief judge, Pacumeni, was slain. Intoxicated with his uninterrupted successes, the Lamanite general crowded yet further north, neglecting to keep up his line of communication in the rear.

Coriantumr's hope was to obtain possession of the narrow isthmus which was the key to both continents. In this he failed. The Nephite commander first checked his progress northward, and then cut off his retreat. In a fierce battle that followed he was killed, his armies surrendered, and the remnants hastened ingloriously home, Moronihah, the Nephite commander, magnanimously permitting them to return unmolested. (B. C. 51.)

CHAPTER XXXVI.

PACUMENI SLAIN—HELAMAN CHOSEN CHIEF JUDGE—THE CONSPIRACY TO SLAY HIM—KISHKUMEN KILLED—THE PROSPERITY OF THE NEPHITES UNDER HELAMAN.

(HELAMAN CHAP. 1 TO 3.)

AS PACUMENI, the chief judge, had been slain at the capture of Zarahemla, no sooner was the war over than an election took place to fill his vacant seat. The choice fell upon Helaman, the more righteous of the people providentially being still in the majority.

Helaman being a God-fearing, just man, his election was very distasteful to the Gadianton band and its sympathizers. They resolved to slay him as they had before slain the younger Pahoran, and place Gadianton on the judgment seat in his stead. To accomplish this the same vile instrument was chosen—Kishkumen. But the protecting hand of the great Jehovah was over and around about Helaman, and he preserved him from the assassin's knife. A servant of Helaman, possibly a detective commissioned in such time of peril to watch the movements of the dangerous classes, by disguise became acquainted with the doings of the robber band, and of their intentions toward his master.

As Kishkumen was on his way to fulfil his bloody work, this servant, whose name is not recorded, met him, and gave him one of their secret signs. This admitted him into the confidence of the assassin, who explained his errand, and asked to be conducted privately into the judgment hall, where Helaman was, then sitting in the performance of his duties. This was agreed upon; the two proceeded to where the murderer expected to find his victim. The strategy of the servant disarmed his suspicions, he was off his guard. At the opportune moment the servant stabbed Kishkumen, and so adroitly did he perform his work, that the robber fell dead without a groan. The servant immediately ran to the judgment hall, and informed Helaman of all that he had heard, seen and done. Without delay, orders were issued for the arrest of the band, but its members, finding that Kishkumen did not return, and fearing he had miscarried in his unholy work, under the guidance of their leader fled precipitately into the wilderness by a secret way, and, in the depths of its luxuriant vegetation, hid in a place where they could not be found. (B. C. 50.)

The succeeding years were of peculiar prosperity, though not of great righteousness, amongst the Nephite people. They spread out and colonized in every direction. Many thousands emigrated to the northern continent, among them great numbers of Ammonites. Numerous new cities were built, and old ones repaired; ship building was largely carried on, and the arts and manufactures encouraged. Temples, tabernacles and sanctuaries were erected in great numbers; in fact, the people spread out and covered both continents north and south, east and west. The sacred historian states that he has not recorded one hundredth part of the doings of the people—their wickedness and righteousness, their wars and contentions, their peace and prosperity; but many records were kept, upon which the history of these things were engraved, and all that is necessary for the world's good will be brought to light in heaven's own time.

The annals of the remainder of Helaman's rule are very short. In the years B. C. 45 and 44 there were many contentions in the land, but in the latter portion of the succeeding year they measurably ceased, and tens of thousands were baptized unto repentance. So great was the prosperity of the church at this time that even the priesthood were surprised thereat, and at the multiplicity of blessings that were poured out upon the people. This happy state of affairs continued until the death of Helaman, though somewhat marred by the increasing pride and vanity that long-continued prosperity had begotten in the hearts of many of the Christians.

Helaman himself was a righteous man: He did observe to keep the judgments, and the statutes, and the commandments of God; and he did do that which was right in the sight of God continually, and he did walk after ways of his father, insomuch that he did prosper in the land. So writes the historian of Helaman; what more can be said of any man?

Helaman had two sons to whom he gave the names of Nephi and Lehi, to remind them, when they heard their own names called, of the faith and goodness of their great ancestors, who, by God's direction, led their fathers to the promised land. When Helaman died he was succeeded by his son Nephi.

CHAPTER XXXVII.

THE SONS OF HELAMAN—NEPHI'S RIGHTEOUS RULE—THE LAMANITES AGAIN INVADE ZARAHEMLA—THEY DRIVE THE NEPHITES INTO THE NORTHERN CONTINENT—THE MINISTRATIONS OF NEPHI AND LEHI—THE MANIFESTATIONS OF GOD'S POWER IN THE CITY OF NEPHI—AMINADAB—THE CONVERSION OF THE LAMANITES—UNIVERSAL PEACE.

(HELAMAN CHAP. 4 AND 5.)

IN NEPHI we have one of the greatest prophets that ever trod the earth, or to whom the God of our salvation revealed his glorious will. He lived during the greater portion of the first century before Christ, and disappeared from the knowledge of mankind but a short time before the advent of the Messiah as a babe in Bethlehem. He is first referred to in the Book of Mormon (B. C. 44) as the elder of Helaman's two sons, Lehi being the younger. These two brothers appear to have been inseparable during their lives. They are nearly always mentioned as associated in the great and ofttimes perilous labors of the ministry undertaken for the salvation of either Nephites or Lamanites. We have no information with regard to the time of Nephi's birth, but when his father died, in the year B. C. 39, he succeeded him as chief judge, the duties of which office he filled with wisdom and justice for about nine years, when owing to the wickedness of the people, he resigned that office, and Cezoram was chosen by the people in his stead (B. C. 30).

The years that Nephi judged his people are some of the darkest in Nephite history. Owing to their great pride and iniquity, the Lord left them to themselves, and they became weak like unto the Lamanites, man for man. When war was declared, the latter, being much the more numerous, carried everything before them. In vain the Nephites struggled for their homes and their liberties. They were forced back by the hordes of the Lamanites from city to city, from land to land. Manti, Gideon, Cumeni, Moroni, and even Zarahemla fell. Nor did the war end when the blood-thirsty Lamanites held high carnival in the midst of its towers and palaces. Onward swept the invading host; backward fled the defenders of the commonwealth, and backward they continued until every town and city, every tower and fort, from Melek to Moroni, from Manti to Bountiful, were filled with the savage, half-disciplined, dark-skinned warriors of Laman. Not a place could be found in the whole southern continent where the soldiers of the Nephites successfully held their ground. Zarahemla, with its hallowed associations, its glorious temples, where the daily sacrifice was unceasingly offered, its proud palaces, its luxurious homes, its courts of justice, where the chief judge sat in the magnificence of almost kingly authority to administer the law—this their queen city, the seat of their government, the centre of their civilization, the home of their highest priesthood, was in the hands of their merciless, vandal-like foes. Nor had the danger stopped; with hurried hands the Nephites built a line of defense across the Isthmus of Panama from sea to sea, for the unnumbered hosts of their conquerors were still pushing forward. This line of fortifications was effectual; it stopped the roll of the barbaric tide northward, and the Lamanite commanders rested with the possession of a continent.

In this war the Nephite dissenters took active part against their white brethren, and to this fact, in part, may be attributed the sudden success that shone on the Lamanite arms. But little by little in succeeding years the half repentant Nephites regained their lost ground, until (B. C. 31) the most northerly half of their possessions had again fallen into their hands; but because of their only partial repentance, their leaders had not strength to lead them further, and Zarahemla still remained in the hands of the warriors of Laman.

When Nephi retired from the judgment seat it was with the intention of devoting his entire time to the preaching of the gospel. He associated his brother Lehi with him, and commencing at Bountiful, he journeyed and preached throughout all the land southward in the possession of the Nephites. From thence the two brothers passed onwards to Zarahemla, where they found many Nephite dissenters, to whom they proclaimed the word of God in great power. Numbers of these confessed their sins, were baptized unto repentance, and immediately returned to their brethren to repair, if possible, the wrongs they had done, and make such restitution as lay in their power.

Numbers of the Lamanites also received the truth gladly, insomuch that eight thousand of that race were baptized in Zarahemla and the regions round about.

From Zarahemla the prophets proceeded to the Lamanite capital in the land of Nephi, where yet mightier power attended them. The voice of God from heaven sustained their testimony; angels ministered to the people who assembled to see them; neither prisons, nor chains, nor bonds could restrain or hold them, and they accomplished an ever blessed and marvelous work amongst the benighted children of Laman (B. C. 30). God's power was manifested at these times in mercy to the darkened condition of the minds of the Lamanites, when only extraordinary manifestations of his divine goodness could reach their hearts. They had no records to which they could appeal, and all their traditions were opposed to the Holy Being whose message of eternal joy the Nephite prophets bore. Thus in their weakness they were strengthened by signs and wonders which a people better educated in the things of God could with but ill grace claim.

The story of the ministration of Nephi and Lehi in the land of Nephi is of the deepest interest. When they reached its chief city they were thrust into that same prison into which Ammon and his companions were cast by the guards of king Limhi. Here they were kept with little or no food for a number of days. At the end of this time the officers of the Lamanites went to the prison with the intention of slaying the two brothers. But to their intense surprise the Lamanites found them encircled about as if by fire. At this strange spectacle fear fell upon the officers. They dared not touch the two prisoners lest they should be burned. Yet when they saw that Nephi and Lehi were not consumed their hearts took courage, though they still stood as if struck dumb with amazement.

At this point the two brethren stood forward and began to explain that what was seen was manifested that the spectators might learn that no one could harm them, and that they were the servants of the Most High, and his all-powerful arm shielded them. Nor was this all: a sudden earthquake, shook the ground, the prison walls tottered to their foundations, a pall of thick darkness covered all whom curiosity or other motives had gathered to the prison. The unburning flame, the tottering walls, the quivering earth, the impenetrable cloud of blackness, all conspired to fill the hearts of the Lamanites with solemn fear and awful dread. They realized the almighty power of God; they were filled with the sense of their own abject insignificance. A voice, the voice of One whom they knew not, sounded in their affrighted ears. Once and again, yea, a third time, and each time that the voice came it was followed by the trembling of the earth and the shaking of the prison walls. All nature quivered at the presence of the Majesty on High, whilst the heavy, palpable, impenetrable darkness still enshrouded them.

From above the voice descended; it was outside the cloud; its tones came not to their quaking hearts with the roar of the pealing thunder; nor was it like the tumultuous flow of angry waters; but a still voice of perfect mildness, almost a whisper, that pierced to their inmost souls. That voice was the voice of the mighty God of Jacob, and he called upon all those who heard him to repent, and to do his servants no hurt. With the third repetition of this command were added marvelous words of salvation that cannot be uttered by men. And because of the darkness that enveloped them, and the fearful dread that filled their hearts, none dared to move. Fear, astonishment, apprehension of what was to come, had riveted each to the spot on which he stood.

Among the crowd was a Nephite dissenter, an apostate from the true church, named Aminadab. This man, happening to turn his face in the direction in which the two disciples stood, beheld that their faces shone with a glorious light, and that they were conversing with some one who appeared to be above them, for their eyes were turned heavenward. Aminadab drew the attention of those who surrounded him to this glorious appearance, and the spell that bound them was sufficiently removed to enable them to turn towards the prisoners and to become witnesses of the fact also. What do all these things mean? they anxiously inquired. They do converse with the angels of God, answered Aminadab. What shall we do that this cloud of darkness may be removed? was their next question. You must repent and cry unto the Voice, even until ye shall have faith in Christ, he replied. They did cry unto God with all the energy that their terrifying surroundings inspired, and so continued to supplicate until the cloud was dispersed. Then, to their great surprise, they discovered that they also were entombed in a pillar of living fire. Yet this fire did not hurt them, it did not singe their garments, it did not consume the prison walls, but their terror was swept away, and they were filled with a joy that was unspeakable, for the Holy Spirit of God filled their souls, and they broke forth in marvelous words of praise and rejoicing. Again a pleasant, searching whisper reached their gladdened ears. It said unto them, Peace, peace be unto you because of your faith in my Well-beloved, who was from the foundation of the world. Now there were about 300 souls who heard and saw these things, and they cast up their eyes unto heaven, which was opened to their vision, and holy angels came down and ministered unto them.

The tidings of this glorious appearing were quickly spread near and far in the lands where the Lamanites dwelt. So powerful was the testimony, and so great were the evidences, that the major portion of the people believed, repented and obeyed the gospel. Then, like all true saints, they manifested the sincerity of their repentance by works of restitution; they laid down their weapons of war, they cast aside their false traditions, their hatred gave place to love, and they restored to the Nephites Zarahemla and the other lands which they had taken from them (B. C. 30).

So great was the reformation in their character that the

Lamanites soon exceeded the Nephites in their faith and good works. Extraordinary as it may appear, instead of Nephite missionaries visiting the Lamanites, Lamanite missionaries were soon ministering the precious truths of the gospel among the Nephites. Then a universal peace, such as had never before been known since the division of the two races, extended over the whole land. Indeed, from this time the history of the two nations, to a great extent, becomes one. Together they worshiped the Lord, together they rose and sank, together they battled with the assassin hosts of Gadianton, together they triumphed over those desperadoes, and together they sought refuge in one vast body when there was no safety but in massing the people in one land, together the more unrighteous portions of both races were destroyed at the crucifixion of the Savior, and together the more righteous ones witnessed his appearing, listened to his words, received his law, and became members of his holy church. Henceforth, for generations, they were no more of Nephi, no more of Laman, no more of Jacob, no more of Ishmael—all were of Christ.

CHAPTER XXXVIII.

GROWTH OF EVIL AMONGST THE NEPHITES—THE INCREASE OF THE GADIANTON ROBBERS—NEPHI'S ANNOUNCEMENT OF THE MURDER OF THE CHIEF JUDGE—THE DISCOVERY—NEPHI ARRESTED—HE IS PROVEN INNOCENT—GOD'S COVENANT WITH HIM—INCREASE OF INIQUITY—A TERRIBLE FAMINE—THE WELCOME RAIN—THE TREND TO DEATH.

(HELAMAN CHAP. 6 TO 11.)

THE GOODLY reign of universal peace, to which we referred in our last chapter, brought stability, stability developed wealth, wealth engendered pride, pride gave birth to numerous sins, to be followed by contentions, dissensions, and then wars. These evils begat sorrow, sorrow softened the hearts of the people to repentance, repentance was followed by the blessing of God, which again brought peace, prosperity and, by-and-by, riches. At this era of Nephite national life, this is the one eternal round which their inspired historians are compelled to chronicle. Within four short years of the happy time of universal peace we have just referred to, the riches of the world had induced stubbornness and rebellion towards God, combined with the insane desire to rob, plunder and murder their fellow-men. If there ever were a people swift to do evil, it was the Nephites of this generation. In the year B. C. 26, Cezoram, the chief judge, was murdered by an unknown hand, as he sat on the judgment seat, and his son, who succeeded him, suffered in like manner within the year. The Gadianton robbers grew in strength, both in numbers and influence, and were actually fostered amongst the Nephites, while the more righteous Lamanites utterly destroyed all they found within their borders. The one people dwindled in unbelief, the other grew in grace and in the power of God's divine Spirit.

Nephi, who had gone to the northern continent, tarried there until the year B. C. 23, when, his teachings and prophecies having been rejected by its inhabitants, he returned in sorrow to Zarahemla; but he found no comfort there. The Gadianton robbers filled the judgment seats, and perverted the law to their own avarice and lust. The life, the property, the liberty, the virtue of righteous men and women were counted but things of naught, their playthings or their spoil.

Nephi's house in Zarahemla was situated on one of the principal thoroughfares. It led to the chief market-place. In his garden, near the highway, he built a tower whither it was his wont to repair for prayer. On one occcasion, shortly after his return from the north, he became so deeply concerned because of the iniquities of the people, that in earnest supplication to the Lord he raised his voice so high that he was heard by the passers by in the street below. A listening crowd soon gathered, and when the prophet had ended his devotions and became aware of their presence, he commenced to teach them. His words were not sugar-coated, to adapt them to the tastes of his congregation. To the contrary, he boldly rebuked their sins, their murders, and their secret wickedness; at the same time, in the love of the gospel, he entreated and plead with them to amend their lives and do better. He also warned them of the terrible judgments that would fall upon them if they did not turn from their sinful ways.

Towards the conclusion of his address, Nephi surprised his hearers by stating that the chief judge, Seezoram, had been murdered by his brother, Seantum, who was anxious to obtain the chief judgeship himself. Both these men were members of the vile band who owned Gadianton as their chief.

The people did not believe Nephi's statement, so five incredulous men ran to the judgment hall to find out the truth of the matter. When they reached there they discovered Seezoram lying dead in a pool of blood near the judgment seat. The five messengers were so overcome with fear at this awful sight that they fell to the earth.

Soon after, other citizens who had not heard Nephi came in. Finding the dead judge and the five men all there they concluded that the latter must be the murderers, who, by some manifestation of the power of heaven, had been prevented from leaving the scene of their shameful deed. The officers therefore took the five and cast them into prison.

When the wicked learned that Nephi's words had proven true, they charged him with being an accomplice. They did not believe in revelation from God, so argued that Nephi must have had a hand in the murder or he could not have known anything about it. He was therefore taken and bound and brought before the multitude. Then they cross-examined him, abused him, and finally offered him money to confess that he had employed some one to commit the dreadful crime. They were anxious to bring reproach and trouble upon him that they might have an excuse for not believing his words nor heeding his teachings.

Nephi to establish his innocence sent his accusers to the house of Seantum, and instructed them what to say. He further told them how the fratricide would act; how he would acquit him (Nephi) of all complicity in the murder, assert his own innocence, until shown stains of blood on his cloak, and then, overwhelmed with terror, he would confess.

The people went and followed Nephi's instructions, and all that he had told them came to pass; for according to his words Seantum did at first deny, and according to the words he did afterwards confess; acknowledging also that Nephi knew nothing of the matter, without it had been revealed to him of God.

Some of the citizens now acknowledged that Nephi was a prophet, others declared that he was a god, whilst many remained hardened in their sins. So violent became the contention that the people gathered in excited crowds upon the streets, wrangling and disputing about the events of the past two days, and in their excitement they entirely forgot Nephi, and left him standing alone in the street.

With a sorrowful heart he wended his way homeward; but before he reached there, the voice of the Lord came to him with many words of comfort and commendation. As with others of his servants, the Lord made a covenant with him, that he would bless him forever; that whatsoever he bound on earth should be bound in heaven, and whatsoever he loosed on earth should be loosed in heaven; that he should have power over the elements to bless and to curse; to smite the earth with famine, and pestilence, and destruction.

Notwithstanding the many proofs the ungodly Nephites had that Nephi was a true prophet, they continued to reject his teachings. They persecuted him, and even went so far as to seek his life. But he was conveyed out of their midst by the power of God, and ministered among other peoples.

The general character of the Nephites continued to grow worse and worse. The Gadianton robbers grew stronger and stronger. For a few years there was increasing commotion, disunion and bloodshed. At last, wearied at beholding so much misery and contention, Nephi prayed that the Lord would not suffer the people to be destroyed by the sword, but rather let a famine desolate the land, and, peradventure, bring the people to an understanding of their awful condition, and cause them to humble themselves and repent. The Holy One heard and answered his petition, the heavens became as brass over the land, the rains ceased, the earth dried up, the crops failed, the people perished for want of food.

Two years passed (B. C. 19 and 18) and the third came, and still the refreshing rain was withheld (B. C. 17). During this year the people, humbled by their sufferings, turned towards the Lord. They endeavored to root out iniquity from their midst. They destroyed the Gadianton robber bands, and established the government on a more righteous foundation. Nephi, observing the change in their conduct and feelings, interceded with the Lord in their behalf. His prayers were answered, the welcome rain descended on the parched-up soil, and a bounteous harvest once more crowned the labors of the husbandman (B. C. 16).

The repentant people now regarded Nephi in his true light; they revered him as a great prophet, and for a few short years they listened to his teachings. While they did so they prospered. But the leaven of unrighteousness had too thoroughly permeated the national life for their faithfulness to God to be of long duration. Two, three, or perhaps half a dozen years they would maintain their integrity, and then corruption would seethe, the vile would snatch the reins of government, the good would be oppressed, and contention and war, with all their horrors, would again reign supreme. Thus it was after the three years of famine. For two years there was peace, in the third there began to be much strife (B. C. 13), in the next, the Gadianton bands reappeared, and carried havoc amongst their more peaceable fellow-countrymen. Going on, year by year they grew in iniquity and ripened for destruction. For many years Nephi strove to stem the tide of vice. At times partial success rewarded his unceasing efforts, and he had joy in the baptism of some honest souls. But the great bulk of the people had rejected the gospel, they had no love for its holy principles, and were unfit for its blessings.

CHAPTER XXXIX.

SAMUEL THE LAMANITE—HIS MISSION AND PROPHECIES—THE VAIN ATTEMPT TO DESTROY HIM—HE RETURNS TO HIS OWN COUNTRY.

(HELAMAN CHAP. 13 TO 16.)

WE COME now to the days of Samuel the Lamanite (B. C. 6). Without any previous reference to him, he appears suddenly in the foreground of ancient American history, bearing a weighty and solemn message; a messenger of God's displeasure, he stands a Jonah to the Nephites. That message is faithfully delivered; then he disappears forever from our sight.

The condition of society in the days of Samuel was somewhat peculiar. The Nephites and Lamanites had, so far as righteousness is concerned, to a great extent changed places. The former were puffed up with worldly pride, were full of vain boastings, envyings, strifes, malice, persecutions, murders and all manner of iniquities. They cast out, they stoned, they slew the servants of God, while they encouraged, exalted and rewarded the false teachers who flattered them in their vileness and sung in their ears the siren's song of "all is well." They reveled in all the luxury that the fatness of the land brought forth; they were ostentatious in the use of gold and silver and precious things; but their hearts never turned in thankfulness to the great Giver of all these bounties. The majority of the Lamanites, on the contrary, walked circumspectly before God; they were full of faith and integrity, were zealous in the work of converting their fellows, and kept the commandments, statutes and judgments of the Lord according to the law of Moses.

Such was the condition of affairs when the Lamanite prophet Samuel appeared among the sin-stained citizens of Zarahemla, and for many days preached repentance in their midst. Their eyes were blind and their ears were deaf, sin filled their souls, and in their anger they cast him out. But the work of his mission was not yet accomplished. As he was preparing to return to his own country, a holy angel visited him and proclaimed the voice of the Lord. That voice commanded that he should turn back and prophesy to the people of Zarahemla the things that should come into his heart.

He returned to the city, but was refused admission at its gates. The iniquitous dwellers therein had no desire to have their peace disturbed by the voice of divine threatenings. But the prophet had the word of the Lord burning within him, and could not be restrained. He mounted the walls of the city, and from this conspicuous vantage ground, with outstretched hands and loud voice, he proclaimed to the wicked the unwelcome tidings of their coming destruction. Many listened to his proclamation, some few were pricked in their hearts, repented of their evil deeds, and sought the prophet Nephi, that they might be baptized. Others were angry, they gathered up the stones in the roadway and hurled them at Samuel; they drew forth their bows and shot arrows at him. But to no effect; the protecting power of the Holy Spirit was around him, and he could not be harmed.

When some beheld how wonderfully the prophet was preserved, it was a testimony to them that God was with him, and they also sought Nephi, confessing their sins. But the great body of the populace grew more enraged at the want of success that attended their murderous efforts. They called upon their captains to seize and bind him. They cried out, He hath a devil, and it is by this power he is preserved; take the fellow, bind him, and away with him! Following the wild satanic cry of the multitude, the officers of the law endeavored to arrest Samuel. But he cast himself down from the wall of the city and fled out of the lands of the Nephites into his own country. There he preached and prophesied among his own people; but among the people of Nephi he was never heard of more.

The prophecies of Samuel are among the most wonderful recorded in holy writ. He especially foretold many things regarding the life and death of our Savior, and concerning the future destiny of his people, and of the Nephites.

With regard to the birth of the Redeemer he said:

Behold, I give unto you a sign; for five years more cometh, and behold, then cometh the Son of God, to redeem all those who shall believe on his name.

And behold, this will I give unto you for a sign at the time of his coming; for behold, there shall be great lights in heaven, insomuch that in the night before he cometh there shall be no darkness, insomuch that it shall appear unto man as if it was day.

Therefore there shall be one day and a night, and a day, as if it were one day, and there were no night; and this shall be unto you for a sign; for ye shall know of the rising of the sun, and also of its setting; therefore they shall know of a surety that there shall be two days and a night; nevertheless the night shall not be darkened; and it shall be the night before he is born.

And behold there shall a new star arise, such an one as ye never have beheld; and this also shall be a sign unto you.

And behold this is not all, there shall be many signs and wonders in heaven.

And it shall come to pass that ye shall all be amazed and wonder, insomuch that ye shall fall to the earth.

Regarding the death of the Lord Jesus he declared:

But behold, as I said unto you concerning another sign, a sign of his death, behold, in that day that he shall suffer death, the sun shall be darkened and refuse to give his light unto you; and also the moon, and the stars; and there shall be no light upon the face of this land, even from the time that he shall suffer death, for the space of three days, to the time that he shall rise again from the dead.

Yea, at the time that he shall yield up the ghost, there shall be thunderings and lightnings for the space of many hours, and the earth shall shake and tremble, and the rocks which are upon the face of this earth; which are both above the earth and beneath, which ye know at this time are solid, or the more part of it is one solid mass, shall be broken up;

Yea, they shall be rent in twain, and shall ever after be found in seams and in cracks, and in broken fragments upon the face of the whole earth; yea, both above the earth and beneath.

And behold there shall be great tempests, and there shall be many mountains laid low, like unto a valley, and there shall be many places, which are now called valleys, which shall become mountains, whose height thereof is great.

And many highways shall be broken up, and many cities shall become desolate.

And many graves shall be opened, and shall yield up many of their dead; and many saints shall appear unto many.

And behold thus hath the angel spoken unto me for he said unto me, that there should be thunderings and lightnings for the space of many hours:

And he said unto me that while the 'thunder and the lightning lasted, and the tempest, that these things should be, and that darkness should cover the face of the whole earth for the space of three days.

And the angel said unto me, that many shall see greater things than these, to the intent that they might believe that these signs and these wonders should come to pass, upon all the face of this land; to the intent that there should be no cause of unbelief among the children of men.

We shall see as we proceed how wonderfully all these

sayings of Samuel the Lamanite were fulfilled.

He closed his prophecy with these emphatic words. First regarding the Lamanites:

Therefore, saith the Lord, I will not utterly destroy them; but I will cause that in the day of my wisdom they shall return again unto me, saith the Lord.

And now behold, saith the Lord, concerning the people of the Nephites, if they will not repent and observe to do my will, I will utterly destroy them, saith the Lord, because of their unbelief, notwithstanding the many mighty works which I have done among them; and as surely as the Lord liveth shall these things be, saith the Lord.

CHAPTER XL.

NEPHI TRANSLATED—HIS SON NEPHI—TIME OF THE SAVIOR'S COMING—THE CONSPIRACY TO SLAY THE BELIEVERS—THE REVELATION TO NEPHI—THE PROMISED SIGNS APPEAR—INCREASE OF THE GADIANTON ROBBERS—WAR—LACHONEOUS GATHERS ALL THE PEOPLE TO ONE LAND—THE END OF THE STRUGGLE.

(III. NEPHI CHAP. 1 TO 6.)

SHORTLY before the birth of Christ, Nephi transferred the plates of brass and other records to his son Nephi, gave him charge concerning them, and departed from the land of Zarahemla. Whither he went, or what became of him, is hidden from the knowledge of mankind. That he did not return to the dwelling-places of humanity is testified to by his son some ten years afterwards.

Six hundred years had now passed since Lehi and his companions left Jerusalem. The time had arrived, of which Samuel the Lamanite and other prophets had borne testimony when the phenomena should appear to bear witness of the birth of the Son of God. As the day drew near, signs and miracles increased among the people. But the hardened in heart, who were ever on the watch to entrap those who believed in the words of the prophets, began to circulate the idea that the time had passed and the prophecies had failed. Not content with mocking and reviling those who were anxiously looking for the promised two days and a night when there should be no darkness, they went as far as to appoint a day when all who believed in the coming of the Savior should be slain, except the sign be first given.

This gross wickedness caused Nephi great sorrow; his only recourse was to heaven. Before God, in mighty prayer, he bowed in behalf of his imperiled people. All the day long he continued his earnest supplications. At last the word of the Anointed One came unto him, saying, Lift up your head and be of good cheer, for behold the time is at hand, and on this night shall the sign be given, and on the morrow come I into the world, to show unto the world that I will fulfil all that which I have caused to be spoken by the mouth of my holy prophets. As was thus declared, so was it fulfilled, for at the going down of the sun it was light as day, and so continued until the morning, when the sun again rose in its usual course. A new star had also appeared in the heavens. Then the faithful rejoiced, their hearts were full to overflowing, they knew that their Redeemer was born, and that the great plan of salvation had entered its most glorious phase; God, the great Jehovah, was tabernacled in the flesh. But the wicked quaked with awful dread, they realized the extent of their iniquity, they sensed that they were murderers at heart, for they had plotted to take the lives of the righteous, and in the terror that this overwhelming sense of their piteous condition wrought, they sank to the earth as though they were dead.

Many now believed who previously had scorned the divine messages that the prophets bore; but others, inspired of Satan, as soon as they recovered from the fright which the appearance of the promised signs had produced, began to explain them away, and, by various lying rumors, endeavored to nullify the good that had been done in the hearts of many. Others again commenced to teach that it was no longer expedient to observe the law of Moses, drawing their conclusions from a false interpretation of the scriptures. Notwithstanding these efforts of the evil one, Nephi and others went forth among the people preaching, baptizing many, and bringing a short period of peace to the land.

But those who were righteous were not strong enough to overcome the vast hosts of Gadianton robbers, who, time and time again, swarmed from their mountain retreats, and carried carnage, rapine and desolation to the homes of both Nephites and Lamanites.

Year by year these marauding bands repeated their incursions. Sometimes one party conquered, sometimes the other. This condition of affairs kept the people in such a state of terror and anxiety that life grew a burden to them. Still they repented not in sincerity of heart, and their many afflictions were permitted by the Lord because of their iniquity.

So great was the misery entailed by these invasions, that the chief judge, Lachoneus, at last determined to gather all the people into one place, and by a policy of masterly inactivity wear out or starve out the invaders. We can scarcely understand how terrible must have been the misery endured by the nation at this time, to have caused the conception and execution of such a measure. Can we picture to ourselves the scenes that must have occurred as the people of two continents converged to one gathering place? From the shores of the great lakes in the north, from the stormy Atlantic seaboard, from the coast where the mild Pacific ebbs and flows, from the regions of the southern Andes, the migrating hosts flowed together to Zarahemla and Bountiful, the lands selected as the temporary gathering place. They came with their flocks and herds, their grain and provisions, leaving nothing that would help to sustain the robber bands while they continued to wage their unhallowed war. (A. C. 17.)

When the people reached the gathering place they fortified it so strongly that it became impregnable to their enemies. Under Gidgiddoni's instructions they also made themselves strong armor and shields as well as all kinds of weapons, so that they might be fully prepared for the day of battle. Lachoneous, in the meantime, preached to them in great power, so much so that they feared his denunciations, forsook all their sins, and turned to the Lord in great humility and devotion.

Game soon became so scarce in the wilderness that the Gadiantons began to suffer for food while besieging the Nephite stronghold. In addition to this, the Nephites made frequent attacks upon them. Seeing his armies wasting away from famine and the sword, Zemnarihah, their commander, gave up all hope of success and withdrew from the siege, and formed the design of marching his followers to the most distant parts of the land northward.

To have permitted the robbers to escape would have increased the difficulties under which the Nephites had so long suffered. Gidgiddoni, the Nephite general, having learned of their purpose, knowing their weakness for want of food and because of the great slaughter made among them through the successful attacks of his own troops, sent his armies to cut off their retreat. During the night they got beyond the robbers, who, when they began their march on the morrow, found themselves between two armies of the Nephites. Many thousands surrendered, and the remainder were slain. Zemnarihah was taken and hanged to the top of a tree; which when he was dead, the Nephites cut down. They then greatly rejoiced and praised God for his mercies and blessings in delivering them from their enemies.

The soldiers of Gidgiddoni succeeded in taking as prisoners all the robbers that were not killed. The word of God was preached to them, and those who repented of their sins and covenanted to cease their evil practices, were set at liberty. The remainder were condemned for their crimes and punished according to law. This entirely broke up these bands of murderers and robbers, and peace and righteousness again prevailed (A. C. 21), but it was not until five years later (A. C. 26) that the Nephites returned to and possessed their old homes.

CHAPTER XLI.

THE LAST CHIEF JUDGE MURDERED AND THE REPUBLIC OVERTHROWN—THE SIGNS OF THE SAVIOR'S DEATH APPEAR—A TERRIBLE STORM—THE UNIVERSAL DARKNESS—THE UNPARALLELED DESTRUCTION — THE TERROR OF THOSE HOURS.

(III. NEPHI CHAP. 6 TO 9.)

THE NEXT year the laws were revised according to justice and equity. They had, doubtless, been violently tampered with during the times that the Gadianton robbers held control of the administration and elected the officers. Good order now prevailed throughout the whole land. Soon new cities were founded and built, and many improvements made. Yet for all this, the peace was short lived. Iniquity and dissension soon began to again raise their hideous heads, and the prophets and servants of God were persecuted and illegally condemned to death.

No officer, according to Nephite law, had power to condemn a person to death without the authority of the governor, but many of the prophets were put to death secretly by the judges. A complaint was entered against these judges to the governor and they were tried for their crimes, according to the law made by the people.

The kindred and friends of the offenders, with certain lawyers and high priests, entered into a secret covenant to destroy the people who were in favor of law and justice, and to save the guilty judges from the just penalty of their misdeeds. This was, in fact, the re-establishment of the order of Gadianton. They proposed to assassinate the governor, set up a king to rule the country, and destroy its liberties. That same year they murdered the chief judge Lachoneus, the younger, as he sat in the judgment seat. The result was not what the plotters anticipated; for the people, being dissatisfied with the condition of affairs, divided into tribes, every man with his family uniting with his kindred and friends. This completely disorganized the government and deranged the plans of the conspirators. Some men had large families and many kindred and friends, and their tribes were correspondingly large. Each tribe appointed its chief, or leader, and it was his special duty to see that the laws they had adopted were properly carried out (B. C. 30).

While these terrible social overturnings were taking place on this continent, how different were the events that were occurring in the midst of the house of Israel on the eastern continent! for it was in this year that Jesus, the Redeemer of the world, was baptized by John in Jordan, as Lehi, Nephi, and others of the ancient prophets had long before foretold; and it was in this year that he commenced his public ministry, and began to teach men the law of his gospel.

There was but little to unite the Nephite tribes except their fear of the Gadianton robbers. This appears to have led to a confederacy for the purpose of defense. They agreed to keep peace with one another, and establish laws to prevent one tribe trespassing upon the rights of the others.

The secret association that had slain the chief judge elected one Jacob to be their leader. Seeing that their enemies, the tribes of the people, were too numerous to contend with, he commanded his followers to flee into the northernmost parts of the land, where they could build up a kingdom to themselves. They carried out his plan, and their flight was too speedy to be intercepted. In the north they built a large city which they called Jacobugath.

In this calamitous condition of affairs Nephi was called, by the voice of the Lord and the administration of angels, to labor diligently in the ministry among this wicked people. At first, but few accepted the truth; but in the following year (A. C. 32) many were baptized into the church. As the succeeding year (A. C. 33) passed away the people began to look anxiously for the fulfillment of the predictions of Samuel, the Lamanite, concerning the important events which would take place at the death of our Savior. Notwithstanding the many predictions of the prophets already fulfilled, there was much doubt and uneasiness among the people concerning that which was yet in the future. They had not long to wait, however, for the fulfillment of his words.

On the fourth day of the thirty-fourth Nephite year the promised signs of the Savior's crucifixion began. A horrible and devastating tempest burst upon the land. All that was ever told of the loudest thunder, and all that was ever seen of the most vivid lightning, would fail to picture the terrific visitation. The earth quivered and groaned and opened in wide, unfathomable chasms. Forests of gigantic trees were uprooted and carried high above the earth to meet in fearful shocks in the air and then to be driven down again and shattered upon the unyielding rocks. Mountains were riven and swallowed up in yawning gulfs, or were scattered into fragments and dispersed like hail before the tearing wind.

Cattle were lifted from their feet and dashed over precipices, or were hurried before the blast to perish in the far off sea. Towers, temples, homes, were torn up, scattered in fragments or crushed by falling rocks, and together with their inmates were ground to dust in the convulsion. Human beings were hurled high into the air and driven from point to point, until, they found graves fathoms deep below the earth's surface. Blue and yellow flames burst from the edges of sinking rocks, blazed for a moment and then all was the deepest darkness again. Boiling springs gushed upwards from sulphurous caverns. Shrieks and howls from suffering animals, awful in themselves, were drowned in the overwhelming uproar. Rain poured down in torrents, cloud-bursts, like floods, washed away all with which they came in contact, and pillars of steaming vapor seemed to unite the earth and sky.

This unparalleled storm raged throughout the land for three hours only—but to those who suffered it seemed an age.

During its short continuance the whole face of nature was changed. Mountains sank, valleys rose, the sea swept over the plains, large stagnant lakes usurped the place of flourishing cities, great chasms, rents and precipices disfigured the face of the earth. Many cities were destroyed by earthquakes, fire, and the tumultuous overflow of the waters of the great seas.

Three days of unnatural and impenetrable darkness followed the horrors of the tempest, and from the heavens the voice of the Lord was heard by the affrighted people, proclaiming in their terrified ears the destruction that had taken place.

Terrible was the catalogue of woes that that heavenly voice rehearsed. The great city of Zarahemla and the inhabitants thereof God had burned with fire. Moroni had been sunken in the depths of the sea and her iniquitous children had been drowned. Gilgal had been swallowed up in an earthquake and her people were entombed in the bowels

DESTRUCTION OF ZARAHEMLA.

of the earth. Onihah, Mocum and Jerusalem had disappeared and waters overflowed the places where they so lately stood. Gadiandi, Gadiomnah, Jacob and Gimgimno were all overthrown, and desolate hills and valleys occupied their places, while their inhabitants were buried deep in the earth Jacobugath, Laman, Josh, Gad and Kishkumen had all been burned, most probably by lightnings from heaven. The desolation was complete, the face of the land was changed, tens of thousands, probably millions of souls had been suddenly called to meet the reward of their sinful lives; for this destruction came upon them that their wickedness and their abominations might be hid from the face of heaven, and that the blood of the prophets and the saints might not come up any more in appeal unto God against them.

CHAPTER XLII.

THE VOICE FROM HEAVEN—THE SAVIOR TESTIFIES OF HIMSELF—SILENCE THROUGHOUT THE LAND—HOW OFT WOULD CHRIST HAVE GATHERED HIS PEOPLE—THE DARKNESS DEPARTS.

(III. NEPHI CHAP. 9 AND 10.)

WHEN the heavenly voice had finished the recital of the calamities that had befallen the land and its inhabitants, the speaker commenced an appeal to those who yet lived, and revealed to them who he was. He declared unto them:

O all ye that are spared because ye were more righteous than they, will ye not now return unto me, and repent of your sins, and be converted, that I may heal you?

Yea, verily I say unto you, if ye will come unto me ye shall have eternal life. Behold, mine arm of mercy is extended towards you, and whosoever will come, him will I receive: and blessed are those who come unto me.

Behold, I am Jesus Christ, the Son of God. I created the heavens and the earth, and all things that in them are. I was with the Father from the beginning. I am in the Father, and the Father in me; and in me hath the Father glorified his name.

I came unto my own, and my own received me not. And the scriptures concerning my coming are fulfilled.

And as many as have received me, to them have I given to become the sons of God, and even so will I to as many as shall believe on my name, for behold, by me redemption cometh, and in me is the law of Moses fulfilled.

I am the light and the life of the world. I am Alpha and Omega, the beginning and the end.

And ye shall offer up unto me no more the shedding of blood; yea, your sacrifices and your burnt offerings shall be done away, for I will accept none of your sacrifices and your burnt offerings;

And ye shall offer for a sacrifice unto me a broken heart and a contrite spirit. And whoso cometh unto me with a broken heart and a contrite spirit, him will I baptize with fire and with the Holy Ghost, even as the Lamanites, because of their faith in me at the time of their conversion, were baptized with fire and with the Holy Ghost, and they knew it not.

Behold, I have come unto the world to bring redemption unto the world, to save the world from sin;

Therefore, whoso repenteth and cometh unto me as a little child, him will I receive: for of such is the kingdom of God. Behold, for such I have laid down my life, and have taken it up again; therefore repent, and come unto me ye ends of the earth, and be saved.

After the people had heard this glad message of forgiveness and redemption, they ceased their mourning for their dead relatives, and there was silence in the land for the space of many hours. Then again was the voice heard, even the voice of Jesus, recounting how oft he had sought to gather his Israel but they would not, and promising in the future that he would again gather them, if they would listen unto him. But if they would not heed him, the places of their dwellings should become desolate until the time of the fulfilling of God's covenant with their fathers. When the people heard this awful prophecy they began to weep and howl again because of the loss of their kindred and friends.

Three days had passed in darkness, in terror and in woe, when the thick mist rolled off the face of the land, revealing to the astonished eyes of the survivors how great had been the convulsions that had shaken the earth. When the darkness passed away the earth ceased to tremble, the rocks were no longer rent, the dreadful groanings ceased, and the tumultuous noises ended. Then nature was again at peace, and peace filled the hearts of the living; their mourning was turned to praise, and their joy was in Christ their Deliverer.

As on the eastern continent, so on this; at the time of Christ's resurrection, numbers of the saints who were dead arose from their graves and were seen and known by many of the living. Christ had suffered for the sin of the world, he had broken the bands of death, he had opened the portals of the tomb, and as soon as he came forth conqueror over death and hell, the faithful ones of many generations, who were prepared for the glories of eternity, came forth also. This was the first resurrection.

CHAPTER XLIII.

CHRIST APPEARS IN THE LAND BOUNTIFUL—THE TESTIMONY OF THE FATHER—JESUS CALLS TWELVE DISCIPLES—HIS TEACHINGS TO THEM AND TO THE MULTITUDE.

(III. NEPHI CHAP. 11 TO 14.)

SOME time after the tribulations that marked the sacrifice of the Lord of life and glory, exactly how long we know not, a multitude assembled near the temple which was in the land Bountiful. The sacred building, it seems, was not destroyed in the late overwhelming convulsions. Possibly many of the high priesthood had assembled there to call upon the Lord, and to officiate in the duties of their calling. At any rate, those whom Jesus deemed worthy to be his twelve disciples, by some inspiration, gathered there. With the rest of the multitude they conversed on the marvelous changes that had been wrought by the desolating earthquakes and their attendant horrors. They also spake one to another with regard to the Savior, of whose death the three days of unexampled, impenetrable darkness had been a sign.

While thus engaged a strange, sweet voice fell upon their ears, yet it pierced them to the centre, that their whole frames trembled. At first they wist not what it said or whence it came nor even when the words were again repeated did they understand. But when they came a third time they understood their glorious import, and knew that it was the voice of God. He said unto them, Behold my beloved Son, in whom I am well pleased, in whom I have glorified my name: hear ye him. Obedient to this heavenly voice they cast their eyes upward, and to their joyous astonishment beheld the Messiah, clothed in a white robe, descending out of heaven.

Even yet they did not comprehend who it was, but thought him an angel. As he descended to the earth and stood in their midst, their wondering eyes were all turned toward him, but for awe not a mouth was opened nor was a limb moved. Then the Redeemer stretched forth his hand and said unto the multitude: Behold I am Jesus Christ, whom the prophets testified should come into the world; and behold, I am the life and light of the world; and I have drunk out of the bitter cup which the Father hath given to me, and have glorified the Father in taking upon me the sins of the world, in the which I have suffered the will of the Father in all things from, the beginning.

Then the whole multitude fell to the earth, they remembered the sayings of the prophets, they realized that their God stood in the midst of them.

Again the risen Redeemer spake: Arise, said he, and come forth unto me that you may thrust your hands into my side, and also that ye may feel the prints of the nails in my hands and in my feet, that ye may know that I am the God of Israel and the God of the whole earth, and have been slain for the sins of the world.

Now they who heard him from the first to the last went forth and assured themselves that it was he of whom the prophets had spoken. Then with shouts of praise they cried: Hosanna! blessed be the name of the Most High God. And they fell down at his feet and worshiped him.

Jesus next called Nephi to him, then eleven others, and gave them authority to baptize the people, at the same time strictly charging them as to the manner in which they performed this ordinance, that all disputes on this point might cease among the believers. The names of the Twelve whom he chose were: Nephi, his brother Timothy, whom he had beforetime raised from the dead, also his son Jonas, and Mathoni, Mathonihah, Kumen, Kumenonhi, Jeremiah, Shemnon, Jonas, Zedekiah and Isaiah. These Twelve are to sit in the great day of judgment as the judges of the seed of Lehi, and be themselves judged by the Twelve Apostles whom Jesus had called from among the Jews.

After Jesus had chosen the Twelve, he commenced to teach the people the principles of the fullness of the gospel. Step by step he led them over the same precious ground of universal truth as he had his followers in the temple at Jerusalem, by the shore of the Sea of Galilee, and on the hillsides of Judea and Samaria. Sometimes, through the difference of the inspired translation of the Book of Mormon from the worldly-wise one of the Bible, a slight difference is noticeable in the wording of the instructions, but as a rule these differences are trivial, the advantage being with the Nephites, whose greater faith drew from the Savior deeper truths than Judah had received, or caused him to display greater manifestations of his omnipotence and boundless love. From the believers he would turn to the Twelve, and give them special instructions as his ministers, then again he would shed forth his words of mercy, truth and divine wisdom upon the multitude; and by and by again address the disciples. So he continued day by day until all was revealed, either to the multitude or to the Twelve, that was necessary for the eternal salvation of the obedient.

Some have wondered why Jesus should have given so many of the same teachings to the Nephites as he did to the Jews. The reason is that those teachings were perfect and could not be improved. They were universal, that is, they were adapted to the wants of all peoples, whether of Israel or of the Gentiles, whether of Judah or Joseph. They were a portion of the everlasting gospel and had to be preached to all the world as a witness, to those who dwelt in America as well as those of Asia, Africa and Europe. Thus we find in the teachings given to the Nephites what we term the first principles of the gospel—faith, repentance and baptism; we also find those divine lessons of love, truth, humility and duty that glorified the Savior's "Sermon on the Mount." These we shall not reproduce but will draw attention to other teachings of the Savior not recorded by the Four Evangelists; that is they are not to be found in their writings as at present contained in the New Testament.

CHAPTER XLIV.

THE FULFILLMENT OF THE MOSAIC LAW—"OTHER SHEEP HAVE I"—THE TEN TRIBES—THE EVENTS OF THE LATTER DAYS.

(III. NEPHI CHAP. 15 AND 16.)

WHEN JESUS had reached a certain point in his teachings wherein he told the people that old things had passed away and that all things had become new he perceived that some of his hearers were wondering what were his intentions regarding the law of Moses. Therefore he next instructed them on this point. He said:

Marvel not that I said unto you, that old things had passed away, and that all things had become new.

Behold I say unto you, that the law is fulfilled that was given unto Moses.

Behold, I am he that gave the law, and I am he who covenanted with my people Israel: therefore, the law in me is fulfilled, for I have come to fulfill the law; therefore it hath an end.

Behold, I do not destroy the prophets, for as many as have not been fulfilled in me, verily I say unto you, shall all be fulfilled.

And because I said unto you, that old things hath passed away, I do not destroy that which hath been spoken concerning things which are to come.

For behold, the covenant which I have made with my people is not all fulfilled; but the law which was given unto Moses hath an end in me.

Behold, I am the law, and the light; look unto me, and endure to the end, and ye shall live, for unto him that endureth to the end, will I give eternal life.

Behold, I have given unto you the commandments, therefore keep my commandments. And this is the law and the prophets, for they truly testified of me.

How simple yet how grand, how plain yet how comprehensive are these teachings, both with regard to himself and to the law which he had given to the forefathers of the Jews and the Nephites! If men would but receive these instructions in the plainness in which they are given, how much controversy would have an end, how much dissension would never have had an existence!

After giving these explanations to the multitude, Jesus again turned to the twelve chosen disciples and told them the meaning of his words when he said unto the Jews: Other sheep I have which are not of this fold; them also I must bring, and they shall hear my voice; and there shall be one fold and one shepherd.

These other sheep of which he spake, Jesus said, were the Nephites themselves, who had been separated from the Jews because of the latter's iniquity; and because of their continued evil doing and lack of faith the knowledge of the existence of Lehi's family on the American continent had been withheld from them. But still more, Jesus had yet other sheep, which were neither of the Jews nor of the Nephites, nor of the lands in which they dwelt. They were a people whom he had not yet visited and who had not yet heard his voice; but he had received a commandment from his Father to visit them, to show himself unto them, and teach them, and then they all would be of the one fold and he would be the one shepherd to them all.

These other sheep, neither Jew nor Nephite, we understand to be the ten tribes of Israel who were carried into captivity, but who, unlike the house of Judah, never returned to their homes in the Promised Land. We are told that they were led away by the power of the Lord to a land of which no one knows anything, only that which God has revealed.

Jesus then told his disciples many things relating to the age in which we live. He explained to them how the Gentiles living on this continent would have the truth presented to them, how they would grow haughty, proud and exceedingly wicked, and how they would oppress the remnants of the house of Israel who dwelt on this broad land. Then how these remnants would have the fullness of the gospel brought to them, and how eventually the house of Israel would be used to punish the disobedient of the Gentiles, who should become as salt that had lost its savor, good for nothing but to be cast out and trodden under foot of men.

CHAPTER XLV.

THE SAVIOR HEALS THE SICK—HE BLESSES THE CHILDREN OF THE NEPHITES—ANGELS MINISTER UNTO THEM.

(III. NEHI CHAP. 17.)

WHEN the Redeemer had finished these teachings he looked around among the multitude and perceived that their minds were not prepared, at that time, to receive any more of the word of the Lord, so he told them to go to their homes, and prepare their minds for the morrow, when he would come unto them again. But as he gazed upon them he noticed that they were in tears, and that they looked beseechingly upon him, as if they would ask him to tarry a little longer with them.

These mute entreaties prevailed with him, his bowels were filled with compassion towards them; and, we are told, he said:

Have ye any that are sick among you, bring them hither. Have ye any that are lame, or blind, or halt, or maimed, or leprous, or that are withered, or that are deaf, or that are afflicted in any manner, bring them hither and I will heal them, for I have compassion upon you; my bowels are filled with mercy:

For I perceive that ye desire that I should show unto you what I have done unto your brethren at Jerusalem, for I see that your faith is sufficient that I should heal you.

And it came to pass that when he had thus spoken, all the multitude, with one accord, did go forth with their sick, and their afflicted, and their lame, and with their blind, and with their dumb, and with all they that were afflicted in any manner; and he did heal them every one as they were brought forth unto him.

And they did all, both they who had been healed and they who were whole, bow down at his feet, and did worship him; and as many as could come from the multitude did kiss his feet, insomuch that they did bathe his feet with their tears.

Jesus next commanded that the little children should be brought.

So the people brought their little children and set them down upon the ground round about him, and the multitude gave way till they had all been brought to him. And when they had all been brought, and Jesus stood in the midst, he commanded the multitude to kneel down upon the ground. And when they had done so, Jesus groaned within himself, and said, Father, I am troubled because of the wickedness of the people of the house of Israel. And when he had said these words, he himself knelt and he prayed unto the Father and the things which he prayed could not be written, but the multitude who heard him bore record: that eye had never seen, neither had ear heard, before, so great and marvelous things as they saw and heard Jesus speak unto the Father. When Jesus had made an end of praying, he arose, but so great was the joy of the multitude that they were overcome. But Jesus bade them arise. Then they arose, and he said unto them, Blessed are ye because of your faith. And now behold, my joy is full. And when he had said these words, he wept; and he took the little children, one by one, and blessed them, and prayed unto the Father for them. And when he had done this he wept again. And he said unto the multitude, Behold your little ones.

And as they cast their eyes upward they saw the heavens open, and angels descending out of the heaven, as it were in the midst of fire, and they came down and encircled these little ones about, and they were encircled with fire; and the angels did minister unto the children. And the multitude, who numbered about 2,500 men, women and children, bore record of the glorious things which they had seen, heard and partaken of.

Can we imagine anything more lovely, more touching, and more glorious than this scene must have been? Can we conceive the joy that must have filled the hearts of these Nephites as they beheld the angels of heaven descending from the courts of glory and ministering to their little ones? How deep must have been their love for the Savior who had brought these blessings to them? how strong must have grown their faith in him? We cannot recall a circumstance in recorded history that draws earth nearer to heaven than this, or that seems to bind the ties so strongly that unite the powers of eternity with the children of mortality.

CHAPTER XLVI.

THE SACRAMENT ADMINISTERED—THE SAVIOR'S TEACHINGS REGARDING IT—HE CONFERS ON HIS DISCIPLES THE POWER TO GIVE THE HOLY GHOST — HE ASCENDS INTO HEAVEN.

(III. NEPHI CHAP. 18.)

JESUS next commanded his disciples to bring him some bread and wine. While they were gone to obtain them, he caused the multitude to sit down upon the earth. When the disciples returned with the bread and wine, he took the bread, and brake and blessed it. This he gave to the disciples and they did eat and were filled. He then commanded them to give unto the multitudes.

When the multitudes had eaten and were filled, Jesus began to instruct the people with regard to the meaning of the bread they had just partaken of. He said:

And this shall ye always observe to do, even as I have done, even as I have broken the bread, and blessed it, and gave it unto you.

And this shall ye do in remembrance of my body, which I have shown unto you. And it shall be a testimony unto the Father, that ye do always remember me. And if ye do always remember me, ye shall have my Spirit to be with you.

After this he gave of the wine to his disciples, and they drank thereof, and then, by his direction, they gave it to the people.

After they had done this Jesus continued his teachings; Blessed are ye, said he, for this thing which ye have done, for this is fulfilling my commandments, and this doth witness unto the Father, that ye are willing to do that which I have commanded you.

And this shall ye always do to those who repent and are baptized in my name; and ye shall do it in remembrance of my blood, which I have shed for you, that ye may witness unto the Father that ye do always remember me. And if ye do always remember me, ye shall have my Spirit to be with you.

And now behold, this is the commandment which I give unto you, that ye shall not suffer anyone, knowingly, to partake of my flesh and blood unworthily, when ye shall minister it;

For whoso eateth and drinketh my flesh and blood unworthily, eateth and drinketh damnation to his soul; therefore if ye know that a man is unworthy to eat and drink of my flesh and blood, ye shall forbid him;

Nevertheless ye shall not cast him out from among you, but ye shall minister unto him, and shall pray for him unto the Father in my name, and if it so be that he repenteth, and is baptized in my name, then shall ye receive him, and shall minister unto him of my flesh and blood;

But if he repent not, he shall not be numbered among my people, that he may not destroy my people, for behold I know my sheep, and they are numbered.

The Lord also gave the people much instruction regarding prayer. Among other things he told them:

Behold, verily, verily, I say unto you, ye must watch and pray always, lest ye enter into temptation; for Satan desireth to have you; that he may sift you as wheat;

Therefore ye must always pray unto the Father in my name;

And whatsoever ye shall ask the Father in my name, which is right, believing that ye shall receive, behold it shall be given unto you.

Pray in your families unto the Father, always in my name, that your wives and your children may be blessed.

And behold, ye shall meet together oft, and ye shall not

forbid any man from coming unto you when ye shall meet together, but suffer them that they may come unto you, and forbid them not;

But ye shall pray for them, and shall not cast them out; and if it so be that they come unto you oft, ye shall pray for them unto the Father, in my name;

Therefore hold up your light that it may shine unto the world. Behold I am the light which ye shall hold up—that which ye have seen me do. Behold ye see that I prayed unto the Father, and ye have witnessed;

And ye see that I have commanded that none of you should go away, but rather have commanded that ye should come unto me, that ye might feel and see; even so shall ye do unto the world; and whosoever breaketh this commandment suffereth himself to be led into temptation.

When Jesus had made an end of his sayings, he touched with his hand the disciples whom he had chosen, one by one. As he touched them he gave them power to give the Holy Ghost. When he had done this a cloud overshadowed the multitude, and they saw Jesus no more that day; but the disciples saw him, and bore record that he ascended into heaven.

CHAPTER XLVII.

JESUS RETURNS AND RENEWS HIS TEACHINGS—HE ADMINISTERS THE SACRAMENT—HE EXPLAINS THE TEACHINGS OF THE PROPHETS—THE WORDS OF MALACHI.

(III. NEPHI CHAP. 19 TO 26.)

WHEN JESUS had ascended into heaven the multitudes dispersed, every one returning home.

All that evening and all that night was the news spread from mouth to mouth that Jesus had come. Many were too excited to sleep, and labored diligently spreading the news far and wide, so that when the morning came the whole people were astir, wending their way to the place where Jesus was expected.

When the multitude had gathered together their number was found to be so great that the disciples divided them into twelve congregations, and one of them taught each of these bodies.

After they had prayed to the Father in the name of Jesus the whole people, led by the disciples, went down to the water's edge. First, Nephi went into the water and was baptized; then he baptized those whom Jesus had chosen. After these had been baptized the Holy Ghost fell upon them, and they were filled therewith also with fire. And the fire encircled them about, and angels came down from heaven and ministered to them.

By and by Jesus himself came, and stood in the midst of his disciples and taught them. He commanded them all, the people and the Twelve, to again kneel upon the earth, and the disciples he instructed to pray.

And they prayed unto Jesus, calling him their Lord and their God.

When Jesus heard these prayers he went a little way off, bowed himself to the earth and said:

Father, I thank thee that thou hast given the Holy Ghost unto these whom I have chosen and it is because of their belief in me, that I have chosen them out of the world.

Father, I pray thee that thou wilt give the Holy Ghost unto all them that shall believe in their words.

Father, thou hast given them the Holy Ghost, because they believe in me, and thou seest that they believe in me, bcause thou hearest them, and they pray unto me; and they pray unto me because I am with them.

And now, Father, I pray unto thee for them, and also for all those who shall believe on their words, that they may believe in me, that I may be in them as thou, Father, art in me, that we may be one.

When our Savior had ended this prayer he returned to his disciples. He found them still praying. Then he blessed them, and smiled upon them. When he smiled the light of his countenance shone upon them, and in reflection of his brightness they became as white as the face or the garments of Jesus;—a whiteness like unto which there was nothing upon this earth.

Jesus, in joy, once more retired a short distance to commune with his Father in heaven. He prayed:

Father, I thank thee that thou hast purified those whom I have chosen, because of their faith, and I pray for them, and also for them who shall believe on their words that they may be purified in me, through faith on their words, even as they are purified in me.

Father, I pray not for the world, but those whom thou hast given me out of the world, because of their faith, that they may be purified in me, that I may be in them as thou,

Father, art in me, that we may be one, that I may be glorified in them.

And when Jesus had spoken these words, he came again unto his disciples, and behold they did pray steadfastly, without ceasing, unto him; and he did smile upon them again; and behold they were white even as Jesus.

And it came to pass that he went again a little way off and prayed unto the Father;

And tongue cannot speak the words which he prayed, neither can be written by man the words which he prayed.

And the multitude did hear, and do bear record, and their hearts were opened, and they did understand in their hearts the words which he prayed.

Nevertheless, so great and marvelous were the words which he prayed, that they cannot be written, neither can they be uttered by man.

And it came to pass that when Jesus had made an end of praying, he came again to the disciples, and said unto them, so great faith have I never seen among all the Jews; wherefore I could not show unto them so great miracles, because of their unbelief.

Verily I say unto you, there are none of them that have seen so great things as ye have seen; neither have they heard so great things as ye have heard.

The Lord Jesus then commanded all to cease from praying, but he also told them they must not cease to pray in their hearts. He next directed them to arise; and at this word they stood upon their feet. Then he administered unto them bread and wine, the emblems of his body and blood given as a ransom for their sins and the sins of the whole world.

Where he obtained this bread and wine no one knew, for neither the disciples nor the people had brought any with them.

When the multitudes had eaten and drank, they were

filled with the Spirit, and with one voice gave glory to Jesus, whom they both saw and heard.

The Savior then commenced to explain to the multitudes many of the sayings of the ancient prophets, more especially those of Isaiah. He dwelt on the great events of the latter days that should precede his second coming; drawing particular attention to those that would concern and be connected with the remnants of the house of Lehi, and in which they would take part. From his words we learn that in the latter times the everlasting gospel will be preached in their midst; that many will receive it; that they will take a prominent part in the building of the New Jerusalem, and in many of the other momentous events that will herald the near approach of that blessed day when the reign of Christ and the triumph of truth and righteousness shall extend from pole to pole, over the whole of this habitable globe.

The Savior also recited to them many of the words which his Father had inspired the Prophet Malachi to utter. Now the Nephites knew nothing of Malachi, as he lived and prophesied to the Jews long after Lehi left Jerusalem. So, for the comfort and instruction of the Nephites, Jesus rehearsed to them the important things which he had revealed. In fact, to use the words of Mormon: And he did expound all things, even from the beginning until the time that he should come in his glory; yea, even all things which should come upon the face of the earth, even until the elements should melt with fervent heat, and the earth should be wrapt together as a scroll, and the heavens and the earth should pass away; and even unto the great and last day, when all people and all kindreds, and all nations and tongues shall stand before God, to be judged of their works, whether they be good or whether they be evil; If they be good, to the resurrection of everlasting life; and if they be evil, to the resurrection of damnation, being on a parallel, the one on the one hand, and the other on the other hand, according to the mercy, and the justice, and the holiness which is in Christ, who was before the world began.

And now there cannot be written in this book even a hundredth part of the things which Jesus did truly teach unto the people.

CHAPTER XLVIII.

THE SAVIOR CONTINUES HIS MINISTRATIONS—HE RAISES A MAN FROM THE DEAD—THE LABORS OF THE TWELVE—THE NAME OF THE CHURCH—THE THREE WHO SHOULD REMAIN.

(III. NEPHI CHAP. 27 TO 30.)

FOR THREE days did the Savior mingle with the Nephites and instruct them; and even after that he met with them oft, and with them partook of the Sacrament of the Lord's supper.

More than this, he ministered to and blessed the children of the Nephites. He loosed the tongues of these little ones, that they spoke great and marvelous things unto their parents, even, we are told, greater things than Jesus had revealed to the people.

Jesus also healed all their sick. The lame, the blind, the deaf, were made whole, and one man he raised from the dead.

From this time the twelve disciples began to baptize and teach as many as came unto them; and as many as were baptized in the name of Jesus were filled with the Holy Ghost. Many of them saw and heard wondrous things which are not lawful to be written.

On one occasion when the disciples were thus traveling, preaching, and baptizing, they united together in fasting and mighty prayer. The subject about which they prayed the most earnestly was, what should be the name of the Church, for its members were not united on this matter.

While they were thus engaged Jesus again showed himself unto them, and in answer to their inquiries regarding the name of his church he told them, Whatsoever ye shall do ye shall do it in my name; therefore ye shall call the church in my name; and ye shall call upon the Father in my name, that he will bless the church for my sake. He further said to them if they called the church by the name of a man it would be that man's church, if by Moses' name it would be Moses' church; but being his church it should be called by his holy name. And many other instructions gave he unto them at this time.

It was during this interview that the Savior asked the Twelve, one by one, What is it that you desire of me, after I am gone to the Father?

Then nine of them said, We desire after we have lived unto the age of man, that our ministry wherein thou hast called us, may have an end, that we may speedily come unto thee in thy kingdom.

And he said unto them, Blessed are ye, because ye desire this thing of me; therefore after that ye are seventy and two years old, ye shall come unto me in my kingdom and with me ye shall find rest.

Then he turned to the three who had not answered, and again asked them what they would have him do for them. But they faltered in their answer; their wish was such a peculiar one, that they were afraid to express it. And he said unto them, behold, I know your thoughts, and ye have desired the thing which John, my beloved, who was with me in my ministry before that I was lifted up by the Jews, desired of me;

Therefore more blessed are ye, for ye shall never taste of death, but ye shall live to behold all the doings of the Father, unto the children of men, even until all things shall be fulfilled, according to the will of the Father, when I shall come in my glory, with the powers of heaven;

And ye shall never endure the pains of death; but when I shall come in my glory, ye shall be changed in the twinkling of an eye from mortality to immortality: and then shall ye be blessed in the kingdom of my Father.

And again, ye shall not have pain while ye shall dwell in the flesh, neither sorrow, save it be for the sins of the world: and all this will I do because of the thing which ye have desired of me, for ye have desired that ye might bring the souls of men unto me, while the world shall stand;

And for this cause ye shall have fullness of joy; and ye shall sit down in the kingdom of my Father; yea your joy shall be full, even as the Father hath given me fullness of joy; and ye shall be even as I am, and I am even as the Father; and the Father and I are one.

These are the three Nephites of whom we sometimes hear and who either singly or together have appeared to believers in this generation.

Then Jesus with his finger touched the nine who were to die, but the three who were to live he did not touch; and then he departed. And behold, the heavens were opened, and the three were caught up into heaven, and saw unspeakable things.

And it was forbidden them that they should utter, neither was it given unto them power that they could utter, the things which they saw and heard;

The sacred record gives no information as to who the three were who were not to taste of death. Mormon was about to write their names, but the Lord forbade him.

Some have supposed that Nephi, the senior of the disciples, was one of these three undying ones, who remained to minister on the earth to the people of the latter days; that is hid from our knowledge, no doubt for a wise purpose. If he was, he lived through that most happy era of Nephite history, when all was righteousness, and joy, and peace throughout America's vast domain; he lived to suffer, with his two brethren, all the persecutions which the wicked, in later days, so frequently imposed upon these three favored servants of the Lord, and in the end he retired from the midst of mankind when overwhelming corruption again paralyzed the life of the Nephite nation. If he was one of the nine who passed away to the presence of their Savior and their God after they had dwelt three score and twelve years in mortality he must have laid aside his earthly tabernacle under as happy circumstances as ever prophet or apostle died, surrounded by a loving, faithful people, amongst whom the practice of iniquity was a remembrance of the past. No ruffian hands cut short his life, or tortured his latest hours, but in the midst of the most holy peace he passed away to the glories of the eternal world.

CHAPTER XLIX.

THE LONG CONTINUED ERA OF PEACE AND RIGHTEOUSNESS—DEATH OF NEPHI—HIS SON AMOS—AMOS THE SECOND.

(IV. NEPHI.)

WHEN Jesus left the Nephites to the care of his disciples he had so thoroughly filled the people with the influences and powers of the eternal worlds that evil utterly ceased in their midst; they were united in all things temporal and spiritual. Universal peace prevailed. Love, joy, harmony, everything desirable to make the life of man a perfect condition of unalloyed, holy happiness reigned supreme. Indeed, it may be said that a type, a foreshadowing of the millennium for once found place and foothold among the erring sons of humanity.

At this blessed period Nephi, the son of Nephi, received the sacred plates. His duty, as the recorder of the doings of his people, was a most happy one; he had nothing but good to relate of their lives and actions, and to record that perfect peace prevailed on all the vast continent. The Nephites increased in numbers (Lamanites there were none), they prospered in circumstances, they grew in material wealth, all of which was held in common, according to the order of God. They colonized and spread far abroad; they rebuilt their ancient capital and many other cities; they also founded many new ones. Above all, they were rich in heavenly treasures; the Holy Spirit reigned in every heart and illumined every soul.

When Nephi died (A. C. 110) this inexpressibly happy, heavenly state still continued in undiminished warmth of divine and brotherly love and strength of abiding faith. All the generation to which Nephi belonged entered in at the strait gate, and walked the narrow way to the eternal city of God; not one of them was lost.

At Nephi's death his son Amos became the custodian of the holy things; and he held them for eighty-four years (from A. C. 110 to A. C. 194). He lived in the days of the Nephites' greatest prosperity and happiness. The perfect law of righteousness was still their only guide. But before he passed away to his heavenly home, a small cloud had appeared upon the horizon, fatal harbinger of the approaching devastating hurricane. A few, weary of the uninterrupted bliss, the perfect harmony, the universal love that everywhere prevailed, seceded from the church and took upon them the title of Lamanites, which ill-boding name had only been known to the Nephites by tradition for more than one hundred years. It may be asked, How was it possible that men and women should withdraw from such a holy order or society where all was perfect peace, where every man dealt justly with his neighbor, where none inflicted wrongs and none suffered from injustice done them—where angels ministered to the children of mortality, and heavenly revelations were their constant guides? If the inquirer will answer why Lucifer, the son of the morning, in heaven itself, rebelled against the Almighty Father, and led astray one-third of the angelic hosts, we will reply by saying that he, Satan, tempted the dissenting Nephites with this same spirit of rebellion to the divine power, and that he succeeded in ensnaring them and leading them away captive to his will.

A second Amos succeeded his father as the keeper of the records. His duties were not the happy ones of his immediate predecessors. Instead of good he had to chronicle much evil.

Amos himself was a righteous man, but he lived to witness an ever increasing flood of iniquity break over the land, a phase of evil-doing that arose not from ignorance and false tradition, but from direct and willful rebellion against God, and apostasy from his laws. The wholesome checks to vice and misery found in the plan of salvation were knowingly and intentionally removed or done away; the voice of reason was disregarded; the promptings of the Holy Spirit were defiantly repelled; men's unbridled passions again bore sway; disunion, dissension, violence, hatred, distress, dismay, bloodshed and havoc spread the wide continents over; and from their high pinnacle of righteousness, peace, happiness, refinement, social advantage, etc., the people were hurled once more into an abyss of misery and barbarism, now more profound, more torturing, and more degrading than ever.

CHAPTER L.

THE COMMENCEMENT OF THE APOSTASY—IT GROWS IN INTENSITY—THE PERSECUTION OF THE DISCIPLES—LAMANITES AGAIN—REAPPEARANCE OF THE GADIANTON BANDS—WAR—AMMARON HIDES THE RECORDS.

(IV. NEPHI.)

BY THE year A. C. 201, all the second generation had passed away save a few; the people had greatly multiplied and spread over the face of the land, north and south, and had become exceedingly rich; they wore costly apparel which they adorned with ornaments of gold and silver, pearls and precious stones. From this date they no more had their property in common, but, like the rest of the world, every man sought gain, wealth, power and influence for himself and his. All the old evils arising from selfishness were revived. Soon they began to build churches after their own fashion, and hire preachers who pandered to their lusts; some even began to deny the Savior.

From A. C. 210 to A. C. 230, the people waxed greatly in iniquity and impurity of life. Different dissenting sects multiplied, infidels abounded. The three remaining disciples were sorely persecuted, notwithstanding that they performed many mighty miracles. They were shut up in prison, but the prisons were rent in twain by the power of God; they were cast into fiery furnaces, but the flames harmed them not; they were thrown into dens of wild beasts, but they played with the savage inmates as a child does with a lamb, and received no harm; they were not subject to many of the laws that govern our mortal bodies, they had passed through a glorious change, by which they were freed from earthly pain, suffering and death. Not only did the wicked persecute these three immortal ones; others also of God's people suffered from their unhallowed anger and bitter hatred; but the faithful neither reviled at the reviler nor smote the smiter; they bore these things with patience and fortitude, remembering the pains of their Redeemer.

In the year A. C. 231 there was a great division among the people. The old party lines were again definitely marked. Again the old animosity assumed shape, and Nephite and Lamanite once more became implacable foes. Those who rejected and renounced the gospel assumed the latter name, and with their eyes open, and a full knowledge of their inexcusable infamy, they taught their children the same base falsehoods that in ages past had caused the unceasing hatred that reigned in the hearts of the children of Laman and Lemuel toward the seed of their younger brothers.

By A. C. 244 the more wicked portion of the people had become exceedingly strong, as well as far more numerous than the righteous. They deluded themselves by building all sorts of churches, with creeds to suit the increasing depravity of the masses.

When 260 years had passed away, the Gadianton bands, with all their secret signs and abominations, through the cunning of Satan, again appeared and increased until, in A. C. 300, they had spread over all the land. By this time, also, the Nephites, having gradually forsaken their first love, had so far sunk in the abyss of iniquity that they had grown as wicked, as proud, as corrupt and as vile as the Lamanites. All were submerged in one overwhelming flood of infamy, and there were none that were righteous, save it were the disciples of Jesus.

Still, active hostilities did not break out for some time; but when war commenced, it scarcely ceased until that great battle near Cumorah, which brought extinction to the Nephite race. This war, or series of wars, was one of peculiar horrors. All the old savagery, ten times intensified, was rekindled, transforming the combatants into fiends. Each race seems to have striven to out-rival the other in its bloody and infernal inhumanity. Mormon, the Nephite prophet-general, in an epistle to his son Moroni, sorrowingly relates the fate of the Nephite prisoners—men, women and children—taken at Sherrizah. He adds: And the husbands and fathers of those women and children they [the Lamanites] have slain; and they feed the women upon the flesh of their husbands, and the children upon the flesh of their fathers; and no water save a little do they give them. And notwithstanding the abomination of the Lamanites, it doth not exceed that of our people in Moriantum. For behold, many of the daughters of the Lamanites have they taken prisoners; and after depriving them of that which was most dear and precious above all things, which is chastity and virtue; and after they had done this thing they did murder them in a most cruel manner, torturing their bodies even unto death; and after they have done this, they devour their flesh like unto wild beasts, because of the hardness of their hearts; and they do it for a token of bravery. Such was the horrible condition into which open, wilful, determined rejection of the gospel had brought both races.

Amos entrusted the records to his son Ammaron in the year 306 A. C.

Owing to the increasing depravity and vileness of the Nephites, Ammaron was constrained by the Holy Ghost to hide up all the sacred things which had been handed down from generation to generation (A. C. 320). The place where he hid them is said to have been in the land Antum, in a hill which was called Shim. After he had hid them up, he informed Mormon, then a child ten years old, of what he had done, and placed the buried treasures in his charge. He instructed Mormon to go, when he was about twenty-four years old, to the hill where they were hid, and take the plates of

Nephi and record thereon, what he had observed concerning the people. The remainder of the records, etc., he was to leave where they were.

CHAPTER LI.

THE LAST LONG SERIES OF WARS — MORMON — THE FINAL CONFLICT AT CUMORAH—THE LAST OF THE NEPHITES.

(MORMON.)

IT WAS in the year 322 A. C. that actual war broke out between the Nephites and Lamanites, for the first time since the Redeemer's appearing. It commenced in the land of Zarahemla near the waters of Sidon. A number of battles were fought, in which the armies of the former were victorious. Four years later the savage contest was renewed. In the interim iniquity had greatly increased. As foretold by the prophets, men's property became slippery, things movable were subject to unaccountable disappearances, and dread and distrust filled the hearts of the disobedient. When the war recommenced, the youthful Mormon was chosen to lead the armies of his nation.

The next year saw disaster follow the Nephite cause. The people retreated before the Lamanites to the north countries. The year following they met with still further reverses, and in A. C. 329 rapine, revolution and carnage prevailed throughout all the land.

In 330 the Lamanite king, Aaron, with an army of forty-four thousand men, was defeated by Mormon, who had forty-two thousand warriors under his command.

Five years later the Lamanites drove the degenerate Nephites to the land of Jashon, and thence yet further northward to the land of Shem. But in the year following the tide of victory changed, and Mormon, with thirty thousand troops, defeated fifty thousand of the enemy in the land of Shem; then he followed up with such energetic measures that by the year 349 the Nephites had again taken possession of the lands of their inheritance.

These successes resulted in a treaty between the Nephites as one party and the Lamanites and Gadianton robbers as the other. By its provisions the Nephites possessed the country north of the Isthmus, while the Lamanites held the regions south. A peace of ten years followed this treaty.

In the year 360, the king of the Lamanites again declared war. To repel the expected invasion, the people of Nephi gathered at the land of Desolation. There the Lamanites attacked them, were defeated, and returned home. Not content with this repulse, the succeeding year they made another inroad into the northern country, and were again repulsed. The Nephites then took the initiative and invaded the southern continent, but being unsuccessful, were driven back to the frontier at Desolation (A. C. 363). The same season, the city of Desolation was captured by the Lamanitish warriors, but was wrested from them the year following.

This state of things continued another twenty years; war, contention, rapine, pillage, and all the horrors incident to the letting loose of men's most depraved and brutal passions, filled the land. Sometimes one army conquered, sometimes the other. Now it was the Nephites who were pouring their forces into the south; then the Lamanites who were overflowing the north. Whichever side triumphed, that triumph was of short duration; but to all it meant sacrifice, cruelty, blood-guiltiness and woe. At last, when every nerve had been strained for conquest, every man collected who could be found, the two vast hosts, with unquenchable hatred and unrelenting obstinacy, met at the hill Cumorah to decide the destiny of half the world. It was the final struggle, which was to end in the extermination of one or both of the races that had conjointly ruled America for nearly a thousand years (A. C. 385). When the days of that last fearful struggle were ended, all but twenty-four of the Nephite race had been, by the hand of violence, swept into untimely graves, save a few, a very few, who had fled into the south country. The powers, the glories, the beauties of this favored branch of Israel's chosen race had sunk beneath a sea of blood; the word of their God, whom they had so long disregarded, was vindicated; the warnings of his servants were fulfilled.

The Lamanites were now rulers of the western world, their traditional enemies being utterly destroyed. But they did not cultivate peace; no sooner were the Nephites obliterated, than they commenced fighting among themselves. The lonely Moroni, the last of the Nephites, tells us, A. C. 400, that the Lamanites are at war one with another; and the face of the land is one continued round of murder and bloodshed; and no man knoweth the end of the war. And again, yet later, he writes: Their wars are exceeding fierce among themselves.

Such was the sad condition of the Lamanite race in the early part of the fifth century after Christ. There the inspired record closes; henceforth we have nothing but uncertain tradition. The various contending tribes, in their thirst for blood so long gratified, sunk deeper and deeper into savage degradation; the arts of civilization were almost entirely lost to the great mass of the people. Decades and centuries rolled by, and after a time, in some parts, a better state of things slowly uprose. In Central America, Mexico, Peru, and other places, the foundations of new kingdoms were laid, in which were gradually built up civilizations peculiarly their own, but in many ways bearing record to the idiosyncrasies of their ancient predecessors. With this we have here little to do; many of their traditions (though disregarded by mankind) bear unequivocal testimony to the truth of the Book of Mormon, and we have the joyous assurance that as the words of their ancient prophets recorded therein have been fulfilled to the letter in their humiliation; and as they have drunk to the dregs from the cup of bitterness of the wrath of God, so is the glorious day now dawning, when the light of the eternal gospel shall illumine the hearts of their descendants; fill them with the love of God; renew their ancient steadfastness and faith, and make them the fitting instruments in his hands of accomplishing all his holy purposes with regard to them, in which also shall be fulfilled all the gracious, glorious promises made by Jehovah to this transplanted branch of the olive tree of Israel.

CHAPTER LII.

THE HISTORIANS OF THE NEPHITES—THE PLATES OF NEPHI— LIST OF THEIR CUSTODIANS—THEIR LENGTHENED YEARS.

SHORTLY after the arrival of Lehi and his little colony on the promised land, Nephi received a commandment from the Lord to make certain "plates of ore" upon which to engrave a record of the doings of his people. Some time later, or between thirty and forty years after the departure of Lehi from Jerusalem, Nephi was further instructed regarding the records. The Lord said unto him, Make other plates; and thou shalt engraven many things upon them which are good in my sight, for the profit of thy people. Nephi, to be obedient to the commandment of the Lord, went and made these other plates, and upon them were engraven the records from which the first portions of the Book of Mormon are translated; or those parts known to us as the First and Second Books of Nephi, and the Books of Jacob, Enos, Jarom, and Omni.

The two sets of plates manufactured by Nephi were both used as records of his people and called by his name; but their contents were not identical. Upon the first set was engraven the political history of the Nephites, upon the second their religious growth and development. The one described the acts of their kings, and the wars, contentions and destructions which came upon the nation; the other contained the story of the dealings of the Lord with that people, the ministry of his servants, the teachings and prophecies. Of the contents of the first we know but little, simply that which we gather from incidental remarks made in the second; but the second is given to us in its completeness in the translation contained in the Book of Mormon.

It would have been very interesting to students of history to have received the detailed account of the reigns of the kings who governed the people of Nephi, that is, to those who would accept these records as of God; but it was far more important that those most sacred truths contained in the revelations of heaven to that people should be made manifest to this generation. The one would be a satisfaction to our intellectual natures, but the other is necessary to our eternal salvation; for the Book of Mormon contains the fullness of the gospel, and also many things plain and most precious that have been taken out of the Jewish scriptures, through the craft or ignorance of apostate Jews and Christians. For this most important reason those portions of the Nephite records that are now contained in the Book of Mormon were first revealed; we should never have been willing to have accepted the others without them, for it is upon the basis of religion, not of history, that the Latter-day Saints accept the Book of Mormon. We also have the promise that other plates will be translated and given unto us in the Lord's due time, and doubtless among them will be those first plates upon which Nephi recorded, with such detail, the travels and labors in the wilderness of his father and associates.

The plates of Nephi containing the sacred annals of his people were not entirely filled with engravings until about two hundred years before Christ. They were made by Nephi between the years 570 and 560 before the advent of the Redeemer; but the record on them goes back to the time when Lehi left Jerusalem, or 600 B. C., so they in reality contain the history of God's dealings with that branch of the house of Israel for about four hundred years.

When Nephi died he transferred these sacred records to the care of his brother Jacob. From that time to the time that Moroni finally hid them in the hill Cumorah, they were in the hands of four families, who had charge of them, as near as can be told from the abridgment that we have in the Book of Mormon, as follows: Jacob and his descendants held them from B. C. 546 to about B. C. 200, when they were transferred to King Benjamin, who, with his son Mosiah, the younger, held them until B. C. 91, at which time they were given into the care of Alma, the chief judge, and he and his posterity retained them until 320 years after the advent of the Messiah. After these, Mormon and his son, Moroni, were the custodians until the close of the record, in the year 421 after Christ.

In the table that follows, B. C. signifies before Christ, and A. C. after Christ, counting from the true date of his birth as given in the Book of Mormon, and not from the accepted Christian Anno Domini (year of our Lord), which is now very generally supposed to be from two to four years wrong. In those places where no date is given, the desired information is not afforded in the Book of Mormon, and therefore can only be guessed at. We therefore prefer to leave such places blank. It will also be remembered that Mormon, just before the great last battle, which resulted in the extinction of the Nephite nation, hid up in the hill Cumorah all the records which had been entrusted to him by the hand of the Lord, save it were the few plates which he gave to his son Moroni.

The following are the names of the Nephite historians, with the times during which they held the records:

Nephi from——to 546 B. C.
Jacob, from 546 to——
Enos, from——to 422.
Jarom, from 422 to 362.
Omni, from 362 to 318.
Amaron, from 318 to 280.
Chemish, from 280 to——
Abinadom, from——to——
Amaleki, from——to 200 (about).
King Benjamin, from 200 to 125.
King Mosiah, from 125 to 91.
Alma (the younger), from 91 to 73.
Helaman (the elder), from 73 to 57.
Shiblon, from 57 to 53.
Helaman (the younger), from 53 to 39.
Nephi, from 39 to 1.
Nephi (the disciple), from 1 to 34 A. C.
Nephi, from 34 to 110.
Amos, from 110 to 194.
Amos (the younger), from 194 to 306.
Ammaron, from 306 to 320.
Mormon, from 320 to 385.
Moroni, from 385 to 421.

In the above table, one thing will most certainly strike the attention of the observant reader. It is the lengthened period that some of the historians held the records. Jacob and his son Enos held them one hundred and twenty-four years. Jarom held them sixty. In this fact we find a very pleasing confirmation of the statement of Nephi that during the time he and his brethren were wandering in the wilderness, living on raw meat and suffering all kinds of hardships, fatigue and privations, the Lord so greatly blessed the women in the company that they were strong, yea, even like unto the men, having an abundance of milk to suckle the babes born unto them. Jacob was born at this time, and doubtless inherited an exceedingly strong constitution, which he transmitted to his posterity.

The second epoch during which the longevity of the custodians of the plates is remarkable is during that reign of universal righteousness which followed the ministry of the crucified Savior. By living unto the Lord in all things their lives were marvelously prolonged; especially were those of the children born during the continuance of this happy and holy period and before the effects of the after apostasy had begun to work on them. Thus Nephi, the son of Nephi the disciple, had charge of the records seventy-six years, his son Amos, eighty-four years, and Amos, the son of the last named, the wonderful period of one hundred and twelve years; or father, son and grandson, three generations, a total of two hundred and seventy-two years. What a powerful sermon this one fact preaches in favor of entire submission of body and soul to the perfect and perfecting law of God!

CHAPTER LIII.

THE WOMEN OF THE BOOK OF MORMON—THEIR CONDITION AND POSITION—ABISH—ISABEL—MARRIAGE—AMULEK—MORONI'S TITLE OF LIBERTY—THE MOTHERS OF THE AMMONITES—TWO EXTREMES.

IT IS somewhat noticeable how little prominence is given to womankind in the historical narrative of the Book of Mormon, and unfortunately when mention is made of them it too frequently grows out of man's sins and their misfortunes. Of all the descendants of Lehi and Sariah, but two women are mentioned by name; one, Abish, a converted waiting woman to a queen of the Lamanites; the other, Isabel, a harlot of the land of Sidon, whose meretricious charms seduced Corianton, the son of Alma, from the work of the ministry among the Zoramites.

Although we have but few individual characters standing out in relief from the historical background, yet from many incidental references as to the story of the Nephites is told we are led to the conclusion that women among that people enjoyed a much greater degree of liberty, and wielded a more powerful influence than they did among contemporary Gentile nations on the eastern hemisphere—say in Babylon, Persia or Greece. We deem this mainly attributable to two causes, first, the Israelitish origin of the race; and again, the power and grace with which the principles of the gospel were preached by a long succession of prophets, who almost uninterruptedly ministered to the seed of Nephi. That this latter cause had much to do with woman's pleasing condition among that people is evident, for we find from the historical narrative that whenever they turned from the Lord it was then that tribulation and oppression came upon their wives and daughters, and they suffered from the iniquities of their husbands and the fury of their enemies. With regard to the first named cause it is generally admitted that the Hebrew women of antiquity enjoyed greater liberty and possessed more privileges than did those of the surrounding nations of the same period. Let the Bible and the history of contemporary nations be compared and the difference is apparent.

The Nephites lived in a dispensation varying considerably from that of the latter days. They observed the law of Moses, to which was added the higher code of the gospel. Our readers know how well both these protect the rights of women, and how sacredly they guard the marriage covenant; infidelity to that sacred bond of union being regarded, whether in the man or in the woman, as a most heinous offense, and worthy of the severest penalties.

At the commencement of the Nephite national life, when they were few in numbers, they seem for a time to have been tainted with some of the social vices of the degenerate people from whom the Lord had separated them. They committed great immoralities and took wives for utterly unworthy purposes, and without the fear of the Lord before their eyes; and after they had taken them, they frequently abused or neglected them, until their suffering cries came up before the Eternal One, and heaven forbade any man among them taking more than one wife, but adding this proviso: For if I will, saith the Lord of hosts, raise up seed unto me, I will command my people; otherwise they shall hearken to these things. This injunction, we are of the opinion, was afterwards removed, and the foreshadowed command given, as it is evident from the later history of the Nephites that in a better era of their national life polygamy was sanctioned by the law and practiced among them, and that, indeed, by the men most favored of God. As an example, we will cite the prophet Amulek, the devoted friend and zealous fellow-laborer of the younger Alma; the only man in all the vast city of Ammonihah to whom an angel was sent, and in whose behalf mighty miracles were wrought. He expressly mentions his women, and as he places them next to himself and before his children, his father and all his other kinsfolk and kindred, and nowhere uses the word wife or wives, it is evident that his wives were meant and not serving-women. No one, surely, would argue that he would give to the latter the place of honor in his address to his fellow-citizens, before his parents and his children. As another instance, the great number of Chief Judge Pahoran's sons is incidentally mentioned.

It was during the brighter days of the rule of the Judges that women, more than at any time before the appearance of the Messiah on this continent, seem to have been most highly regarded and esteemed. The Nephites were then living under that excellent code of laws drawn up by the inspired King Mosiah, which bear evidence of having been most admirably adapted to a people worthy of a large amount of liberty. This age was adorned with the presence of such men as Alma, Moroni (the prophet-general of the Nephite armies), Ammon and the other sons of King Mosiah, Helaman, Amulek and others conspicuous for their devotion to the laws of God and the rights and liberties of the people. General Moroni, than whom a more devoted man to the cause of truth and humanity never lived, is especially conspicuous in his untiring efforts for the safety and happiness of the wives and little ones of his people. On the standard to which he rallied the patriot warriors of the republic, which he named the Title of Liberty, he inscribed, In memory of our God, our religion and freedom, and our peace, our wives and our children. This seems to have been his watchword throughout the long and sanguinary succeeding campaigns, in which he defended the Nephites from the savage onslaughts of their Lamanitish foes. Again and again we find him rallying the hosts of Nephi with this soul-stirring cry, and under the ardor it wrought in their hearts carrying triumph to their banners and freedom to their land. One series of events that occurred during this long war sheds a most pleasing light upon the inner life of the faithful among the Nephites; it is found in the story of Helaman and his two thousand striplings, who, though very young, were so full of the spirit of faith implanted in their hearts by the wise counsels of their loving and God-fearing mothers, that in the might of Jehovah they went forth against the enemies of their adopted country (for they were Lamanites by birth), and no power could withstand them. Their mothers' teachings and their mothers' prayers were weapons of destruction to their foes and shields of defense to themselves. They went forth conquering and to conquer, and the All-seeing One only knows how much the teachings of those saintly women effected towards the preservation of the Nephite commonwealth from imminent destruction.

And what shall we say of the condition of woman in that blessed Sabbatic era succeeding the glorious appearing of the Redeemer on this western land, when for nearly two hundred years this continent enjoyed undisturbed and heavenly peace; when all men devoutly worshiped the Lord and dealt justly with their fellows—men or women? It was an age in which no woman was wronged, no deserted children pined in the streets, no abused wives mourned in secret, or lifted their sorrowing hearts in anguish to the Great Father of mankind; no brazen courtesans flaunted on the broad highways, or ruined maidens hid their sorrow and shame wherever seclusion was the most profound. The inspired historian tells us that if ever there were a happy people on this earth, there they were found; and most happy must have been the gentler ones, who bear in the stubborn battle of life so large a share of its sorrows and misfortunes.

But this golden age was soon followed by its opposite, when every virtue seems to have been supplanted by a vice, and all good was turned to evil. At almost lightning speed, the people having once taken the downward track, the nation rushed to ruin, until this continent became one vast field of carnage, rapine, and misery, over which devils gloated and hell enlarged itself. Indeed, the whole land seemed peopled with a race of demons who perpetuated cruelties that could alone be conceived in the hearts of the damned. During these lengthened years of untold horror the fair daughters of the land suffered unspeakable barbarities. Life, virtue, everything was the plaything of the victor, be he Nephite or Lamanite, until in the hate of revenge and the fury of despair they joined their national leaders on the battlefield, and with their husbands, sons and brothers, dyed their hands in the blood of the foe. Nor did they arm themselves alone, but with feelings turned to those of monsters, they put weapons into the hands of their children and inflamed their young minds with the savage love of slaughter. The war was not one for supremacy alone; it was for national and individual existence; and, midst a sea of carnage, unparalleled on any land save ours, the Nephite nation was swept out of existence, leaving scarce a trace behind, a most terrible instance of divine mercy scorned and divine laws abused.

CHAPTER LIV.

DOMESTIC LIFE AMONG THE NEPHITES—HOUSEHOLD DUTIES—DRESS—ORNAMENTS—HOMES—FOOD—MANUFACTURES—TRANSPORTATION.

FROM the casual references found in the historic portions of the Book of Mormon, we are led to infer that the domestic life of the Nephites was patterned, as it very naturally would be, after the manners and customs of their forefathers in the land of Jerusalem, modified, of course, by time and their surroundings. The changed material conditions, the absence of older though co-existent peoples and powers, the new and sometimes strange animal and vegetable productions, etc., all had an influence in the formation and growth of their civilization; trivial, perhaps, when considered separately, but when taken together, and working for centuries, having a marked effect on their public polity and home life. It is, however, necessary to explain that the details of the latter are very meagre, and only obtained incidentally, as they may form a link in the chain of some historical narrative, or be introduced as an illustration in some doctrinal teaching or prophetic warning.

In the midst of a people guided or reproved through their entire national life by an almost continuous succession of inspired teachers, it is but reasonable to conclude that the domestic virtues were assiduously cultivated, and all departures therefrom severely rebuked. Industry, economy, thrift, prudence, and moderation in dress were evidently as much the subject of the prophet's commendation then as in these latter days. Zeniff and others directly refer to the labors and toils of the Nephite women in spinning and making the material with which they clothed themselves and their households; and the same fabrics which delight the modern daughters of Israel also appear to have pleased the eyes of their Nephite sisters in the long ago. We must, however, say to the praise of these ancient worthies, the mothers of Mosiah, Alma, Moroni, Helaman, and of the two thousand striplings who loved to call the latter father, that the beauty of their apparel was the workmanship of their own hands. Steam looms, spinning jennys, and their like, were unknown, so far as we can learn, to the enterprising, vigorous, God-blessed race that for nearly a thousand years filled the American continent with the favored seed of Jacob's much-loved son.

The materials of which the clothing of this race were

made are frequently mentioned in the inspired record. Fine silk, fine twined or twisted linen, and cloth of every kind are often spoken of. In one place good homely cloth is mentioned. By the word homely we must not understand the writer to mean ugly; the work is there evidently applied in its original significance, as it is used today in England, for homelike or fit for home—such material as was suited to the everyday life of an industrious, hard-working people.

The love of ornaments has ever been a characteristic of Abraham's chosen race. The golden earrings and bracelets that gladdened the eyes of Rebecca, when sought as the wife of the patriarch's son, have had their counterpart in many a more modern instance. It was so with Sariah's myriad daughters. Time and again we read of pride and vanity entering the hearts of the people, and of their affections being set upon their costly apparel and their ornaments of gold, of silver, of pearls, of precious things, (gems?) their bracelets, ringlets, etc.

Nor would it be just to convey the idea that the gentler sex were alone guilty of these extravagances; the sacred record admits of no such conclusion. We cannot judge by the sober drabs, greys and browns with which the civilized gentleman of today clothes himself, of the colors, the styles or the fashions of the raiment of the Nephite beaux. The only safe conclusion that can be drawn is that they probably copied to some extent the gorgeousness of tropical nature by which they were surrounded. Nor is it reasonable to suppose that a single description would apply to the styles in the days of Lehi, of Benjamin and of Mormon, any more than the varied fashions of the days of the Williams, the Edwards, the Jameses and the Georges of English history could all be condensed into one sentence. It is not conceivable that dress, or anything else, remained entirely unchanged throughout a thousand years, though it is quite possible that those changes were nothing like so sudden or so radical as have been those that have taken place among the leading nations of western Europe. On these points, however, so far as the record of Mormon is concerned, we can simply surmise, as the military accoutrements, armor, etc., of the warrior are the only habiliments with regard to which he gives any particular details. It is this poverty of information on this and kindred subjects that makes it so difficult for our artists to illustrate, with any assurance of approximate correctness, scenes and incidents from Book of Mormon history.

Nor can we learn much more with regard to their residences than we can concerning their dress. The most detailed account given of any man's home is that of Nephi, the son of Helaman. His house was situated on the main highway which led to the chief market place of the city of Zarahemla. In front of his house was a garden, and near the gate opening upon the highway was a tower, upon the top of which the prophet was accustomed to pray. These towers, from the numerous references made to them, either as private property or attached to their places of worship, as watch towers or as a part of their system of fortification, must have formed quite a conspicuous feature in the Nephite landscape.

The residences of the rich were elegant and spacious, adorned with exceedingly fine wood work, carving, etc., and with ornaments of gold, silver, copper, brass, steel and other metals. From the importance attached to the fact that but little timber existed in the northern continent when the Nephites began to spread over it, and consequently that the immigrants had to build their houses of cement, it is presumable that wood entered largely into the composition of the buildings. This idea is strengthened by the frequent reference made to the skill of their artisans in wood working, and in the excellence they had attained in the refining of ores and the manufacturing of metal ornaments for their houses and persons. Regarding one monarch it is written: King Noah built many elegant and spacious buildings; and he ornamented them with fine works of wood, and of all manner of precious things, of gold and of silver, and of iron, and of brass, and of ziff and of copper; and he also built him a spacious palace and a throne in the midst thereof, all of which was of fine wood, and was ornamented with gold and silver, and with precious things. And he also caused that his workmen should work all manner of fine work within the walls of the temple, of fine wood, and of copper, and of brass, etc. This was in the land of Lehi-Nephi.

We next turn to the food of this people. Here, also we are without definite information, but we can measurably judge of their staple articles of diet by noticing the grains they cultivated most extensively: to wit, wheat, corn and barley, the latter appearing to have been the standard by which they gauged the price of other commodities. Great attention was also given to the planting of fruit trees and grape vines. From the fruit of the grape abundance of wine was manufactured, of which (we think we do the Nephites no injustice by saying it) they were as fond as are the generality of mankind. They were not as attached to a meat diet as were the Lamanites, who were great flesh-eaters, but they apparently kept large flocks and herds as a source of food supply, as well as for wool, leather, etc., and to provide for the numerous sacrifices enjoined by the law of Moses, which they carefully observed, until the offering of that greatest of all sacrifices on Mount Calvary, of which all the rest were but types and shadows.

Thus we may conclude that bread made from corn, wheat or barley, the flesh of their flocks and herds, together with that of wild animals caught in the chase, fruit, wine, milk and honey, formed the basis of their daily food, differing no doubt in details, according to the location, climate and other circumstances.

Their methods of locomotion and modes of transportation are not described. They were very rich in horses, and doubtless made use of them as beasts of burden. The fact that large bodies of this people made extended journeys in their various migrations and colonizings, is beyond dispute. From one family they filled a continent, or more properly two continents. The use of ships is not mentioned until the middle of the last century before the Christian era. These were then used in conveying immigrants, lumber, provisions, etc., to the northern continent; the first ship-building, of which we have an account, having been done at the settlements near the Isthmus of Panama, to which point good roads had by that time been constructed. In the earlier history of the Nephites it is probable that most of their material was transported on pack animals, as is done to-day in the regions then inhabited by them. In the dense tropical vegetation of the wilderness, and along the mountain slopes of the Andes, road-making was difficult and expensive, and packing on the backs of animals (say the horse, the mule, the llama, the alpaca, etc.,) was the cheapest and most convenient to a comparatively poor and small people.

Chariots are mentioned but seldom. The Lamanite monarch, Lamoni, had his horses and chariots, to which reference is more than once made; and in after years, when the Nephites gathered with all they possessed into one place, to defend themselves against the Gadianton robber (A. C. 17), they removed their provisions, grain, etc., by means of vehicles called chariots. These are the only instances, which the writer remembers where vehicles of any kind are spoken of in the Book of Mormon, in connection with the inhabitants of this continent.

CHAPTER LV.

AGRICULTURE AMONG THE NEPHITES—GRAINS—STOCK RAISING—IRRIGATION.

NO SOONER had Lehi and his little colony arrived on the promised land than they commenced the cultivation of the soil, planting therein the seeds they had brought with them from the land of Judea, which, to their great joy, yielded abundantly. The grains and fruits of the Asiatic continent were found to flourish as luxuriantly in the soil of America as in their native land. This not only held good in the land of the Nephites' first inheritance, but also in the lands of their later possession—Nephi, Zarahemla, etc., as all through the Book of Mormon we have occasional references (incidental to the story of their history) to the success that attended their farming operations. Nor must it be imagined that their business was carried on in the primitive manner that characterizes the labors of Laman's degenerate descendants to-day. Agricultural machinery, and all manner of tools of every kind to till the ground, are mentioned by more than one writer.

Of cereals, corn, wheat and barley appear to have been, as in the land of their forefathers, the staple crops. If we mistake not, oats are never mentioned in the Bible, nor is rye spoken of more than once or twice. In the Book of Mormon we have no recollection of the mention of either of these grains. On the other hand they appeared to have cultivated grains with which we are unacquainted, known to them by the names of neas and sheum. Had there been any English equivalents to these words, we should doubtless have had these equivalents as in other cases, instead of the original Nephite names.

All kinds of fruit flourished under their careful cultivation. Special reference is several times made to vineyards and grape culture, as well as to the manufacture of wine. Like the moderns, they understood the secret of fortifying or. strengthening it with liquor or alcohol, of which knowledge they took advantage when paying tribute to the Lamanites, in cases when they intended to escape from their taskmasters while the latter were under the influence of this intoxicating drink.

It is evident from the sacred record that the Nephites carried on their farming very much in the same manner and for very much the same reasons, as the early settlers in Utah. When a new colony was planted, a town or village was built in a suitable location, somewhat after the style of our early forts. This city or settlement was generally named after the founder or leader of the colony. The farming land contiguous was called by the same name. The land was tilled in every convenient place around the city, and when the Lamanites appeared, or other danger threatened, the people retreated into their place of refuge, in the center of their lands. As an example, we will cite the case of the followers of Alma, in the land of Helam. When the army of the Lamanites made their unwelcome appearance, the people were mostly engaged in tilling the soil. At the coming of the dreaded foe they gathered with all haste into the city to await developments and to receive the counsel their wise, brave and good leader might give them. By his advice the men went out of the city in a body, and made a treaty with the Lamanites, which the latter, as soon as their purpose was accomplished, failed to keep.

It is probable that in many parts of the continent some system of irrigation was adopted to raise the crops. But this was not necessary in all portions of the Nephite possessions; we are inclined to think it was not so in the cultivated portions of the valley of the Sidon. Certain it is that when the righteous Nephi (the father of one of the Twelve Disciples chosen by Jesus from among the Israel of this western continent) called upon the Lord, at his request a famine desolated the land. The sacred historian records: For the earth was smitten that it was dry, and did not yield forth grain in the season of the grain. But when the people had repented and Nephi had pleaded in their behalf, it is written, And it came to pass in the seventy-sixth year (B. C. 16), the Lord did turn away his anger from the people, and caused that rain should fall upon the earth, insomuch that it did bring forth her fruit in the season of her fruit. And it came to pass that it did bring forth her grain in the season of her grain. We judge from this that in those days the Nephite agriculturist depended on the direct rains from heaven; for it appears that in the same year that they fell, the grain harvest was reaped and the fruit harvest gathered. But it is unsafe to form positive theories on these points, until we fully understand the great changes that took place on the face of the land, with consequent alterations of climate, etc., at the time of the awful convulsions that attended the crucifixion of our Lord and Savior.

Except in the days of their excessive pride and ungodly arrogance, the calling of the agriculturist among the Nephites was a most honorable one, as in truth it should be among all people. King Mosiah, the beloved, reminded the people that, to prevent their taxes being grievous, he himself did till the earth for his support, and to maintain the expenses of the monarchy. With this royal example, it is no wonder that the farmer and the horticulturist were esteemed among the greatest of nature's noblemen.

The Nephites were also successful stock-raisers; their flocks and herds formed no inconsiderable portion of their wealth. The abundance of their horned stock, sheep, goats, wild goats, horses, fatlings, etc., is frequently referred to. To this industry the Lamanites, who were great meat-eaters, also gave considerable attention. It was a business that suited their semi-civilization. It did not tie them down so completely to one spot, as did agriculture and manufacture. But it is a notable fact that whenever any bodies of Lamanites passed over to the Nephites, they not only adopted the latter's religion and faith, but also their mode of living, and became skilled in the pursuits of industry. As an example, we read, in the days of the Judges, of many of these people joining the people of Ammon (their former brethren), when they did begin to labor exceedingly, tilling the ground, raising all manner of grain, and flocks and herds of every kind.

CHAPTER LVI.

SCIENCE AND LITERATURE AMONG THE NEPHITES — THEIR ASTRONOMY AND GEOGRAPHY—THE LEARNING OF EGYPT.

THE Nephites were unusually happy in having, as the founders of their nation, men who were not only wise in the ways of the Lord, but also learned in the knowledge of the world. Most races that have made a mark in history have had to grope their way for centuries from darkness to light, from ignorance to knowledge. Little by little such races have advanced in the path of civilization, falling into manifold errors, and committing grievous blunders. With Lehi and his posterity it was not so. They were taken from the midst of a people who were surrounded by the most powerful and refined nations of antiquity, with whose wisdom and learning Lehi was undoubtedly well acquainted. We can readily conceive that the Lord, in planting this mighty and vigorous offshoot of the house of Joseph, on the richest and most favored land of all the earth, would not only choose one of his most faithful, but also one of his most intelligent servants, to commence the work. Indeed, on the very first page of the Book of Mormon, Nephi incidentally refers to the learning of his father; which learning, we infer from many passages in the sacred record, was obtained by Lehi in Egypt, as well as in Palestine; the association between the inhabitants of these two countries being, in his day, very close, and the inter-communication frequent.

As the foundation of their literature. Lehi and his colony carried with them a copy of the sacred scriptures, which contained not only an account of God's dealings with mankind, from the creation to the age of Jeremiah, but also the only complete history in existence of the people who lived before the deluge. The Egyptians, Chaldeans and other nations had mangled, mythic and jumbled-up accounts of man's history from the creation to the flood; but the Nephites possessed the details of this epoch in much greater completeness than even Christendom does today. These scriptures—historical and doctrinal—being numerously reproduced and scattered among the people, formed the basis of Nephite literature, giving them the immense advantage over all other people of possessing the unpolluted word of God in every age then past, supplemented by a correct and undisputed history of the results, to the world, of man's obedience or disobedience to these heavenly messages. How much more complete these scriptures were than the Bible of Christendom is shown by the numerous references to the lives, and quotations from the teachings, of ancient worthies, Melchisedek, Jacob, Joseph and others; to the acts and infamies of Cain, etc., not found in the Bible, as well as by lengthy quotations from ancient prophets, whose names—Zenos, Zenoch, Neum, Ezias—are not even mentioned in its pages. How much modern Christianity has lost by these omissions may be partially inferred from the beauty and grandeur of the extracts given in the Book of Mormon, from the writings and prophecies of Zenos alone. Take, as a single instance, his inspired parable of the wild and tame olive trees, given in the Book of Jacob; no more important, no more sublime prophecy can be found in the whole contents of the holy scriptures.

The connection of Lehi with Egypt, whose language he appears to have adopted, doubtless gave him a practical knowledge of the condition of the whole civilized world in his day, when the glories of Chaldea had departed, and those of Assyria and Egypt were passing away; when Babylon was at the zenith of its power, and the growing strength of Persia and Greece was as yet scarcely felt. To this personal information he, like Moses, added an acquaintance with the learning of the Egyptians, a people wise above all other uninspired races in the numerous branches of science and art in which they excelled. With this knowledge, combined with the information of immeasurable value contained on the sacred plates, the foundation was laid for a stable civilization, guided by past revelation and present inspiration; to which was added the experience of other nations, as beacon-lights to warn the Nephites of the dangers to which all communities are subject, and to guide them to havens of governmental and political safety.

The Nephites, then, from their earliest day had at least all the important historical and geographical knowledge possessed by the most favored communities of the eastern hemisphere, with as much more as it pleased heaven to reveal. They had one advantage over the peoples they had left—they were well acquainted with them and their condition; but of the Nephites the dwellers in the old world knew nothing. With regard to the knowledge received through revelation, it is evident, from several incidental expressions scattered through the record, that the Lord did give to his faithful servants information with regard to historical and geographical matters. We will cite one instance: Jacob, the brother of Nephi, in one of his impressive exhortations, while encouraging his brethren (often somewhat downcast on account of their lonely condition, so far from the rest of mankind), remarks: We have been led to a better land, for the Lord has made the sea our path, and we are upon an isle of the sea. But great are the promises of the Lord unto they who are upon the isles of the sea; therefore, as it says isles, there must needs be more than this, and they are inhabited also by our brethren.

How could Jacob have known, except by revelation, that the vast continent which the Nephites inhabited was entirely surrounded by the waters of the great oceans? He and his companions had, but a few short years before, first landed on its shores, and had now explored but a very small portion of its wide extent, and there were no others in communication with them who could supply the information that North and South America were one immense island. Evidently the Lord had revealed this fact to them. And, by the way, this simple statement is strong testimony of the divine authenticity of the Book of Mormon. At the time that this portion of the sacred plates was translated (A. D. 1827-8), or even when the whole book was published and the Church of Jesus Christ was organized (A. D. 1830), it was not known to modern science that the American continent was indeed an island. Joseph Smith could not have received knowledge of this fact, so unhesitatingly affirmed, from any learned geographer or practical navigator. The hope of centuries, in Europe, had been to discover a north-west passage to India, but to that date all attempts had met with disastrous failure, so far as the chief object was concerned. Little or nothing was then known of the North American coast, west of Hudson's Bay. It was not until, after repeated expeditions, that in May, 1847, the truth of the statement of Jacob could be affirmed from actual knowledge of the geographical features of the country, as at that date the explorations and surveys by land and sea, from east and west, were brought sufficiently near to leave the matter without a doubt. It was not until 1854 that the first ship's crew (that of Captain McClure), which ever sailed across the Arctic Ocean from the Pacific to the Atlantic, along the northern coast of America, returned from their perilous voyage. We thus find that human geographical knowledge could not have aided the prophet Joseph Smith in making this statement, had it originated with him and not with the son of Lehi.

While ancient Greek and other philosophers were groping among the fallacies of the absurd system of astronomy given to the world by Ptolemy, and teaching that the sun with all the stars revolved around the earth, the Nephites were in possession of the true knowledge with regard to the heavenly bodies, etc. Possibly they were the only people of their age blessed with a comprehension of these sublime truths. It is altogether probable that among their scriptures were copies of the Book of Abraham, from which they could acquaint themselves with the beauties and harmonies of celestial mechanism. They undoubtedly had the writings of Joseph, the son of Jacob, as these are quoted in the Book of Mormon; and, as the prophet Joseph Smith found the writings of Abraham and Joseph together in the Egyptian mummies, it is far from improbable that the Nephites, as well as the early Egyptians, possessed both. To show the astronomical knowledge possessed by the Nephites, we will draw attention to the words of two of their prophets. The first extract is from the reply of Alma to Korihor, the Anti-Christ (B. C. 75), when the latter asked for a sign to prove the existence of a God. His words are: Thou hast had signs enough; will ye tempt your God? Will ye say, Show unto me a sign, when ye have the testimony of all these thy brethren, and also all the holy prophets? The scriptures are laid before thee, yea, and all things denote there is a God; yea, even the earth, and all things that are upon the face of it, yea, and its motion; yea, and also all the planets which move in their regular form, doth witness that there is a Supreme Creator. The next quotation is from the reflections of one of the servants of God (probably Mormon) inserted into the Nephite history of about seventy years later. The writer is speaking of the greatness and goodness of God, and among other things declares: Yea, by the power of his voice doth the whole earth shake; yea, by the power of his voice doth the foundations rock, even to the very center; yea, and if he say unto the earth, move it, it is moved; yea, if he say unto the earth, thou shalt go back, that it lengthen out the day for many hours, it is done; and thus according to his word, the earth goeth back; and it appeareth unto man that the sun standeth still; yea, and behold, this is so; for sure it is the earth that moveth, and not the sun. Thus we find that in these points, the astronomical knowledge of the Nephites was, at least equal to that of the moderns.

CHAPTER LVII.

THE ART OF WAR AMONG THE NEPHITES—THEIR WEAPONS, ARMOR AND FORTIFICATIONS — MORONI'S LINE OF DEFENSE.

NO SOONER had the separation taken place between the families of Nephi and Laman, and the foundation been laid for the two nations that for a thousand years contended for supremacy on this continent, than Nephi, to protect his people from the threatened attacks of the Lamanites, found it necessary to prepare for war. He took the sword of Laban, and using it as a pattern, fashioned many others, which he distributed among his subjects as a means of defense.

These swords, with cimeters, spears, javelins, darts, bows and arrows, slings and stones, appear to have been the principal weapons of war used by the Nephites throughout their entire national existence, though reference is more than once made to unnamed and undescribed weapons. We have no reason to imagine from any of the descriptions of their battles that gunpowder or any like composition was known to them. It is more probable that the unnamed weapons were something of the same kind as the ancient ballista and catapult, (machines made by the ancients for throwing stones, arrows, etc.,) and used for the same purposes. From the abundance of metallic ore in the regions most densely populated by the Nephites, and the oft-mentioned skill possessed by their artisans in the working of iron, steel, brass and copper, we have no reason for supposing that less satisfactory substitutes were brought into use in the manufacture of their weapons. There was no necessity for using bone, flint, etc., when metal was so abundant and its preparation so well understood.

The accounts we have of the early wars between the two races are but mere notices of the fact of their occurrence and results. It is not until the days of the Judges that anything like details are given. At that time the Nephites had adopted the use of defensive plate armor for their heads, bodies and thighs; they also carried shields and wore arm plates. These arts for the protection of the soldiers were carried to their greatest excellence under Moroni, during the first half of the last century before Christ. This officer, one of the greatest generals the Nephite race ever gave birth to, appears to have made a great revolution in their military affairs. He re-organized their armies, compelled more stringent discipline, introduced new tactics, developed a greatly superior system of fortification, built towers and citadels, and altogether placed the defensive powers of the commonwealth on a new and stronger footing. The Lamanites, who appear to have developed no capacity for originating, but were apt in copying, also, in course of time, adopted defensive armor, and when they captured a weak Nephite city they frequently made it a stronghold by surrounding it with ditches and walls after the system introduced and put into execution by Moroni.

The foundation of Moroni's system of fortification was earthworks encircling the place to be defended. The earth was dug from the outside, by which means a ditch was formed. Sometimes walls of stone were erected. On the top of the earthworks strong defenses of wood, sometimes breastworks, in some cases to the full height of a man, were raised; and above these a stockade of strong pickets was built, to arrest the flight of the stones and arrows of the attacking forces. Those arrows, etc., that passed above the pickets fell, without doing injury, behind the troops who were defending the wall. Besides these walls, towers were raised at various convenient points, from which observations of the movements of the enemy were taken, and wherein corps of archers and slingers stationed during the actual continuance of the battle. From their elevated and commanding position these bodies of soldiers could do great injury to the attacking force.

To make this subject yet plainer we insert a few extracts, from the Book of Mormon, that have a bearing thereon.

In the year B. C. 73 a severe war was being waged, in which Moroni had command of the Nephite armies and Amalickiah of those of the Lamanites. It is written that at this time Moroni erected small forts, or places of resort: throwing up banks of earth round about, to enclose his armies, and also building walls of stone to encircle them about, round about their cities and the borders of their lands; yea, all round about the land; and in their weakest fortifications he did place the greater number of men; and thus he did fortify and strengthen the land which was possessed by the Nephites.

The year following Moroni caused his soldiers to dig up heaps of earth round about all the cities, throughout all the land which was possessed by the Nephites; and upon the top of these ridges of earth he caused that there should be timbers; yea, works of timbers built up to the height of a man, round about the cities. And he caused that upon these works of timbers there should be a frame of pickets built upon the timbers round about; and they were strong and high; and he caused towers to be erected that overlooked those works of pickets, and he caused places of security to be built upon those towers, that the stones and the arrows of the Lamanites could not hurt them. And they were prepared, that they could cast stones from the top thereof, according to their pleasure and their strength, and slay him who should attempt to approach near the walls of the city. Thus Moroni did prepare strongholds against the coming of their enemies, round about every city in all the land.

Again, in the same war, the Lamanite prisoners were set to work digging a ditch round about the land, or the city Bountiful; and Moroni caused that they should build a breastwork of timbers upon the inner bank of the ditch; and they cast up dirt out of the ditch against the breastwork of timbers; and thus they did cause the Lamanites to labor until they had encircled the city of Bountiful round about with a strong wall of timbers and earth, to an exceeding height. And this city became an exceeding stronghold ever after.

The forces of both races appear to have been composed very largely, if not entirely, of infantry. We have failed to notice any passage that gave a definite assurance that either cavalry or war chariots were used in their campaigns.

Like nearly all rude or semi-civilized races, the Lamanites depended on the strength of numbers and brute force for victory in the open field. They massed their troops in solid bodies, and with wild cries rushed to the assault in the hope of bearing down all resistance by their superior numbers, as in almost every war they greatly outnumbered the Nephites. Indeed it is doubtful if even the last-named people used much scientific strategy previous to the days of Moroni; before this time it was a hand-to-hand conflict, wherein the Nephites, though fewer in numbers, had many advantages over their half-naked foes, by reason of superior weapons and defensive armor, and, above all, through the blessing and guidance of the Lord.

In the year B. C. 72 the armies of Moroni drove the Lamanites out of that portion of the east wilderness bordering on the land of Zarahemla into their own lands. The northern line or boundary of the latter ran in a straight course from the sea east to the west. The Lamanites having been driven out of those portions of the wilderness north of the dividing line, colonies of Nephites were sent to occupy the country and build cities on their southern border, even to the Atlantic coast. To protect the new settlers, Moroni placed troops all along this line and caused them to erect fortifications for the better defense of the frontier. This fortified line ran from the west sea (the Pacific Ocean) by the head of the river Sidon (the Magdalena) eastward along the northern edge of the wilderness.

Some of the readers of the Book of Mormon have imagined this line of defense to have been one continuous rampart or wall—after the style of the great wall of China—reaching from ocean to ocean, and on this surmise have argued that the completion of such an immense work in a few years was an impossibility to a people of the limited numerical strength of the Nephites. To get over this difficulty of their own creation they have resorted to various theories with regard to its locality, inconsistent with the geographical details, on purpose to shorten its distance to what they deemed a reasonable length, possible for the Nephites to have built in a few years. The writer holds the opinion that the Book of Mormon conveys no such idea, it simply states that Moroni erected fortifications along this line; or, as he views it, Moroni took advantage of the natural features of the country, its wide rivers, far-stretching swamps and ranges of high mountains, and built fortifications at every point where the Lamanites would find ingress, such as at the fords of the rivers and the passes between the mountains. He there stationed bodies of troops sufficiently strong to hold their posts, and, if necessary, defend the surrounding country. This system of defense would be more powerful and effective than an artificial wall; high mountains and deep rivers largely taking the place of earthworks, masonry and heavy timbers.

A number of years later (B. C. 34), the Lamanites having temporarily driven the Nephites from the southern continent, Moronihah, the son of Moroni, fortified the Isthmus of Panama from sea to sea, and in this way prevented the Lamanites from pushing yet further north. This defensive line was again fortified by Mormon (A. C. 360) in the last great series of wars between the two races.

It does not appear, so far as can be gathered from the record, that any very great improvements, either in the system of fortification, the style of defensive armor, or the manufacture of their weapons, were made by the Nephite commanders who lived after the days of Moroni.

There is another kind of defensive clothing, beside plate armor, mentioned as being worn by the ancient American warriors. It consisted of very thick clothing, possibly made of cotton or woolen cloth, thickly padded. Moroni uniformed some of his troops in this manner when he first took command of the Nephite armies (B. C. 74), and the next year the Lamanites followed his example and not only prepared themselves with shields and breastplates, but also with garments of skins; yea, very thick garments to cover their nakedness.

The various enemies that the Nephite armies had to meet, from time to time, on the field of battle—Lamanites, Amulonites, Amalekites, Zoramites, Gadianton robbers, etc.—

were very differently equipped for their bloody work. Those who had dissented from the Nephites naturally held to the same tactics, used the arms and protected their bodies with the same armor as the people to whom they had turned traitors. With the original Lamanites it was different. At first, when they came against the Nephites they were clothed with a short skin girdle about the loins, and with their heads shaven; and their skill was in the bow and the cimeter and axe. The dissenters, while armed and equipped like the Nephites, set a mark upon themselves by which they might be known and distinguished on the battle field. In doing this they unconsciously fulfilled the word of the Lord to their fathers. Thus, the followers of Amlici, the would-be king, marked themselves with red in their foreheads after the manner of the Lamanites, though they did not shave their heads as did the direct descendants of Laman (B. C. 87).

The description of the Gadianton robbers, as they appeared when prepared for war (A. C. 18), is a very terrible one: They were girded about after the manner of robbers; and they had a lamb-skin about their loins, and they were dyed in blood, and their heads were shorn, and they had head-plates upon them: and great and terrible was the appearance of the armies of Giddianhi, because of their armor and because of their being dyed in blood.

CHAPTER LVIII.

THE LAWS OF THE NEPHITES—THE ROMAN AND NEPHITE CIVILIZATIONS—THE LAWS UNDER THE KINGS—POSITION OF THE PRIESTHOOD—SLAVERY—CRIMINAL OFFENSES.

IF THE existence of wise, just and liberal laws, administered in righteousness, be the rule by which we can judge of the true greatness of a nation and of the happiness and prosperity of its citizens, then the Nephites were a far happier and more prosperous people than were their contemporaries on the eastern continent. If this be not so, then we have not read history aright.

The Nephite nation was co-existent with the great Roman power that for so long triumphed over and crushed the surrounding people in Europa, Asia and Africa. True, Rome was founded more than a century before Lehi left Jerusalem,* but at the time of his exodus its growing power had scarcely begun to be felt outside of Italy. At the time that Moroni's record closed, the Nephites, as a nation, had become extinct, and the glory of the mistress of the world was rapidly fading away. Rome had been sacked by barbarians, the empire had been divided into two governments, the legs of Nebuchadnezzar's great image were forming; peoples and nations were rebelling and throwing off the iron yoke, and the idea of universal empire had become a thing of the past.† But how different the theory and genius of the two nations! The Nephite rulers governed by the power of just laws, the Romans by the might of the unsheathed sword. Among the

---

*The generally accepted date for the foundation of Rome is 753 B. C.
†The eastern and western empires were divided A. D. 395. Alaric, the Goth, sacked Rome A. D. 410. Britain broke away from the empire A. D. 418. Gaul, Spain and Africa were soon afterwards lost.

former, every man was a free man, with his rights as a citizen guaranteed and protected by just laws. Among the latter, few could assert, as did the Apostle Paul, *Civis Romanus Sum*—I am a Roman citizen. The vast majority of the millions who formed its people were either abject allies, vanquished enemies or degraded slaves.‡ Neither of these had many rights that the Roman citizen felt himself called upon to respect. We are apt to be awed by the grand military exploits of the Roman generals, and to be dazzled with the magnificence of Rome in art and architecture, but we must recollect that the history of that city is the history of tyranny. Its power, during the greater portion of its continuance, was in the hands of the few, who used it for the interest of their class. The masses of the population were the subjects of oppression and violence.

No language could so well describe the spirit of Roman aggrandizement as that used by the Prophet Daniel when interpreting to the Babylonish king the import of the terrible image he had seen in his dream. These are his words: And the fourth kingdom shall be strong as iron: forasmuch as iron breaketh in pieces and subdueth all things: and as iron that breaketh all these, shall it break in pieces and bruise. (Daniel ii. 40.) And thus did Rome rule the eastern world as with a rod of iron. We need not refer to the other nations that existed on the eastern continent, for the people that Rome neither conquered nor destroyed were barbarians, who, during the existence of the Nephites, filled but a small page in the world's history.

These facts are presented as worthy of the consideration of all who study the social and political condition of the great and highly-favored people who flourished on this continent for so many centuries; and we imagine the student cannot

---

‡In Sicily alone, goaded by ill-treatment, the slaves rebelled. Their army numbered 200,000 (B. C. 134-132.)

fail to be impressed with the thought that they were at least a thousand years in advance of their fellow-men in the science of true government; and in their policy find a type of the most advanced and most liberal forms of government of the present age. That this should be so, will not surprise us when we consider that they were a branch of the house of Israel, a people who enjoyed more political liberty (until their own follies had cut them off therefrom) than any of the other nations of antiquity, and that to the law of Moses they had added the divine teachings of the everlasting gospel, which in themselves are a perfect law of liberty. Further, it is a noteworthy fact which stares us in the face from the beginning to the end of the Book of Mormon, that when the people departed from gospel principles, it was then and then only that they fell into bondage, of whatever nature that bondage might be.

The political history of the Nephites may be consistently divided into five epochs:

First.—When they were governed by kings.

Second.—The republic, when they were ruled by judges and governors.

Third.—A short period of anarchy when they were divided into numerous independent tribes.

Fourth.—The Messianic dispensation, when they were controlled entirely by the higher law of the holy priesthood.

Fifth.—The chaotic state of intestine war which preceded their final extinction as a nation and as a race.

The first portion of the history of the Nephites when they were governed by kings, covers almost exactly one-half of their national existence, or from the time of the landing of the colony on the coast of Chili to 509 years after the departure of Lehi from Jerusalem. Of the laws by which the people were governed during this period, which, however, we are told were exceedingly strict, we have few details, for the reason that the plates from which the greater portion of the Book of Mormon which relates to this period was taken contain the records of their prophets rather than the annals of their kings. With regard to these kings, they of whose lives we have any particulars, viz: Nephi, the first king, and Mosiah I., Benjamin and Mosiah II., the three last, were eminently virtuous, just and merciful men, who reigned as all monarchs should, but few do—with an eye single to the good of their subjects. Of their kings in general the prophet Jarom, about 400 years before Christ, remarks: Our kings and our leaders were mighty men in the faith of the Lord: and they taught the people the ways of the Lord. Indeed, we recollect no intimation, in any place in the sacred record, of tyranny on the part of those who reigned over the main body of the nation. The government may, we think, be justly considered to approximate nearest to a limited monarchy, in which, as in ancient Israel, the prophet often exercised more power than the king. Though this is true of the central government, it unfortunately cannot be so stated of the colony which returned to the land of Nephi in the days of King Benjamin; that people suffered beyond description from the tyranny and wickedness, and the consequences resulting therefrom, of their second king, Noah, the murderer of the Prophet Abinadi.

Of the life and character of the first king of the Nephites, the father of his people, Nephi, the son of Lehi, we need say nothing here. History affords no better model of the true prince. So thought his people, and they, to retain in remembrance his name, and to perpetuate the recollection of his virtues, called his successors, second Nephi, third Nephi, etc., no matter what their original name might have been.

The right of choosing his successor appears to have been vested in the reigning sovereign. When Nephi became old, and saw that he must soon die, he anointed a man to be a king and a ruler over his people. King Benjamin chose his son Mosiah to reign in his stead, and then gathered the people to receive his last charge and ratify his selection. Mosiah gave the people yet greater liberty, and instead of nominating his successor directed them to make their own choice. The people highly appreciated this act of grace on the part of their beloved king, and selected Aaron, his son. Aaron, whose heart was set upon the salvation of the Lamanites, declined the kingly authority, when Mosiah very wisely advised his subjects not to select another to fill the throne, lest it give rise, in the future, to bloodshed and contention, but to elect judges to be their rulers, instead of kings, which proposition they accepted with great joy.

With regard to the Nephite laws in the days of the kings, and the manner of their execution, we can learn most from the parting addresses of kings Benjamin and Mosiah II. to their subjects. We are frequently told by the sacred writers, from Nephi, the founder, to Nephi, the disciple, that the people observed the law of Moses, modified, we judge, in some of its details to suit the altered circumstances of the Nephites from those of their brethren in the land of Palestine. As an instance we draw attention to the fact that, as there were none of the tribe of Levi in the colony that accompanied Lehi, from Judea, the priestly office must necessarily have been filled and the required sacrifices and burnt offerings offered by some of the members of the tribes who were with them. Nephi (doubtless by the direction of the Lord) appointed his brothers Jacob and Joseph to be the priests for the people, they being of the tribe of Manasseh, and the care of the sacred records remained with the descendants of the first named for several generations. The members of the various orders of the priesthood, when not actually engaged in the work of the ministry, in the duties of the temple, or the service of the sanctuary, were required to labor for their own support, that they might not prove burdensome to the people. A merciful provision was, however, made for the sustenance of members of the priesthood in cases of sickness or when in much want.

Though the laws were strict, they were mercifully and equitably administered, which gave much greater stability to the government and respect for the law than if they had been adjudged loosely, and with partiality towards classes or persons. It has been wisely observed that it is not the severity of the law but the sureness of the punishment that deters the evil-doer, and in this respect the Nephite nation had cause for thankfulness. All men were alike before the law, there were no privileged classes as in Rome, or in feudal Europe in later years. Mosiah says, Whosoever has committed iniquity, him have I punished according to the law which has been given to us by our fathers.

From the charge of king Benjamin to his son Mosiah we learn that slavery was forbidden. All the inhabitants of the continent being of the house of Israel, they could not observe the law of Moses and enslave their brethren.

Murder, robbery, theft, adultery and other sexual abominations were punished by law, as also was lying or bearing false witness.

Mormon states that in king Benjamin's days the false Christs, etc., were punished according to their crimes; but we are not informed if those crimes consisted in false personation, etc., or in fomenting, aiding and abetting treason and rebellion, as was almost universally the habit of those who apostatized from the gospel and sought to establish false religions in its place. King Benjamin also states that he had not permitted the people to be confined in dungeons; but we are uncertain whether to infer from this remark that the king intended his hearers to understand that he had not done this, as so many tyrants do, without cause and without trial, or that some other more effectual means had been found of punishing those transgressors not deemed worthy of death. We incline to the former opinion.

When the Nephite kingdom was first established the people were so few that they could not possibly sustain the expenses incidental to royalty. Thus it became the rule for the kings to sustain themselves. This unique, though most excellent custom continued as long as the monarchy lasted, even when the nation had grown rich and numerous. King Benjamin reminds his subjects that he had labored with his own hands that they might not be laden with taxes. Of Mosiah, his successor, it is written that he had not exacted riches of the people and that he had granted unto his people that they should be delivered from all manner of bondage.

We must not forget that, in connection with the civil law, the law of the gospel was almost unceasingly proclaimed during the whole period of the monarchy. Various false Christs and false prophets had arisen at different times, but the power of the priesthood had remained, ministering in holy things, rebuking iniquity and aiding in the suppression of vice. The kings of the Nephites, as we before observed, were, as a rule, men of God, holding the priesthood, and were often prophets and seers as well as temporal rulers. To this happy circumstance we must greatly attribute the peace and good order that so generally prevailed; the respect for the law that was so widespread; the large amount of liberty accorded to the people and the few abuses they made of that freedom. To use the idea of the prophet Joseph Smith, for long years, they were taught correct principles, and they (to a great extent) governed themselves.

In the course of the centuries, as the people increased and spread far and wide over the land, they appear to have introduced local customs to suit their differing circumstances, or in some cases their whims and notions. Thus, until king Mosiah II. established uniformity by law, nearly every generation and each section of the country had its own moneys, weights, measures, etc., which were altered from time to time according to the minds and circumstances of the people.

This custom naturally caused confusion, annoyance and distrust, and to obviate these, and possibly greater evils, Mosiah consented to newly arrange the affairs of the people; and, if we may so express it, to codify the law. This code became the constitution of the nation under the rule of the Judges, which limited the powers of the officials and guaranteed the rights of the people. This compilation was acknowledged by the people, whereupon the historian remarks, Therefore they were obliged to abide by the laws which he had made. And from that time they became supreme throughout the nation. It is stated in another place that this change was made by the direct command of Jehovah.

CHAPTER LIX.

THE LAWS UNDER THE JUDGES—THE VOICE OF THE PEOPLE—ELECTIONS—RIGHTS OF THE PEOPLE—CHURCH AND STATE—THE CRIMINAL PROCEDURE.

WE NEXT enter into the consideration of the law as it existed under the Judges, gathering our information from various passages in which it is directly referred to, or wherein some historical incident is narrated which throws light on its powers and manner of execution.

From the death of king Mosiah II. (B. C. 91), the governmental authority was vested in a chief judge and other subordinate judges and officers, all of whom were elected by the voice of the people, to judge according to the laws which had been given to and accepted by the people. Their authority was defined by the law (the code of Mosiah), but within the bounds therein prescribed they appear to have held unrestricted powers. This was especially so in the case of the chief judge. No civil council or parliament divided with the chief executive the authority to make war or conclude peace, to decide the terms of treaties, or frame enactments for the regulation of public affairs. No direct statement is made of the length of the term that a judge remained in office, but from the historical narrative we gather the idea that he was elected for life or during good conduct. We have instances of judges resigning, but none of their removal by the people because their term of office had expired. Each city or land appears to have had its chief judge or ruler as well as its inferior magistrates, all of whom were responsible to the chief judge of the whole nation, whose seat of government was located in the Nephite capital, Zarahemla, when the city was not in the hands of Lamanites or traitors.

The manner of conducting elections is not clearly defined. The result is always spoken of as the voice of the people. The mode of procedure was uniform, that is, it was the same throughout the land. In the election of the first chief judge (Alma the younger), the people assembled in bodies throughout all the land to cast in their voices, which conveys the impression that they declared their choice *viva voce,* or by acclamation rather than by lot or ballot. It is quite possible that the methods were entirely dissimilar to any known at modern elections; this, however, is but conjecture.

When the sentiments of the people were greatly divided and party feeling ran high, the opposing factions assembled in separate bodies throughout the land to cast in their voices, as in the attempt to make Amlici king. The decisions of the people in these assemblies or mass meetings were laid before the judges, who proclaimed the result. In cases where the petition was made for any particular object, or for a change in the law, the judge directed that a special election (if we may so term it) be held, and the results were proclaimed according to the voice of the people, as a whole, or if they were divided, according to the voice of the majority.

Under the code of Mosiah, the judges received wages according to the time which they labored to judge those who were brought before them; and their wages were a senine of gold, or its equivalent a senum of silver, for each day that they were thus employed. As the Nephites had changed the names and values of their coins from the old Hebrew standards, we have no direct way of judging from the record how liberally these officers were remunerated. Lawyers, also, were hired and appointed by the people to administer the law at the time of their trials; it is presumable that these acted in behalf of the republic somewhat in the capacity of prosecuting attorneys in the United States. If trial by jury was in vogue among the Nephites, we have not been able to find any reference to that method; indeed the evidence is altogether in favor of the idea that the judge decided as to the guilt or innocence of the accused, and, if adjudged guilty, passed sentence on the culprit. The corruption of these lawyers and judges early became, in some portions of the land, a foundation for the destruction of the government.

When the chief judge was elected he took an oath of office, and it is presumable that the lesser officers did the same. The nature of that oath can be easily understood by referring to the case of Pahoran. He was appointed chief judge and governor over the people, with an oath and sacred ordinance to judge righteously, and to keep the peace, and the freedom of the people, and grant unto them their sacred privileges to worship the Lord their God; yea, to support and maintain the cause of God in all his days, and to bring the wicked to justice, according to their crimes.

The punishment of corruption, or malfeasance in office, was specially provided for. King Mosiah explains the provisions of the law on this subject in the following language: And now if ye have judges and they do not judge you according to the law which has been given, ye can cause that they may be judged by a higher judge: if your higher judges do not judge righteous judgments, ye shall cause that a small number of your lower judges should be gathered together, and they shall judge your higher judges according to the voice of the people. These safeguards became strong bulwarks for the protection of the rights of the individual and the preservation of the liberty of the whole people.

When Alma, the first chief judge, resigned that office, so that he might devote all his time and energies to the work of saving the souls of men, he nominated or suggested his successor; but whether this was simply a courtesy extended to him by the people on account of their great love for his person and respect for his judgment, or whether it was a provision of the law, is not plain. The passage states that Alma chose Nephihah as his successor, and gave him power, according to the voice of the people to enact laws according to the laws which had been given, and to put them in force according to the wickedness and crimes of the people.

The rights of the people were:*

Personal Liberty:—It was contrary to the law of Mosiah that there should be any slaves among the Nephites.

Equality before the Law:—No privileged classes. All men to enjoy their rights and privileges alike.

Uniformity of Taxation:—The burden of supporting the government fell on all the citizens, that every man might bear his part.

The Elective Franchise:—Whether the suffrage was confined to men, or universal, or limited by any particular restrictions, does not plainly appear.

The Rights of Petition:—As examples of the exercise of this right we introduce the following: At the time when

---

*The people had doubtless other rights which we have failed to notice, or that are not mentioned by the writers in the Book of Mormon.

Pahoran was chief judge a part of the people desired that a few particular points of the law should be altered. The chief judge refused to alter the law, whereupon a portion of the people petitioned him, and he directed that an election be held, or rather that the voice of the whole nation be appealed to. This being done, the result proved that the majority of the people objected to a change. Again, Moroni, the commander-in-chief of the Nephite armies, sent a petition to the chief judge for power to compel certain dissenters to help defend their country against the national enemies, or to put them to death. His request being according to the voice of the people, the desired power was given to him. Here we have instances of the right of petition exercised, in one case by a large body of the people, and in the other by a single, though important, individual. Both were extraordinary circumstances, and in the latter case it appears to have required the all-powerful *vox populi* to give validity to the action of the executive.

The statement is frequently made, though in slightly different phrases, that the law had no power to punish a man for his belief; for it was strictly contrary to the commands of God that there should be a law which should bring men on to unequal grounds. If a man believed in God it was his privilege to serve him; if he did not believe in him, there was no law to punish him. * * A man was punished only for the crimes he had done; therefore all men were on equal grounds. Unbelief was handled by the church, not by the civil law. The names of those whose hearts were hardened were blotted out and they were remembered no more among the people of God. During the days of the Judges there was no church established by law; when the people served God they elected righteous men for their rulers; when the masses fell into unbelief and transgression they chose Gadianton robbers and such like to administer their laws.

If the rights of women, under the law, were any different, more or less, than those of men, we have no information; in fact, the inspired record is entirely silent on this subject.

The criminal law inflicted the death penalty for murder, rebellion and treason; for robbery, theft, adultery, sexual abominations, fraud and lying, lesser punishments were inflicted.

The first recorded case of execution for murder under the rule of the Judges is that of Nehor, for killing the aged patriot, Gideon. Another noteworthy case is that of Paanchi, the son of Pahoron, of whom it is written that he was tried according to the voice of the people, and condemned unto death; for he had raised up in rebellion, and sought to destroy the liberty of the people.

No high priest, judge or lawyer had power to inflict capital punishment. When a man had been tried and condemned to death by the law his condemnation had to be signed by the governor of the land, before the sentence could be carried out. The mention of governor in this relation, with other passages in which the chief judge and governor are spoken of as different persons, suggests the idea that as the Nephites grew in numbers and spread over distant regions, the duties of the chief judge became excessive, and a separation was made between the executive and judicial responsibilities, and divided between two officers.

The mode of inflicting the death penalty is not stated, but we incline to the idea that hanging was often resorted to. Military offenders were, as a rule, put to death with the sword. Of Nehor it is said that he suffered an ignominious death at the top of the hill Manti, and that, before his death, he acknowledged between heaven and earth that he had taught false doctrine. Zemnarihah was hanged upon the top of a tree until he was dead, and then the Nephites felled the tree to the earth. Many of the martyrs were burned to death by unjust judges, or stoned, as was Timothy, afterwards one of the Twelve Disciples; but we regard this last act as resulting from the violence of a mob, rather than from any pretended execution of the law.

The law with regard to debtors seems to have been somewhat severe. On this point it is stated, Now if a man owed another, and he would not pay that which he did owe, he was complained of to the judge; and the judge executed authority, and sent forth officers that the man should be brought before him; and he judged the man according to the law and the evidences which were brought against him, and thus the man was compelled to pay that which he owed, or be stripped, or be cast out from among the people as a thief and a robber. If a man desired to pay, but from misfortune could not, doubtless the law contained some merciful provision in his behalf.

It is more than probable that the mode of procedure in all criminal cases very much resembled the one cited above, and from it we can gather a very clear idea of the practice of their courts, which differs but little from that of our own day. The complaint was first made, the proper officer was then authorized by the court to arrest the accused and bring him before the judge, the trial next took place, the witnesses gave their testimony, the law and the evidence were examined, the opposing lawyers were heard, the judgment was given, the sentence pronounced and lastly carried out. In times of war the military code seems to have varied according to the exigencies of the situation. As a rule, the Nephite armies were composed of volunteers. In times of great danger to the republic, enlarged powers were given to the commander-in-chief. In one place we find the statement that Moroni, having been appointed by the chief judge and the voice of the people, had power according to his will with the armies of the Nephites, to establish and to exercise authority over them; also, he caused to be put to death those of the Amalickiahites (rebels) who would not enter into a covenant to support the cause of freedom and the rights of their fellow-countrymen.

Prisoners of war were evidently treated much the same as in modern civilized nations. Indeed, in one place, the fact that the necessities of his position compelled Moroni to set his Lamanite prisoners to work, is referred to in somewhat of an apologetic tone. When such prisoners attempted to escape, they were slain by their guards. We have numerous instances where prisoners were released on parole, or on their giving such promises to the Nephite general as were thought necessary.

It frequently happened, during the days of the Judges, that the Nephites, in some of their periodical spasms of apostasy and wickedness, would clamor for changes to be made in their just and wise laws, in a manner to better suit their degraded habits and course of life. When the majority of the people were on the side of righteousness, these attempts were in vain. When wickedness abounded, the corrupt majority carried their points. The record of their history shows that in the sixty-second year of the Judges (B. C. 30) they had altered and trampled under foot the laws of Mosiah, or that which the Lord had commanded him to give unto the people; and that their laws had become corrupted, and they had grown wicked like unto the Lamanites. Seven years later the corruption of the people had become pitiable. The Gadianton robbers were filling the judgment seats, having usurped the power and authority of the land: Laying aside the commandments of God, and not in the least aright before him; doing no justice unto the children of men; condemning the righteous because of their righteousness; letting the guilty and the wicked go unpunished, because of their money; and moreover to be held in office at the head of government to rule and do according to their wills, that they might get gain and glory of the world; and moreover that they might the more easily commit adultery, and steal, and kill, and do according to their own wills.

Such a condition of affairs, in the course of time, wrought

national disintegration, and would have brought about that result much sooner than it did, had it not been that, influenced by the mighty preaching of the inspired servants of God, the Nephites (or portions of them) had now and again returned to the service of heaven. But such happy periods were short-lived, and matters went from bad to worse until thirty years after the birth of Christ, when the republican form of government was entirely broken up, and the people split up into numerous tribes, each tribe caring only for its own interests, and giving obedience to its own particular chief. This state of things only continued for about four years, as during the terrible convulsions at the time of the crucifixion of our Lord Jesus Christ, the more wicked portion of the people were destroyed.

CHAPTER LX.

LAWS OF THE NEPHITES CONTINUED — THE DIVISION INTO TRIBES—THE MESSIANIC DISPENSATION—THE FINAL CONVULSION.

WE CAN well understand that the originating or primal cause of the destruction of the Nephite republic was the corruption of the people, especially of those whose duty it was to administer the law. This class, being greedy for power, formed a secret combination (as those of old time) to establish a kingdom; and as a means to this end, they had the chief judge assassinated, while they selected a man named Jacob for their king. These royalists, or kingmen, were not as successful in obtaining the sympathy of the majority of the people as they anticipated; they therefore decided to remove in a body to the northernmost part of the land, and there establish the monarchy. This design they successfully carried out. Those who remained at home favored the division of the people into tribes, and there being none strong enough to effectually oppose this suicidal policy, the republic became a thing of the past.

The organization of these tribes was evidently on the patriarchal principle; the head, or most influential member of a family, gathered his kinsmen around him. The historian states: And the people were divided one against another, and they did separate one from another, into tribes, every man according to his family, and his kindred, and friends.

Each of these tribes chose a chief, leader, or ruler, as it is written: And every tribe did appoint a chief, or leader over them; and thus they became tribes and leaders of tribes.

Now behold, there was no man among them, save he had much family, and many kindreds and friends.

The laws of the various tribes were not uniform, but there was a general understanding by which they prevented the outbreak of actual war. It is stated that in the thirty-first year (after Christ), They had come to an agreement that they would not go to war one with another; but they were not united as to their laws, and their manner of government, for they were established according to the minds of those who were their chiefs and their leaders. But they did establish very strict laws that one tribe should not trespass against another, insomuch that in some degree they had peace in the land.

The destruction of the wicked, the visits of the crucified Redeemer, the ministry of his disciples, the universal acceptance of the fullness of the gospel by the people throughout the length and breadth of the land, brings us to a time when there was no need of civil law; for all men lived above the law, being controlled and guided at all times by the higher law of heaven. There was no need of courts of law, for there were no disputations or contentions. No judges or magistrates were required, for there were no offenders or offenses. There were neither envyings, nor strifes, nor tumults, nor whoredoms, nor lyings, nor thefts, nor violence, nor murders. For the love of God dwelt in the hearts of the people; they all dealt justly one with another; temptation was removed; they had all things in common; they were one, the children of Christ, and heirs of the Kingdom of God.

It has been said, Happy are the people who have no history, and thrice happy were the Nephites of this era, whose history was one of continued peace and joy. Well may it be written of them, There could not be a happier people among all the people who had been created by the hand of God. We can scarcely conceive of such a people on this fallen world of ours; an entire continent on which dwelt perfect peace; people among whom there were no rich, no poor—all were alike; a race in whose hearts dwelt the sweet influence of the Spirit of God, the wisdom of which illumined every mind. How they must have increased; how they must have prospered; how they covered the land with millions of human souls; how the arts and sciences must have been developed; and how greatly must true and heavenly knowledge been spread abroad! The law of Moses was no longer observed, but the holy priesthood, after the order of the Son of God, ministered in might in their midst; the faith of the people made angels their frequent visitors; the purity of each life caused the Holy Spirit to be the constant companion of every soul. This happy, glorious state of holiness continued nearly two hundred years, and then commenced the decline of the nation; rapid indeed was its descent, and great was its fall.

The first signs of the decrease in the righteousness of the people, recorded in the Book of Mormon, were: That some became lifted up in pride; these took to wearing costly apparel, jewels, and the fine things of the world. The people ceased to have their goods and their substance in common. They began to be divided into classes; rich and poor appeared. They commenced to deny portions of the gospel, and to build up churches to suit their peculiar ideas; others began to deny the true Church of Christ. They administered that which was sacred (temple ordinances) to the unworthy; and before long they devised all manner of wickedness, and commenced to persecute the servants of God, even to death, when permitted to do so by the powers that rule in the heavens.

Thus matters went on, growing worse every year, until the people were again divided into two nations, Nephites and Lamanites, with their old traditions and ways; which, as was natural, ultimately culminated in war; and such a war! For savageness, brutality, and utter devilishness, we doubt if it was ever equalled in this suffering world. But it is not our province in this chapter to enter into historical details. The law is our subject, and of that we can say little. If it were possible to conceive of such a contradiction, we should say that the law of anarchy reigned supreme. Might made right; and the more numerous Lamanites ultimately overcame and annihilated their Nephite brethren. We can well conceive of the nature of the laws during the fierce struggle that preceded this dire calamity, from the light of this nation's previous history; they were no doubt framed, enacted and administered for the benefit of the rich and the strong, and to the injury of those in whose bosoms burned one lingering spark of righteousness. The history of the Nephites, from beginning to end, fully justifies the saying of the wise man, Righteousness exalteth a nation, but sin is a reproach to any people.

CHAPTER LXI.

THE MONEY OF THE NEPHITES—THEIR COINS—BARLEY THE STANDARD OF VALUE.

IN THE early days of the Nephite nation, when its people were struggling to develop their own peculiar and distinctive civilization, each province, district or even city had its particular standards of weights, measures and money. This state of affairs frequently prevails in young communities, and is an evidence that the growth of Nephite civilization was much the same as in the nations of the eastern hemisphere. As the population of a nation increases, its powers of government consolidating and its commerce developing, these various and conflicting standards of exchange give rise to much unnecessary confusion, many perplexing difficulties and frequent misunderstandings and complications, which hamper trade and commerce, retard material progress, and delay the unification of the nation. It thus becomes the work of the far-seeing statesman or wise ruler to bring all these various local rates to one national standard, recognized as legal and equitable in all parts of the realm.

This work the second Mosiah accomplished for the Nephites. When he revised and codified the national law for the government of the people under the Judges, he abolished the local distinctive rates and introduced one universal standard. Of the ratios of the various weights and measures, either before or after the enactment of Mosiah's wise law, we are told nothing in the Book of Mormon; it is simply stated that the Nephites had not adhered to the standards in use among the Jews, but had altered their reckoning and their measures, very frequently as caprice, convenience, or local exclusiveness inspired. As to the ratios of the coins legalized by Mosiah's code they are highly artistic, evince a large acquaintance with monetary matters and point to a high degree of civilization as then existing among the Nephites.

The following is the table of these coins as given in the Book of Mormon:

GOLD COINS.		SILVER COINS.
1 Senine	equal to	1 Senum.
1 Seon, 2 Senines,	"	1 Amnor.
1 Shum, 4 "	"	1 Ezrom.
1 Limnah, 7 "	"	1 Onti.

Of smaller coins—

1 Shiblon was equal to half a Senine or Senum.
1 Shiblum was equal to a quarter of a Senine or Senum.
1 Leah was equal to an eighth of a Senine or Senum.
While an Antion of gold was equal to three Shublons.

Though not directly so stated, we judge from the context that the Shiblon, the Shiblum and the Leah were silver coins.

The names of these coins seem to be identical with, or derived from those of familiar persons or places. Thus we have a Leah, a Shiblon,* and an Amnor,† all names of persons. Also an Antion, which word is found in Antionah‡ and Antionum,§ a Shiblum which differs from Shiblom§ only in one letter, and a Shublon from Shiblon,* and a Limnah from Limhah,§ to the same extent.

This custom of naming coins after well-known or distinguished persons is a practice not confined to the Nephites. Other nations have done the same; as for instance, in France a twenty-franc gold piece is called a Napoleon.

---

*A son of Alma the younger.
†A Nephite officer under Alma.
‡A chief ruler in the city of Ammonihah.
§Three Nephite generals killed at Cumorah.

One little item that in itself may appear trivial is not without its weight in the consideration of the minor or incidental evidences of the truth of the Book of Mormon. A measure of barley is especially mentioned as the unit of value on which the monetary system, or the value of the coins of the Nephites was based. One senine was worth one measure of barley, and its multiples were, of course, multiples of this measure of barley, but we have no information as to what the contents of this measure may have been.||

Now the old English unit of measurement was a barley-corn, or grain of barley. Three barley-corns make one inch, is the way the table commenced.

Believing, as the Latter-day Saints do, that the Nephites were a branch of the house of Israel, and also that the races whence the English have most largely sprung had much of the blood of Israel in their composition, the agreement of these two units on the grain so frequently mentioned in the Bible (as with the Nephites all grain seems to have been of equal price) is not without its value in either argument. The fact, also, that the Nephites made grain the standard of value shows how highly agriculture must have been esteemed among that people.

||The payment per day, fixed by law, for a Nephite judge when actually engaged in his official duties was one senine, otherwise one measure of barley.

CHAPTER LXII.

PERSONAL APPEARANCE OF THE NEPHITES—THEIR BEAUTY—TESTIMONY OF REMAINS FOUND—THE DARK SKINNED LAMANITES.

EVER and anon throughout the Book of Mormon, we are reminded by the inspired historians of the beauty of the Nephite race, especially in the days when the glory of righteousness beamed in their eyes, and shone in their countenances; then they were fair, very fair—a white and a delightsome people.

And well might it be so, for were they not descended from that kindred couple, Abraham and his half-sister, whose great beauty has been proverbial in every generation, since they graced the earth with their comeliness? So lovely was Sarah, the fairest of womankind of her generation, that when she was sixty-seven years of age, the royal Pharaoh, disregarding the charms of the darker daughters of Egypt, desired her for his wife; and his admiration was doubtless in good taste, for the Bible tells us that she was then very fair. And still more remarkable, when yet another twenty-two years had passed away, and she had seen nearly ninety summers and winters come and go on this earth, another monarch, Abimelech, sought to take her to himself. Nor was her husband's manly beauty less striking; obedience to God, the observance of the laws of life, and the cultivation of the generous virtues so ennobled his existence, that strength and manhood tarried with him in its force, long after that age when the sons of modern generations are feebly tottering to their graves.

Of the commanding beauty of Abraham's descendants, we have many recorded instances, but none that exceed that of his great-grandson Joseph, whose surpassing manliness placed him in the greatest jeopardy, but whose uncompromising virtue and unaffected innocence brought him off conqueror over temptation, and raised him to the highest pinnacle of earthly splendor and heavenly favor. It was from this well-favored Joseph that the Nephites sprang.

God has set the mark of his displeasure on the Lamanites, whom he has cursed, because of the iniquities of their fathers, with a darkened skin, uncomely features, and straight, black, coarse hair. In the beginning it was not so with either Judah or Manasseh.

In confirmation of the testimony of the Book of Mormon, that the inhabitants of this continent were once a white and beautiful people, it may be stated that when very ancient burial places in North and South America have been opened, the remains of two races—one dark and the other fair— have been exhumed. The question may arise: How could this be told, when the skin had long rotted off the bones, and left only the skeleton behind, which fell in powder as soon as it was exposed to the action of the air? In this way: The dry, gravelly soil in which some of these bodies were buried, had so little affected the mummy, that portions of the hair still remained in good preservation, and in numerous instances it was such as is only found on heads of light races. We will cite a few examples given by different inquirers in this field of research.

One writer, speaking of the ancient mummies found in Peru, says: The hair in general is of a lightish brown, and of a fineness of texture which equals that of the Anglo-Saxon race. Again: The ancient Peruvians appear, from numerous examples of hair found in their tombs, to have been an auburn-haired race. Another gentleman, a Mr. Haywood, has described the discovery, early in the present century, of three mummies, in a cave near the Cumberland river, in Tennessee; and the color of their skin was said to be fine and white, and their hair auburn and of a fine texture. The same investigator mentions several other cases where mummies were found in the limestone and saltpetre caves of Kentucky and Tennessee, with light yellowish hair. One scientist, to account for this peculiarity, suggests that it is possible that the light color was due to the action of the lime and saltpetre; but this suggestion will not affect those buried in other formations of rock, nor will it account for the fineness of the texture of the hair. Reasoning from other data, other writers have concluded that the cities whose ruins still stand in Yucatan and Central America were the work of two races, a light and a dark-skinned race respectively.

The reference to the Anglo-Saxon race, above made, is not without its value. To us it seems highly probable that the righteous Nephites, in very many particulars of form and feature, resembled this people and its kindred races. Our reasons are: first, that there was a striking similarity in the appearance of the ancient Israelites and the olden Anglo-Saxons. This likeness has been remarked and commented upon by various authors. Again, it is well known to the Latter-day Saints that there was a large percentage of the blood of Ephraim in the stock whence the Angles and Saxons sprung. So much admitted, it is easy to understand how the two half tribes, descended from the comely Joseph—the one from Ephraim, and the other from Manasseh—would bear a strong family likeness.

Were we introduced to a typical Nephite, we should expect to find him well proportioned, ruddy of countenance, auburn haired and light eyed. This, of course, is simply conjecture, and is entitled to consideration only as such.

From reliefs found sculptured on the walls of the ruined cities of Central America, it seems probable that the ancient Lamanites esteemed flat, receding foreheads the highest type of beauty. Most of the figures on which the greatest artistic skill is displayed appear to represent persons on whom some artificial means had been used, in infancy, to flatten the front part of the head, as their debased descendants, the Flatheads, do in our day. It is a noteworthy fact, that other races of Israelitish descent, or who have come in close contact with the Hebrews, show this same tendency.

Skulls thus flattened have been taken out of tombs in the neighborhood of Ancient Media, where the Israelites were once in captivity; also from sepulchres in Circassia, Scandinavia, Great Britain, etc., and one was even exhumed from outside the walls of Jerusalem. It is true the Book of Mormon does not refer to this custom, but it often speaks of the Lamanites shaving their heads, which in all probability may have afterwards grown into the still more hideous practice of flattening the skull, under the idea that it made them courageous. Indeed, it is quite possible that it did make them recklessly bloodthirsty, by injuring their intellectual powers, and thus tending to develop their more savage instincts.

CHAPTER LXIII.

LANGUAGE OF THE NEPHITES—THE INFLUENCE OF THE EGYPTIANS—NEPHITE WORDS—RAMEUMPTOM—LIAHONA—RABBANAH—THE LAMANITE TONGUE—WORD BUILDING.

THERE appears to be a slight difference of opinion among students of the Book of Mormon with regard to the language of the ancient Nephites. We will endeavor to give a sketch of both ideas.

One class of inquirers affirm that it is evident, from a careful study of the Book of Mormon, that the people of Nephi were greatly influenced by the language and ideas of the Egyptians. That language was the language of their every-day life, altered or reformed (whether corrupted or improved cannot be told) so greatly in the course of time, that in his day Moroni informs us no other people knew it. In the thousand years that had elapsed between the exodus of Lehi from Jerusalem and the abridgement of the record, the Nephites had altered the Hebrew also, so that neither their sacred nor their common modes of speech could be understood by other races.

At the very opening of the inspired record Nephi writes: I was taught somewhat in all the learning of my father. A little further on he explains what that learning was. He says: I make a record in the language of my father, which consists of the learning [literature] of the Jews and the language of the Egyptians. It is not strange that Lehi should have been acquainted with the Egyptian tongue, as from the days of king Solomon, for some hundreds of years, it was the polite language of the world, as French was in Europe during the eighteenth century. King Mosiah in after years confirmed this statement, that Lehi was taught in the language of the Egyptians. It would be rather unreasonable to suppose that the knowledge of that language carried no further influence than to enable the Nephites to converse in it. It brought them *en rapport* so to speak, with those who used it in its native home in Africa, evidences of which yet exist in the Egyptian types of architecture and hieroglyphics found in the midst of the ruins of the ancient cities, scattered far and wide over this western continent. This similarity has been noticed again and again by explorers and students, but its cause still remains to them an unsolved problem.* To the believers in the Book of Mormon the mystery stands revealed.

Other students incline to the opinion that when the Egyp-

---

*No claim has been advanced, we believe, which advocates an actual Egyptian colonization of the New World, but strong arguments have been used to show that the architecture and sculpture of Central America and

tian language is mentioned it probably only means its orthography. They say the Jews seem to have understood the Egyptian language or writing. For he [Lehi] having been taught in the language of the Egyptians, therefore he could read these engravings [the brass plates]. Laban and his forefathers must have understood the Egyptian, and recorded their sacred writings, from generation to generation, in that language. The words "language of the Egyptians" very probably means little more than Egyptian characters or an alphabet for spelling Hebrew words. There seemed to be two sets of characters—the Egyptian and the Hebrew (see Mormon ix., 32 and 33) for spelling; but it is doubtful whether the words written were words of two distinct languages, or words of one language written in the Egyptian and Hebrew characters. Which was the fact is not clearly specified.

We here reproduce two cuts to show our readers that there is a distinct family likeness between the engravings on the plates from which the Book of Mormon was translated and ancient Egyptian characters. One is a copy of the noted passage from the Book of Mormon taken by Elder Martin Harris to Professor Anthon in New York; the other a reproduction of some very ancient Egyptian characters engraved on the rocks not far distant from Mount Sinai.

There are but few Nephite words handed down to us in the Book of Mormon, as wherever an English equivalent

---

Mexico have been influenced from Egypt, if not attributable directly to Egyptian artisans.—J. T. Short.

The hieroglyphics, symbols and emblems which have been discovered in the temples bear so strong a resemblance to those of the Egyptians as to encourage the supposition that a colony of that nation may have founded the city of Palenque or Culhuacan.—Jaurros.

Giordan found the most striking analogies between the Central American and Mexican remains and those of the Egyptians. The idols and monuments he considers of the same form in both countries, while the hieroglyphics of Palenque do not differ from those of ancient Thebes.

could be found, it has been given by the Prophet in his inspired translation. These words are:

Neas and Sheum—Kinds of grain.
Ziff—A metal.
Rameumptom—A holy stand.
Gazelem—A name given to a servant of God.
Liahona—A director or compass.
Rabbanah—A title, meaning powerful king.

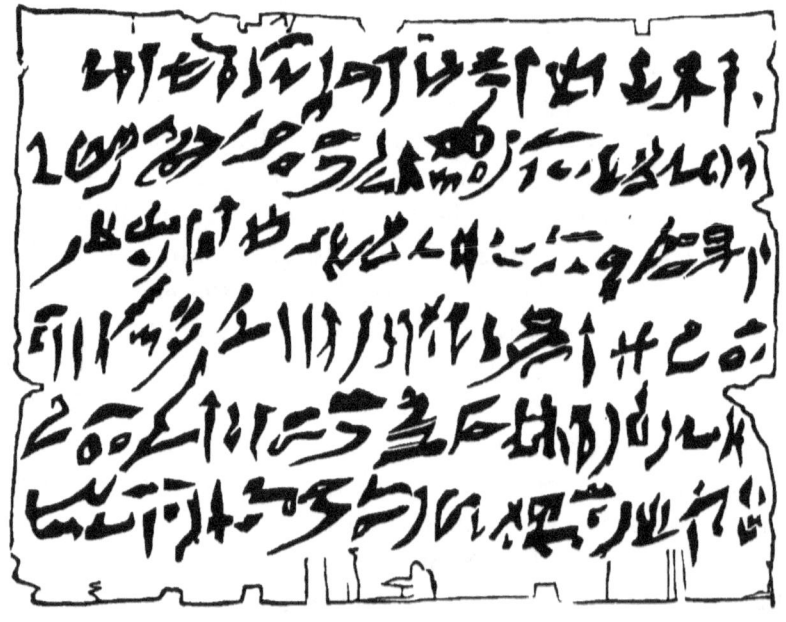

ANCIENT EGYPTIAN CHARACTERS.

Also the names of their coins, and proper names of persons, places, etc.

Some would-be-wise folks have seen fit, at different times, to amuse themselves at the expense of these words, applying to them various contemptuous terms and styling them gibberish. But we propose to show that these words are derived from the Hebrew and Egyptian tongues, neither of which, all men admit, were known to the Prophet Joseph Smith at the

COPY OF CHARACTERS ON THE PLATES FROM WHICH THE BOOK OF MORMON WAS TRANSLATED.

And it shall come to pass, that the Lord God shall bring forth unto you the words of a book, and they shall be the words of them which have slumbered.

But the book shall be delivered unto a man, and he shall deliver the words of the book, which are the words of those who have slumbered in the dust; and he shall deliver these words unto another;

But the words which are sealed he shall not deliver, neither shall he deliver the book. For the book shall be sealed by the power of God, and the revelation which was sealed shall be kept in the book until the own due time of the Lord, that they may come forth: for behold, they reveal all things from the foundation of the world unto the end thereof.—*II. Nephi xxvii. 6, 9, 10.*

time he published the Book of Mormon (A. D. 1830). Had he been worldly wise, he might by his own learning have fashioned these words; but as he was not, when we can adduce evidence that they have true Hebrew or other ancient roots, we have brought forward another strong argument in favor of the inspiration of the translation.

It has been wisely said, It is very evident that pure words of either the Hebrew or Egyptian tongue could hardly be expected in the Book of Mormon, for the reason that the Nephites had altered the Hebrew, and their language was so completely changed that their speech could not be understood by other races. But although the structure of their language had thus changed, it does not follow that all the words had been replaced by others entirely unlike the former language spoken and written by them. It is logical to expect many remnants of the ancient roots, which, however much changed, may retain so much of their original types as to be capable of identification. Thus, in the word *Ziff,* which the Prophet Joseph tells us was a metal, we find a word of the same sound as the Hebrew word ziph or seph, which means a metal. The metal laid over statues was so called. It is true that the word ziff is not spelled the same, but in its orthography is like the name of the Hebrew month, Ziff. But the word ziff means brightness—metallic brightness. (The word is used in Daniel ii., 31, also in Isaiah xxx., 22, where it means overlaying metal.)

Ramcumptom was the name given by the Zoramite apostates to the elevated place in their synagogues, from whence they offered up their vain-glorious and hypocritical prayers. Alma states the word means a holy stand. It resembles, in its roots, Hebrew, and also Egyptian, in a remarkable manner. *Ramoth,* high (as Ramoth Gilead), elevated, a place where one can see and be seen; or, in a figurative sense, sublime or exalted. *Mptom* has probably its root in the Hebrew word translated *threshold,* as we are told that the Philistine god, Dagon, had a threshold in Ashdod (see I. Samuel v., 4, 5). Words with this root are quite numerous in the Bible. Thus we see how Rameumptom means an exalted place to stand upon, a pulpit or holy stand.

Sheum, a kind of grain, is singularly like the Hebrew Shum (garlic), as found in Numbers xi., 5.

Gazelem appears to have its roots in Gaz—a stone, and Aleim, a name of God as a revelator or interposer in the affairs of men. If this suggestion be correct, its roots admirably agree with its apparent meaning—a seer. The text reads: And the Lord said, I will prepare unto my servant Gazelem, a stone, which shall shine forth in darkness unto light, that I may discover unto my people who serve me, that I may discover unto them the works of their brethren: yea, their secret works, their works of darkness, and their wickedness and abominations.

Rabbanah is another wonderful word. It is the title applied by the servants of king Lamoni to Ammon, the son of Mosiah, after his miraculous exploits at the waters of Sebus. It is translated powerful or great king. Whether it was a Nephite or Lamanite word is uncertain, as the Lamanites of that age (B. C. 91) had been taught by royal command in the language of the Nephites. It is, however, of little moment to which of these kindred tongues it belonged, but its Hebrew derivation is most unmistakable. Its origin is evidently in *abba,* father. Max Muller, the great modern authority on such points, says the word king originally meant father; having doubtless taken this form in the earliest patriarchal days when the king ruled by right of his fatherhood, and represented God, the Great Father of us all. This ancient American word confirms Professor Muller's statement; while it manifests how remarkably the unities of the Book of Mormon are preserved, consistent only with its claim to Divine inspiration. It would be the height of folly to ascribe such a coincidence to chance; a man must be far more credulous to so believe, than it can possibly be claimed such are who place implicit confidence in the realities of Nephite and Lamanite history.

From the few examples of words and names before us, we judge the Lamanite language to have been quite musical. Such names as Rabbanah, Lamoni, Lehonti, Middoni, Antionum, Onidah, etc., are certainly specimens of a soft, flowing, pleasing form of speech.

One practice, that of word building, or adding several words together to form a new word, which combination gave expression to the desired idea, obviously obtained among the Lamanites. As examples we have the city of Lehi-Nephi. the village of Ani-Anti and the people of Anti-Nephi-Lehi. Such a practice is frequent among many families of their modern representatives. It was found to exist among the Mexicans—the Aztecs—by the early Spanish invaders, and today is practiced by our near neighbors the Shoshones. This habit explains the reasons for the existence of so many words of great length found in both of these tongues.

CHAPTER LXIV.

NEPHITE PROPER NAMES—BIBLE NAMES—SARIAH—NEPHI—SAM—MELEK—JERSHON—ISABEL—AHA, ETC.,—PREFIXES AND SUFFIXES.

THE number of Bible proper names found in the Book of Mormon has been now and again urged as an argument against its divine origin. If those making these objections were to calmly consider the matter, we believe they would quickly acknowledge that it would be very inconsistent to expect the opposite. Nearly all devout races are in the habit of naming their children after the holy men—patriarchs, martyrs and sages—whose lives they reverence, and whose virtues they desire to see reproduced in their offspring. It is so with ourselves; nearly all our most familiar names are English forms of Bible names. For example: John, James, Jacob, Joseph and Thomas among men, and Mary, Anna, Elizabeth and Sarah among women. So it was with the Nephites. The Hebrew was the language of their sacred literature; while their fondest recollections, their holiest pride ran back to the days of Joseph and Joshua, Samuel and Isaiah, and, like other races, they named their children after the ancient worthies they reverenced most. Hence, we find the following Bible names borne by the descendants of Lehi* and Sariah: Aaron, Aminadab, Ammon, Amnah; Amos, Benjamin, Enos, Gideon, Gilgal, Helam, Helem, Isaiah, Ishmael, Jacob, Joseph, Jeremiah, Jonas, Laban, Lemuel, Noah, Samuel, Shem, Timothy and Zedekiah. A few others are evidently slightly altered Hebrew names, as Chemish from Chemosh, Sherem from Shaaraim, and Zenos from Zenas. Indeed, there may be no actual difference; the apparent change may arise from the English translators inserting a wrong vowel sound in words where, according to the ancient custom, the consonants only were written.

We will now consider a few proper names found in the Book of Mormon, but not in the Bible; for, notwithstanding the changes made by the Nephites in their language, the derivation and significance of many of these names are evident, when considered in connection with the languages of the races with whom the ancient Hebrews were brought most closely in contact.

Sariah is obviously Hebrew. It is a name of extreme beauty and force. Its roots are in Sara, a princess, and Jah

---

*The name Lehi itself, is to found in *Judges xv., 9.*

or Iah, Jehovah, thus meaning a princess of Jehovah; a most fitting name for the mother of a multitude of nations.

Nephi is another very remarkable name. Its roots are Egyptian; its meaning, good, excellent, benevolent. From very ancient times the Egyptians believed that all who died had to have their acts upon earth scrutinized by a council of inquisitors, before they could be proclaimed fit to enter the eternal abodes of bliss and stand in the presence of the god Osiris, the chief lord of the land of the departed. One of the names given to this god, expressive of his attributes, was Nephi or Dnephi (the D being silent, as Dniester, Dnieper, etc.), or the good, and the chief city dedicated to him was called N-ph, translated into Hebrew as Noph, in which form it appears in Hosea, Isaiah and Jeremiah. Its modern English name is Memphis. In the Coptic, the language of the modern Egyptians, the word has the form of Menfi or Mnefi. Plutarch, the ancient historian, says that Dnephi was a benevolent person, and an epithet for Osiris, and was also applicable to Memphis, the sepulchre of that god. The word Neph frequently appears in Egyptian proper names before the Christian era, as Amoneph, Amuneph, Me-Nephta From these facts we conclude that Nephi was a common name in the Egyptian tongue; and, as far as the founder of the Nephite nation was concerned, most applicable to his character, which was pre-eminently good and benevolent.

The English word, Nephites, that is the people or family of Nephi, occurs twice in its Hebrew form in the Old Testament; once in *Ezra* (ii., 50) as Nephisim, and again in *Nehemiah* (vii., 52), as Nephishesim, which show that the name was common among the Hebrews of the age of the captivity.

Sam is a name which some shallow-pated opponents of the Book of Mormon have been disposed to ridicule. But it is pure Egyptian. It was the distinctive name of one of the highest orders of their priesthood. The great *Rameses* himself belonged to the order of Sam. The fact that Lehi gave to two of his sons such peculiarly Egyptian names shows how great an influence the literature of that country must have had on his life.

Melek is the name given to a region of country situated west of the river Sidon. No reason is given why it was so called, but its meaning is evident. It was the king's land. The ancient Phœnician word for king is spelled letter for letter the same as in the Book of Mormon (Melek), and the Hebrew word is almost identical.

Jershon, the name applied to the land given by the Nephites to the exiled Ammonites, means the land of the expelled, or of the strangers. We think it altogether probable that this significant name was given to it at the time it was set off for the habitation of these expatriated Christian Lamanites, as it defines their condition as exiles, and their relation to the Nephites as strangers. The name is not mentioned before this event, and would possibly be the only local name by which it was known to the compiler of the Book of Mormon. Before the date of this exodus, it was, we think, considered a portion of the land of Zarahemla.

Isabel is either a form of Jezebel, the chaste, a name given in derision to the character who bore it, or it has its derivation like Isaiah, which means the delight of Jehovah, and thus signifies the delight of Bel, that is to say, of her lord, husband or possessor. It may have been assumed to suggest the supposed joys of her society. It is a remarkable fact that the land wherein she dwelt is styled the land of Siron, that is, the land of the deserters, or apostates. It was situated at the extreme edge of the Nephite possessions, and on the borders of the Lamanites, beyond the land of Antionum, in which dwelt the Zoramite apostates. The experience of the Saints in this age teaches them how apt apostates are to draw off to remote corners, where they fancy the reproofs of the priesthood are the least likely to be heard. In such a place, far from the Nephite capital, outside the reach of the rigors of the law of Moses, the enticing Isabel could carry on her vile vocation with the greatest safety and impunity.

Aha, we suggest means laughter. Sarah, the wife of Abraham, called her son Isaac—laughter. The sound of the word also resembles a laugh, and again it is the name for laughter in the language of the modern Sioux, as Minne-aha —laughing water.

Without being able to express a positive opinion, but simply as a suggestion, we insert the supposed meaning of the following words:

Nephihah,	Jehovah's consolation.
Ammon,	A worker of Jehovah.
Shazer (or Shazeh),	Gladness.
Nahom,	Comfort.
Zarahemla,	From a rising of light, or whom he (God) will fill up.
Laman,	White (another form of Laban).
Manti,	Relating to Prophets or oracles.

Many others could be inserted, but might possibly prove irksome.

Before closing this branch of inquiry we will draw attention to the ancient Nephite prefixes and suffixes. These matters may not be of great interest to the general reader, but to the students of the Book of Mormon they may prove an incentive to further interesting research.

Among the most numerous prefixes found in Book of Mormon proper names, are Am, Anti, Gid and Hel, of which the first is by far the most frequent. We find Am in Ammon, Amaron, Ammaron, Ammoron, Amoron, Amulon, Amnor, Ammonihah, Amalickiah, Amnah, Amlici, Aminadi, etc.; Anti in Antionah, Antiomno, Antipas, Antipus, Antionum and Anti-Nephi-Lehi. It was also used as a suffix, an Ani-Anti. The prefix Gid we find in Giddianhi, Gidgiddoni, Giddonah and Gidgidonah; and Hel in Helem, Helam, Helaman and Helorum.

Not to make this portion of our investigations tedious, we will only give two or three examples of the suffixes that appear to have been most in use.

>ah, as Zerahamnah, Giddonah, Cumorah.
>am, as Zoram, Lauram, Seezoram.
>iah, as Amalickiah, Mosiah.
>ihah, as Nephihah, Moronihah, Cumenihah.
>om, as Sidom, Shiblom, Jarom.
>on, as Mormon, Emron, Corianton.
>or, as Amnor, Korihor, Nehor.
>en, as Kumen, Kishkumen.
>um, as Teancum, Helorum, Moriantum.
>us, as Antipus, Archaentus, Lachoneus.
>oni, Moroni, Lamoni, Mathoni.
>di, Aminadi, Abinadi.
>hi, as Nephi, Zenephi, Limhi.
>ti, Lehonti, Manti.
>doni,* as Gidgiddoni, Middoni.

*We suggest that this is a form of the Hebrew word Adonai—Lord.

CHAPTER LXV.

THE LANDS OF THE NEPHITES—MULEK AND LEHI—ZARAHEMLA AND NEPHI—THE WILDERNESS—THE LAND OF FIRST INHERITANCE — THE JOURNEYS NORTHWARD — THE WATERS OF MORMON—LEHI-NEPHI.

TO THE ancient Nephites the whole of North America was known as the land of Mulek, and South America as the land of Lehi; or, to use the exact language of the Book of Mormon, the land south was called Lehi; and the land north was called Mulek.

The reason why these names were so given was because the Lord brought Mulek into the land north, and Lehi into the land south, when he led them from Judea to this greater land of promise.

From the days of the first Mosiah to the era of Christ's advent, South America was divided into two grand divisions. These were the land of Zarahemla and the land of Nephi. During this period, except in times of war, the Lamanites occupied the land of Nephi, and the Nephites inhabited the land of Zarahemla.

That these two lands occupied the whole of the southern continent is shown by the statement of the sacred writer: Thus the land of Nephi, and the land of Zarahemla, were nearly surrounded by water; there being a small neck of land between the land northward and the land southward. The width of this narrow neck of land which connected the two continents is in one place said to have been the distance of a day and a half's journey for a Nephite. In another place it is called a day's journey. Perhaps the places spoken of are not identical, but one may have been slightly to the north of the other along the line of the isthmus.

Both the lands of Nephi and Zarahemla were sub-divided, for governmental purposes, into smaller lands, state or districts. Among the Nephites, these lands, in the days of the republic, were ruled by a local chief judge, subject to the chief judge of the whole nation; and among the Lamanites by kings, who were tributary to the head king, whose seat of government was at the city of Lehi-Nephi or Nephi.

The land of Nephi covered a much larger area of country than did the land of Zarahemla. The two countries were separated by the wilderness which extended entirely across the continent from the shores of the Atlantic Ocean to the Pacific. The northern edge of this wilderness ran in a line almost due east and west, and passed near the head of the river Sidon. The Sidon is generally understood to be the river in these days called the Magdalena.

All north of this belt of wilderness was considered the land of Zarahemla; all south of it was included in the land of Nephi. We are nowhere told its exact breadth, and can only judge thereof from casual references in the narrative of the Book of Mormon.

The river Sidon flowed through the centre of the Nephite civilization of the days of the republic. After the convulsions that attended the crucifixion of the Holy Messiah, the physical and political geography of the continent was greatly changed, and the new conditions are very vaguely defined by the inspired historians.

On the western bank of the river Sidon was built the city of Zarahemla. From the time of its first occupancy by the Nephites, to the date of its destruction by fire at the crucifixion, it was the capital or chief city of the nation, the centre of its commercial activities, and the seat of government. It was the largest and oldest city within their borders, having been founded by the people of Zarahemla before the exodus of the Nephites, under the first Mosiah, from the land of Nephi.

When the Nephites, by reason of increasing numbers, the exigencies of war, or for other causes founded new cities the cities so built were generally called after the name of the leader of the colony or of some illustrious citizen, and the land immediately surrounding, contiguous or tributary to the new city was called by the same name. As an example we will take the city or land of Ammonihah, regarding which it is written: Now it was the custom of the people of Nephi to call their lands and their cities, and their villages, yea, even all their small villages, after the name of him who first possessed them; and thus it was with the land of Ammonihah.

Some of these lands appear to have been relatively small, more resembling a county, or possibly a township, than any other division at present prevailing in this country. Such we suppose to have been the lands of Helam and Morianton. Others, such as the lands of Bountiful and Desolation, embraced wide, extended tracts of country.

The exact place where Lehi and his little colony first landed on this continent is not stated in the Book of Mormon: but it is generally believed among the Latter-day Saints to have been on the coast of Chili in thirty degrees south latitude. In fact, the Prophet Joseph Smith so stated.

We do not think it possible, without divine revelation, to determine with accuracy the identical spot where Lehi and his colony landed. We believe that the coast line of that region has entirely changed since those days. Even if we do not take into consideration the overwhelming convulsions that took place at the crucifixion of our Lord, which changed the entire face of nature, there remains the general elevation or subsistence of the land which is continually taking place the world over. Some coasts are rising, some are falling. The land in South America, on its western or Pacific shores, has long been rising, some think for centuries.

If this be so the rise of an inch a year would entirely change the configuration of the sea shore, and give this generation shallows and dry land, where but a few centuries ago there were deep waters. But so far as the results growing out of the terrible earthquakes that occurred at the death of the Savior are concerned, we can form no conclusions, for they were variable. In some regions the waters usurped the place of the land, in others the land encroached upon the waters. Which way it happened near the place where Lehi landed we have no record, and consequently can say nothing. For all we know a huge mountain may now cover the spot, or it may be hidden beneath the blue waters of the Pacific, scores of miles away from any present landing place.

In the region that Lehi landed there he also died. Soon after his death, Nephi, and those of the colony who wished to serve the Lord, departed for another country. They did so by direct command of heaven. The reason for this command was the murderous hatred shown by Laman and Lemuel towards Nephi and his friends. These vicious men determined to kill Nephi, that he might not be a king and a ruler over them. Their hearts were wicked, they loved sin and were resolved that they would not be governed by their virtuous and heaven-favored brother.

Nephi and his company journeyed in the wilderness for many days. By the expression "the wilderness," we understand the inspired writer to mean the uncultivated and uninhabited portion of the land. This word appears to be frequently used in after years, with this signification. At other times it is applied to the desert and uninhabitable regions, the tropical forests, and jungles infested with wild beasts. The journey of the Nephites was northward, as is shown by their later history; but Nephi, in his very brief account of this migration, says nothing with regard to the direction in which they traveled.

At the end of many days a land was found which was deemed suitable for settlement. There the company pitched their tents, and commenced the tillage of the soil. In honor of their leader, it was called the land of Nephi; or to use the modest language of Nephi, My people would that we should call the name of the place Nephi, wherefore we did call it Nephi.

No doubt the choice of location was made by divine inspiration. It was a highly-favored land, rich in mineral and vegetable productions, and yielded abundant crops to the labors of the husbandman.

In this happy country the Nephites dwelt, prospered and increased until they again moved northward. Perhaps not once nor twice they migrated, but several times; for we hold it to be inconsistent with the story of the record and with good judgment to believe that in their first journey they traveled as far north as they were found four hundred years afterwards, when they again took up their line of march, and finally settled in the land of Zarahemla. In the first place there was no necessity for Nephi and his people taking such a lengthy, tedious and hazardous journey; in the second place, in their weak condition, it was nigh unto an impossibility. To have taken a journey of a few hundred miles would have placed them out of the reach of the Lamanites; there was no need for them to travel thousands. Again, in a few years the Lamanites had followed and come up to them; it is altogether inconsistent to think that that people, with its racial characteristics, would in so short a time have accomplished so marvelous a triumph as to follow, hunt up and attack their late brethren if the latter had placed all the distance from Chili to Ecuador between them and their pursuers When we consider the difficulties of travel through the trackless wilderness, the obstacles interposed by nature, the lack of all roads or other guides to indicate where the Nephites had gone, it seems out of the question to imagine that in twenty years or so, the shiftless, unenterprising Lamanites had accomplished such a feat. To the contrary, we believe that Nephi and those with him traveled until they considered themselves safe, then settled down in a spot which they deemed desirable. By and by the Lamanites came upon them; the Nephites defended themselves as long as they could, and when they could do so no longer they again moved to the northward. Their early history was one of frequent wars; and as the Lord used the Lamanites as thorns in their sides when they turned from him, we judge for this reason, and that they were found so far north in the days of Amaleki and Mosiah, that the savage descendants of Laman had frequently defeated them and driven them farther and farther away from the land of their first possession.

The inquiry will naturally arise, as a result of these suggestions: In what portion of the South American continent lay the home of the Nephites in the days of Mosiah? This cannot be answered authoritatively. We are nowhere told its exact situation. Still, there are many references in the Book of Mormon from which we can judge, to some extent, of its location. Elder Orson Pratt suggests that it was in the country we now call Ecuador. The writer entirely agrees with Elder Pratt's suggestion. Other brethren have placed it considerably farther south; but in our reading of the Book of Mormon we have found no evidence to confirm their suppositions, but much to contradict them.

We believe that the lands occupied by the Nephites before they went down into the land of Zarahemla were situated among the table lands or high valleys of the Andes, much as Utah is located in the bosom of the Rocky Mountains and parallel chains. For these reasons:

First:—They were lands rich in minerals, which all through the American continents are found most abundantly in mountain regions. We may (so far as mineral proximity is concerned) compare the country east of this portion of the Andes—the unexplored, alluvial silvas of the Amazon—to the great plains or prairies east of the Rocky Mountains. These silvas, stretching from the Andes to the Atlantic, we regard as the great wilderness south of Zarahemla so often spoken of in the annals of the Judges.

Secondly, the climate of the torrid lowlands, almost directly under the equator, would be intolerable for its heat, and deadly in its humidity; while the country in the high valleys and table lands would be excellently adapted to human life, especially (we may presume) before the great upheavals and convulsions that marked the death of the Redeemer. As the Nephites spread over the country they located in regions where fevers were common, possibly in those parts rendered unhealthy by the overflowing of the rivers, which, when they receded, left large bodies of stagnant water covering the surface of the ground for the greater portion of the year.

It is also probable that in their journeys the Nephites would follow the most available route, rather than plunge into the dense, untrodden, primeval forests of the wilderness; the home of all manner of savage animals, venomous snakes and poisonous reptiles; where a road would have to be cut every foot of the way through the most luxuriant and gigantic tropical vegetation to be found on the face of the globe. Therefore we regard its accessibility as another reason for believing that the Nephites did not leave the great backbone of the continent to descend into the unexplored depths of the region whose character they aptly sum up in the one word, wilderness.

Our readers must not forget that there were two lands called by the name of Nephi. The one was a limited district immediately surrounding the city of Lehi-Nephi or Nephi. There Mosiah and the Nephites dwelt, about two hundred years before Christ. The other land of Nephi occupied the whole of the continent south of the great wilderness.

As this wilderness, though of great length east and west, was but a narrow strip north and south, and its northern edge ran close to the head waters of the river Sidon, it is evident that the land of Nephi covered by far the greater portion of

South America. Within its wide boundaries was situated the original land of Nephi; as well as many other lands called by various local names, just in the same way as there are many States in these United States, all together forming one great nation.

It is very obvious how there came to be these two lands of Nephi. At first, the small district around the capital city comprised all the territory occupied by the Nephites. As they spread out, whatever valley, plain, etc., they reclaimed from the wilderness was considered a part of that land; and thus, year by year, its borders grew wider and wider, while for convenience sake or governmental purposes, the newly built cities and the lands surrounding were called by varied names, according to the wishes of the people, most frequently after the leader of the out-going, colony or founder of the city. Thus we have a land of Nephi within the land of Nephi; just as we have now-a-days Utah County within the State of Utah; and the city of New York and the County of New York within the state of New York. To distinguish the smaller land of Nephi from the whole country, it is sometimes called the land of Lehi-Nephi.

We have stated that the small land of Nephi was a very limited district. We think this is easily proven. It was so limited in extent that we are told king Noah built a tower near the temple so high that he could stand upon the top thereof and overlook not only the land of Lehi-Nephi where it was built, but also the land of Shilom and the land of Shemlon, which last named land was possessed by the Lamanites. No matter how high the tower, these lands must have been comparatively small (or at any rate the land of Lehi-Nephi was) to have enabled a man to overlook the whole three from the top of one building.

It was on the borders of this land, at the outer edge of its cultivated grounds, in the forest (or thicket) of Mormon, that Alma used to hide himself in the day-time, from the searches of the king, while he ministered among the people when the shades of evening gave him security. It was there he gathered the believers in his teachings, baptized them in the waters of Mormon, and organized the Church of Jesus Christ. From the waters of Mormon to the city of Zarahemla it was twenty-one days' actual travel for an emigrant train.

Alma having been warned of the Lord that the armies of king Noah would come upon his people, the latter gathered together their flocks, and took of their grain and departed into the wilderness which divided the lands of Nephi and Zarahemla. They fled eight days' journey into the wilderness when they rested and commenced to build a city, which they called Helam. Being afterwards compelled to leave this city, on account of the persecutions of the Lamanites and Amulonites, they again took their journey northward, and reached the homes of the main body of the Nephites in Zarahemla in about thirteen days.

Here we have a people encumbered and delayed by flocks and herds, heavily laden with grain, etc., making the journey (in two separate stages) in twenty-one days. It is scarcely supposable that they traveled in a direct line; mountains, rivers and swamps would render the journey somewhat circuitous or winding. But even supposing that they did advance in an almost direct line from point to point, it would only make the distance between Nephi and Zarahemla 210 miles, if they traveled ten miles a day; 315, if they traveled fifteen miles; and 420 if they journeyed twenty miles a day.

Our readers must decide for themselves which distance per day is the most likely that a company, driving their flocks and herds before them, would advance through an unexplored wilderness, full of natural hindrances, and without roads, bridges, ferries and other helps to the traveler.

Zarahemla was situated on the Sidon, certainly a considerable distance from its head waters, as other lands and cities (such as Minon and Manti) are mentioned as lying far above it. If we measure the distance from such a point southward, either 200, 300, or 400 miles, all these measurements will bring us into the country now called Ecuador.

We are of the opinion that the land of Lehi-Nephi was situated in one of the higher valleys, or extensive plateaus of the Andes. In the first place, admitting it was in Ecuador, it would lie almost immediately under the equator, and the lowlands, as before suggested, would be unbearable for an industrious population on account of the great heat; as well as exceedingly unhealthy by reason of chills, fever, and like complaints.

Again, the crops of which the Nephites raised most abundantly—barley and wheat—are not those that flourish in a tropical climate, but can be grown most advantageously in a temperate region, such as could be found in these higher valleys.

It was also a land rich in mineral wealth, which is not probable would have been the case if it had been situated among the wide-spreading alluvial plains east of the Andes.

It is likewise spoken of as a hilly or mountainous country. The hill north of the land of Shilom is frequently mentioned in the historical narrative. For instance:

Ammon came to a hill, which is north of the land of Shilom (*Mosiah* vii. 5).

King Limhi caused his guards to go to the hill which was north of Shilom (*Mosiah* vii. 16).

King Noah erected a great tower on the hill north of the land of Shilom (*Mosiah* xi. 13).

For another reason, the expression "up" is almost always used when reference is made to persons going towards the land of Nephi. Not only did they travel from Zarahemla up the Sidon and across the wilderness to Nephi, but also *up* from the land of Ishmael and other portions of the land of Nephi to the city of Nephi and its surroundings. In contradistinction to this, persons leaving Nephi went down to the land of Zarahemla and to other places.

The only time in which the word down is used, when referring to persons going towards Nephi, is when certain persons came down to the city from off the hill mentioned above.

Some of our readers may object to the statement that the city of Nephi and the city of Lehi-Nephi were one and the same place; and that the land round about was sometimes called the land of Lehi-Nephi, and sometimes the land of Nephi only. But we think that a careful perusal of the record of Zeniff, in the Book of Mormon, will convince them of the fact; especially if they will compare it with the last few verses of the book of Omni. Zeniff in one place speaks of possessing, by treaty with the Lamanites, the land of Lehi-Nephi (*Mosiah ix.* 6), and a few verses later on (verse 14), he talks of the thirteenth year of his reign in the land of Nephi.

If we mistake not, the name of Lehi-Nephi occurs only seven times in the Book of Mormon, everywhere else the name Nephi is used when referring to this land.

CHAPTER LXVI.

NEPHI IN THE HANDS OF THE LAMANITES—THE LANDS OF SHEMLON, SHILOM, HELAM, AMULON, ISHMAEL, MIDDONI, JERUSALEM, ETC.

IN THE second generation the Nephites began to grow numerous, and iniquity made its appearance among them. It was then that Jacob their priest, prophesied: The time speedily cometh, that except ye repent, they [the Lamanites] shall possess the land of your inheritance, and the Lord God will lead away the righteous out from among you. This prophecy was completely fulfilled, if not on previous occasions, about 300 years or so afterwards, when Mosiah, by the command of God, led the righteous Nephites out of the land of their inheritance—the land of Nephi—down into the land of Zarahemla.

From that time the land of Nephi was possessed and ruled by the posterity of Laman, Lemuel and Ishmael; or by Nephite apostates, who, with superior cunning, worked themselves on to the Lamanitish throne.

During the era that the Nephites dwelt in the land of Nephi they built several cities. These the Lamanites eagerly took possession of when Mosiah and his people vacated them. We are not told when and by whom these cities were founded; such particulars, doubtless, appear on the plates of the kings. It is only incidentally that we learn anything regarding them; reference to them is found in the record of Zeniff's return from Zarahemla, and re-occupancy, by treaty with the Lamanites, of a portion of the old Nephite home.

The Lamanites of that age were a wild, ferocious, bloodthirsty and nomadic race, who did not build cities, for the simple reason that they had neither the inclination nor the skill. But when they found the Nephite cities deserted by their inhabitants they immediately occupied them. Even then, they did not enlarge or repair them, but let them fall into gradual decay.

No sooner had the Lamanites surrendered the cities of Lehi-Nephi and Shilom to Zeniff than his people set to work to build buildings and to repair their walls. In the next generation king Noah caused many fine buildings and towers to be built in both the lands of Lehi-Nephi and Shilom.

The two cities above mentioned are the only ones directly spoken of in the Book of Mormon up to this time. There was most probably a city built in the contiguous land of

Shemlon, which was held by the Lamanites, but it is never mentioned by name.

We judge Shilom lay to the northward of Lehi-Nephi, and in the same valley or plateau; otherwise it could not have been so completely viewed from king Noah's tower, mentioned in our last chapter. Its relative position to Lehi-Nephi appears from the fact that those who went to or from the land of Zarahemla, generally did so by way of Shilom; it seems to have lain in the direct route between the two capital cities. Ammon, the Zarahemlaite, and his company entered in that way, and Limhi and his people escaped in the same direction.

The next city that we read of is called Helam. It was located eight days' journey from Nephi towards Zarahemla, and was founded by Alma, the elder, and his followers, when they fled from the murderous persecutions of king Noah. This city and the surrounding country were called after the first man baptized by Alma in the waters of Mormon. His name was Helam, and he doubtless was a leader among that people.

In the same direction from Nephi as Helam, and apparently adjoining thereto, lay the land of Amulon. It was first peopled by the fugitive priests of Noah, when they fled from the vengeance of the justly incensed Nephites. The leader of this band of wicked men was named Amulon, and in his honor the land was so called. The king of the Lamanites afterwards made Amulon the tributary king or chief local ruler over the lands of Helam and Amulon. From this we judge that they lay side by side, their boundaries extending indefinitely into the great wilderness.

Our next information regarding the condition of the land of Nephi is gleaned from the history of the mission of the sons of king Mosiah to the Lamanites in that region. This mission commenced B. C. 91, and lasted fourteen years.

We find the Lamanites of that age considerably advanced in civilization, many of them inhabiting populous cities. The country was divided into several distinct kingdoms, each ruled by its own king; but all subject to the head monarch whose court was at Nephi.

The lands specially mentioned in connection with this mission are those of Nephi, Middoni, Ishmael, Shilom, Shemlon, Helam, Amulon and Jerusalem.

Shilom and Shemlon we have already shown to be in the neighborhood of Lehi-Nephi; Helam, eight days' journey for loaded teams to the north, and Amulon not far distant therefrom. We may next inquire what can be learned of the lands of Jerusalem, Ishmael and Middoni.

The location of the land of Jerusalem is clearly stated. It was away joining the borders of Mormon, that is, on the other side, probably east or north from Nephi. There, somewhere about 100 B. C., the Lamanites, with Amulonites and other apostate Nephites, built a great and thriving city, which they called Jerusalem, after their father's ancient home in Judea.

There Aaron, the son of Mosiah, unsuccessfully preached the gospel. Its apostate citizens were too sin-hardened to accept the message he bore. This city was afterwards destroyed on account of its great wickedness and persecution of the saints, in the terrors that attended the crucifixion of the Savior, and waters came up in the place thereof. A stagnant sea, akin to that which covers Sodom and Gomorrah, occupies the place where once its proud palaces and rich synagogues stood.

The first land visited by the missionary prince, Ammon, was Ishmael; its situation is not clearly stated. It was *down* from Nephi. This leads to the thought that it lay in the alluvial plains considerably east of the Andes. It does not seem compatible with the narrative of Ammon's mission to believe it was situated in the narrow strip of wilderness that lay between the mountains and the Pacific Ocean. Its relative position to other lands precludes this idea.

Near the highway that connected Ishmael and Nephi lay the land of Middoni. This is shown by the fact that when Ammon and king Lamoni were traveling from Ishmael towards Middoni they met Lamoni's father, the head king of all the land, coming from Nephi. This leads to the conclusion that the same road from Ishmael led to both Nephi and Middoni.

Nephi is called *up* from both these lands; we, therefore, suggest that, like Ishmael, Middoni occupied a portion of the lower lands on the eastern borders of the Andes, but somewhat nearer the capital city.

CHAPTER LXVII.

THE LANDS OF THE NEPHITES, CONTINUED—ZARAHEMLA—JERSHON—ANTIONUM—MANTI—GIDEON.

AS THERE were two lands of Nephi, the greater and the less, so, for exactly the same reason, there were two lands of Zarahemla; the one occupying the whole of South America, from the great wilderness, which formed its southern border, northward to the land Bountiful; the other, the district immediately surrounding the capital city.

That there was a Zarahemla within Zarahemla is shown by various passages in which persons are spoken of as journeying to the land of Zarahemla, when they were already within the borders of the greater land of that name. For instance, Minon, on the river Sidon, is said to have been situated above the land of Zarahemla (*Alma ii.* 24); again, Alma took Amulek and came over to the land of Zarahemla from Sidon (*Alma xv.* 18). While in many other places, notably where the boundaries of the possessions of the Nephites are given, the name Zarahemla is applied to the whole of the lands of that people, even sometimes including Bountiful, which is generally spoken of separately.

In the days of the first Mosiah and his son, Benjamin, the greater portion of the Nephites appear to have been located in and immediately around the city of Zarahemla. King Benjamin, when about to resign the royal authority into the hands of his son Mosiah, commanded him to gather his people together, For, he adds, on the morrow I shall proclaim unto this my people out of mine own mouth, that thou art a king and a ruler over this people (*Mosiah i.* 10). The proclamation was sent forth and the people were gathered in an unnumbered host; a thing that could not have been done in so short a time had their habitations been widely scattered over an extended territory.

In the reign of the younger Mosiah, the people stretched out in all directions, and colonies were planted in distant regions. This vigorous policy was continued, only on a much larger scale, during the days of the Judges.

After carefully perusing the Book of Mormon, we suggest that the lands or cities (which in Nephite geography appear to be frequently used interchangeably, or one for the other), included within the borders of the Nephites, in the days of the Judges, were:

In the extreme north, the land of Bountiful, which extended southward from the Isthmus of Panama. On its southern frontier lay the land of Jershon.

On the River Sidon: Zarahemla, Minon, Gideon and Manti.

In the interior, eastward of the Sidon: Antionum, Siron, and probably Nephihah.

On the shores of the Atlantic Ocean and Caribbean Sea: Mulek, Morianton, Lehi, Omner, Gid, Aaron and Moroni.

In the interior, west of the Sidon: Melek, Noah, Ammonihah and Sidom.

Between the upper waters of the Sidon and the Pacific Ocean, or in the extreme southwest: Cumeni, Antiparah, Judea and Zeezrom.

Besides the above the following cities are mentioned, but only in connection with their destruction at the time of the terrible convulsions that marked the sacrifice at Jerusalem of the world's Redeemer:

The great city of Moronihah, covered with earth.

Laman, Gad, Josh and Kishkumen, burned with fire.

Gilgal, Gadiandi, Gadiomnah, Jacob and Gimgimno, sunk in the depths of the earth; and

Onihah and Mocum, in whose place waters came up.

We imagine from the names, that some of the above were built by the Lamanites or Gadianton robbers. But this is simply a conjecture, as the sacred record is entirely silent on the point.

We will now very briefly examine, one by one, some of the more important divisions of the country.

JERSHON.—This was the name given to the regions set apart by the Nephites (B. C. 78), as the home of the Ammonites, or Christian Lamanites. It was situated far to the north, and was evidently chosen for the reason that the strength of the Nephite nation might lie between the fugitives and their former countrymen, the Lamanites, who then thirsted for their blood. It was bounded by the Caribbean Sea and the land Bountiful on the north and east, and by the land of Antionum on the south. Its western boundary is not defined, but we are inclined to believe, from the context, that it was the river Sidon. Its geographical situation is partly described in *Alma xxvii*. 22, thus: We [the Nephites] will give up the land of Jershon, which is on the east by the sea, which joins the land Bountiful, which is on the south of the land Bountiful. With regard to its southern boundary, *Alma xxxi.* 3 (which we shall hereafter quote), states that Antionum lay to the south of it.

ANTIONUM, the land where the Zoramite apostates gathered (B. C. 75), was an extensive and thinly settled region, extending from the land of Jershon to the great southern wilderness. Its boundaries are thus defined (*Alma xxxi.* 3): Antionum, which was east of the land of Zarahemla, which lay nearly bordering upon the sea shore, which was south of the land of Jershon, which also bordered upon the wilderness south. By this we understand that it stretched north from the great wilderness, which passed by the head of the Sidon, almost to the Atlantic Ocean; that its western boundary was the land of Zarahemla, and Jershon its northern limit. Nothing is said of its eastern borders, for the simple reason that at the time this passage was originally written, the country east was yet uninhabited, except possibly by a few wandering Lamanites. At its extreme southern or southeastern corner, "among the borders of the Lamanites" of the wilderness, was the outlaying land of Siron. This place is mentioned but once in the Book of Mormon (*Alma xxxix.* 3).

MANTI.—During the days of the republic, Manti was a district of great importance to the Nephites. It was situated contiguous to the wilderness at the head waters of the Sidon (*Alma xvi.* 6), and lay on the line of march generally taken by the armies of the Lamanites when they invaded Zarahemla. Its exact boundaries are not defined; indeed, it is altogether probable that they varied considerably at different periods of Nephite history. However, it is evident that it was the most southerly of all the lands inhabited by the Nephites, in the western half of the South American continent, after they had moved from the land of Nephi.

GIDEON.—In a valley on the east of the Sidon was built, during the early days of the republic, an important city, which was named after the martyr Gideon. The valley itself was also known by the same name, and is frequently called the land of Gideon, for we find no evidence to lead to the conclusion that the land extended beyond the valley. Nearly all that we know of this region is contained in a single passage (*Alma vi. 7*), which states that Alma left Zarahemla and went over upon the east of the river Sidon, into the valley of Gideon, there having been a city built which was called the city of Gideon, which was in the valley that was called Gideon, being called after the man who was slain by the hand of Nehor with the sword.

From the references in the historical narrative we incline to the opinion that this valley lay either directly east, or somewhat to the south of the city of Zarahemla. Travelers coming from the north are never mentioned as passing through it on their way to Zarahemla, without they had a purpose in so doing, as in the case where Moroni marched from the northeast to the relief of chief judge Pahoran (*Alma lxvii*).

CHAPTER LXVIII.

LANDS OF THE NEPHITES, CONTINUED—MINON—MELEK—AMMONIHAH—NOAH—SIDOM—AARON—LEHI—MULEK—BOUNTIFUL—THE SOUTHWEST BORDER.

MINON is mentioned but once in the Book of Mormon. Its location is then directly stated. It is spoken of as the land of Minon, above the land of Zarahemla, in the course of the land of Nephi (*Alma ii. 24*). Elder Orson Pratt, in a note to this chapter, places Minon about two days' journey south of the city Zarahemla. This is the obvious conclusion to be drawn from the details contained in the chapter; from these details and the above quotation, we also judge it to have been on the western banks of the Sidon, and in the direct road between Nephi and Zarahemla. At this date (B. C. 91) it was inhabited by an agricultural population, who, at the approach of the Lamanites, fled before them into the capital city.

As the course of the river Sidon was from south to north, it is but reasonable to conclude that when the words above and below are used, when reference is made to places on its banks or in its neighborhood, that above means south and below, north. This is a very common mode of expression in such cases.

MELEK.—The boundaries of this land are very indistinctly stated by the inspired writer of the Book of Alma, for it is in that book alone that it is mentioned. However, two things are positively stated (chapter viii.), namely, that it was west of the river Sidon, and that it extended westward as far as the narrow strip of wilderness which ran north and south between the mountains and Pacific Ocean. We imagine that its eastern borders touched the land of Zarahemla and from thence it stretched out as far as the country proved habitable, as it appears to have had a large population, judging from the account given of Alma's ministrations (B. C. 82). That it embraced a large district of country is proven by the fact that when Alma had finished his labors in the city of Melek, he traveled three days' journey on the north of the land of Melek before he came to the city of Ammonihah (*Alma viii.* 6). In later years, when it was considered unsafe for the Ammonites to remain longer in Jershon they were removed to Melek, the proximity of which to Zarahemla, as well as its remoteness from the lands of the Lamanites, rendered it admirably adapted as a place of safety for that persecuted people.

AMMONIHAH.—When Alma had made the three days' journey spoken of above, he reached Ammonihah the country around which city was called by the same name. From the text of the passage some conclude that Alma traveled northward from Melek, but to us it conveys the idea that the prophet journeyed three days westward along or near the northern boundary of that land. We are confirmed in this opinion by the statement made in another place regarding Ammonihah's proximity to that portion of the wilderness which ran along the sea shore (*Alma xxii.* 27). In Alma (*xvi.* 2), it is stated: The armies of the Lamanites had come in upon the wilderness side, unto the borders of the land, even into the city of Ammonihah. If Ammonihah had been situated three days' journey north of Melek, we suggest that it could not have been near that portion of the wilderness which the Lamanites so easily reached without discovery; for a march due north would have taken them close to, or actually through the lands of Minon, Noah, Melek and Zarahemla, the most thickly populated portions of the country; or, to have avoided these, they must have taken a circuitous route of immense length and great danger. Then when they attempted to retire, their retreat, owing to their great distance from Nephi, would have most assuredly been cut off, as was the case with the Lamanite general Coriantumr under these conditions.

NOAH.—Of this land we simply know two things: First, that it was west of the Sidon; second, that it was not far distant from Ammonihah and Melek.

SIDOM is only mentioned in the 15th chapter of Alma. When the persecuted members of the true church were driven out of Ammonihah by its vicious citizens, they fled to Sidom. It is not supposable that these persecuted people were in a condition to travel far. They would necessarily gather to the first available place of refuge. It is, therefore, reasonable to conclude that Sidom was not far distant from Ammonihah.

AARON.—When Alma was first cast out of Ammonihah he turned his face towards a city called Aaron (*Alma viii.* 13).

It is natural to suppose that Aaron was not far distant from Ammonihah; at any rate, not on the other side of the continent. Yet the only other time when a city called Aaron is referred to, it is spoken of as adjoining the land of Moroni, which was the frontier district in the extreme southeast of the lands possessed by the Nephites. Our only way out of this difficulty is to suggest that there were two cities called Aaron; not at all an unlikely thing when we reflect how important a personage Aaron, the son of Mosiah, was among his people. When chosen to be king he declined this great honor, and the republic was established. It requires no stretch of the imagination to believe that a free and grateful people would name more than one city in honor of this self-denying prince. When we consider how many places there are in the United States called Washington, Lincoln, etc., our only wonder is that we do not find more than two cities called Aaron.

This same difficulty exists with regard to NEPHIHAH. We fancy there were also two cities of this name; one situated on the southern frontier, some distance east of Manti and the Sidon (*Alma lvi.* 25); the other on the Atlantic seaboard, north of Moroni (*Alma l.* 14). Of this latter city it is written that in the year B. C. 72 the Nephites began a foundation for a city between the city of Moroni and the city of Aaron, joining the city of Aaron and Moroni, and they called the name of the city or land, Nephihah. This is the region again referred to in chapters 51, 59 and 62 of the Book of Alma. Elder Orson Pratt, in a foot note to chapter 56, draws attention to the fact that the Nephihah there mentioned is not the one spoken of in the other chapters.

THE ATLANTIC SEA-BOARD.—It appears, though it is not altogether certain, that the lands and cities of the Nephites on the Atlantic sea-board were situated in the following order, commencing at the north: Mulek, Gid, Omner, Morianton, Lehi, Aaron, Nephihah and Moroni (*Alma li.* 26).

MORONI was situated by the seashore, on the borders of

the great wilderness, being the farthest from the city of Zarahemla of all the settlements of the Nephites in the southeast. Or, to use the language of the inspired historian, it was by the east sea; and it was on the south by the land of the possessions of the Lamanites (*Alma l. 13*). As the wilderness ran in a straight line from east to west, and the Sidon arose near its northern border, on which border Moroni was also situated, if the convulsions at the time of the crucifixion of our Lord did not so alter the face of the country as to change the locality where this river took its rise, then Moroni was in the country now called Guiana, or in the extreme north of Brazil. The city Moroni now lies covered by the waters of the Atlantic (*III. Nephi viii. 9*). In Guiana, there is a river still called Moroni, or, as it is generally printed on the mapes, Maroni or Marony. There is also a river Morona in Ecuador.

LEHI.—The land of Lehi on the Atlantic coast must not be confounded with the whole of South America, also called the land of Lehi by the Nephites. This lesser land of Lehi was the district surrounding the city of Lehi, and immediately adjoining the land of Morianton, whose people indeed claimed, though unjustly, a portion of its territory.

MULEK was the most northern of the settlements of the Nephites south of the land Bountiful, close to the borders of which it was built. It is positively stated to have been located on the east sea (*Alma li. 26*); west of it was a wilderness, or uninhabited region (*Alma lii. 22*).

BOUNTIFUL.—We believe that there is an idea held by some that the city Bountiful was situated on the Pacific shore. This opinion we think is not warranted by any statement in the Book of Mormon. Mulek, as we have already shown, was on the Atlantic, or east sea; Bountiful was northward of Mulek. When Teancum retreated before the hosts of the Lamanites, who poured out of the city of Mulek to capture his small force, he began to retreat down by *the sea shore northward* (*Alma lii.* 23). This course brought him to Bountiful. From the details contained in this chapter we opine that he and his soldiers reached that city on the same day that they started from outside of Mulek. Now, unless the configuration of the coast line has been entirely and completely changed, no march of one day, or indeed of any length of time along "the sea shore northward" would bring a person to the Pacific Ocean. Our only conclusion can be that Bountiful was situated on the sea shore on the eastern side of the Isthmus, if on the Isthmus at all. Other passages than the one above show that Mulek and Bountiful lay in close proximity.

We fancy the reason why some suppose that the city Bountiful lay on the west coast is because Hagoth built his ship yards there. But the record does not say he built them in or near the city Bountiful. What is stated is that Hagoth went forth and built him an exceedingly large ship, on the borders of the land Bountiful, by the land Desolation, and launched it forth into the west sea, by the narrow neck of land which led into the wilderness northward (*Alma liii.* 5). This narrow neck of land was the dividing line between the land Desolation on the north, and the land Bountiful on the south. We think it is evident, from the above, that the city Bountiful and Hagoth's settlement lay on opposite sides of the Isthmus, the first, on the east near Mulek, the second, in the northwest near Desolation.

Before the land Bountiful was settled by the Nephites, it was a wilderness filled with all manner of wild animals of every kind; a part of which had come from the land northward for food (*Alma xxii.* 31). But the Nephites, to prevent the Lamanites creeping up through the wilderness along the coasts, and thus gaining a foothold in the land northward, at as early a date as possible inhabited the land Bountiful, even from the east to the west sea (*Alma xxii.* 33).

The city called Bountiful is not mentioned until B. C. 64

(*Alma lii*), though the land of that name is frequently referred to at earlier dates.

THE SOUTHWEST BORDER.—All we know of the cities and lands in the southwest is contained in Helaman's report to Moroni of the military operations in that department (*Alma lvi, lviii*). Four cities are mentioned west of Manti: Judea, Antiparah, Zeezrom and Cumeni. Of these, Antiparah appears to have been situated nearer the coast than Judea, while there was yet another city still nearer the ocean, and apparently to the north of Antiparah. But we can simply guess at their relative positions, no positive information being given us.

Besides the foregoing there was a land called DESOLATION. Before the time of the Nephites it was thickly inhabited by the Jaredites. In the days of the latter people Bountiful formed its southern border. The two lands apparently joined at the Isthmus. At first, like most frontier districts, it extended indefinitely into the uninhabited regions. When other lands were colonized its boundaries became more definitely fixed. It is generally supposed to have embraced within its borders the region known to moderns as Central America. Its capital was a city of the same name probably built in later years, as it is never mentioned but by Mormon in the account of the long series of wars in which he took so prominent a part.

CHAPTER LXIX.

THE LANDS OF ANTUM, TEANCUM, JOSHUA, DAVID, ETC.—CUMORAH—THE HILLS OF THE NEPHITES—THE RIVER SIDON.

IN THE history of the final wars between the Nephites and Lamanites we find lands and cities mentioned that are nowhere else spoken of. It is presumable that most of them were built during the blest sabbatic era that followed the visit of the Redeemer. The greater portion of these places were situated in North America, but the exact locality can in scarcely any instance be determined. Among those named are the lands or cities of Antum, Angola, David, Joshua, Jashon, Shem, Teancum, Boaz, Jordon, Cumorah, Sherrizah and Moriantum.

ANTUM.—A land of North America in which was situated a hill called Shim. In this hill Ammaron deposited the sacred records. Mormon afterwards, by Ammaron's direction, obtained the plates of Nephi from this hiding place and continued the record thereon. The land of Jashon appears to have bordered on the land of Antum; as the city of Jashon is said to have been near the land where Ammaron deposited the records.

The city of TEANCUM was situated by the sea shore near to, and apparently north of, the city Desolation.

The land of JOSHUA was on the borders west by the sea shore, but whether in the northern or southern continent is not clear.

The land of DAVID appears to have been located between Angola and Joshua.

One of the most noted places in ancient American history was the land in which was situated the hill known to the

Jaredites as Ramah and to the Nephites as Cumorah. In its vicinity two great races were exterminated; for it was there that the last battles were fought in the history of both peoples. There also the sacred records of the Nephites found their final resting place. When iniquity began to increase in their midst Ammaron hid the holy things in the hill Shim (A. C. 321). About fifty-five years after (say in A. C. 376) Mormon, seeing that his people were fast melting away before the Lamanites, and fearing that the latter would get possession of the records and destroy them, removed all that had been placed in his care by Ammaron, and afterwards hid up in the hill Cumorah all that had been entrusted to him by the hands of the Lord, save the few plates which he gave to his son Moroni. Moroni afterwards concealed the treasures committed to his keeping in the same hill, where they remained until they were, by heaven's permission, exhumed and translated by the Prophet Joseph Smith for our edification. We presume all our readers are acquainted with the fact that this hill is situated about three or four miles from Palmyra, in the state of New York.

Besides Cumorah, several other hills come prominently to the foreground in Nephite history. There were the hills Riplah and Amnihu, near the river Sidon, in the neighborhood of which desperate battles were fought in the days of Alma, resulting, in both instances, in victory to the hosts of the Nephites. Again there was the hill Manti. It also was near the Sidon; on its top Nehor was executed for the murder of the aged Gideon. Then there was Mount Antipas on whose summit Lehonti and the recalcitrant Lamanites gathered when they refused to give heed to their king's war proclamation. It was situated somewhere within the borders of the Lamanites, near Onidah, the place of arms. There was also a hill Onidah in the land of Antionum, upon which Alma preached to the Zoramite apostates.

When perusing the Book of Mormon we have sometimes inclined to the opinion that before the time of the crucifixion of Christ the Andes and other ranges of mountains existed in a much more modified form than at present. We have been led to this conclusion from the fact that no high mountains or stretches of rugged mountain country such as at present exist in Chili, Peru, Ecuador and the United States of Columbia, are suggested by the narrative. Individual hills such as we have drawn attention to, are occasionally mentioned, showing that the country was of diversified altitude; but we have little or nothing to lead our minds to the contemplation of the stupendous peaks and everlasting hills that characterize this region now-a-days. It is also somewhat singular that no reference is made to any rivers in the regions where the Orinoco and Amazon now course in their vast volume to the Atlantic. Our only answer is that the Book of Mormon is primarily a religious record, that the geographical and topographical references are only incidental, and consequently no special importance can be placed on what is not mentioned. Perhaps, also, these rivers, as suggested in the case of the Sidon, ran in different channels, and possibly with a less volume of water then than now.

One of the most important places in Nephite history, for four or five hundred years, was the river Sidon. It was their great highway, more to them than the Mississippi is to this country or the Thames to England. Along its banks were situated their capital and other prominent cities. Its valleys were the most densely populated portions of the land. It was also the grand trunk road to the land of Nephi, and adown its banks poured the hosts of the dark skinned invaders when they forced their way into the land of Zarahemla. To tell all that took place on its borders would be to rewrite the history of the Judges, and to include much of the annals of the kings and the story of the Messianic dispensation.

As stated in other places in this book it is understood that the Sidon of the Nephites is the Magdalena of today;

but it is open to question if its course was not considerably changed during the convulsions that attended the death of the Savior. We incline to the opinion that in the ages before those terrible upheavals of the lands the Sidon was a far nobler, more placid river than the Magdalena is now. Nor do we think it emptied into the ocean at the same spot as at present. The coast line, we believe, has much changed and with that change the point of outflow of this river has been moved.

While journeying on their way through Arabia, Lehi and his party gave such names to the localities they passed or at which they rested as they pleased. The Red Sea is the only place we can distinguish by the name given to it. At their first temporary abiding place on its borders, Lehi, in honor of his elder sons, called the valley where they camped the valley of Lemuel, and the river that coursed through it the river Laman. As they proceeded on their journey we read of Shazer, Nahom, and Bountiful. The last named must not be confounded with the Bountiful in the northern part of South America where the Savior, more than six hundred years afterward, appeared and taught the Nephites. It was a portion of Arabia Felix, or Arabia the happy, so called in contradistinction to Arabia the stony and Arabia the desert, on account of its abundant productiveness and great fertility. It was in this blessed region, on the shore of the Arabian sea, that Nephi built the ship that carried the colony to the promised land. To the sea itself they gave the name of Irreantum, meaning many waters.

The course traveled by Lehi and his people has been revealed with some detail. The Prophet Joseph Smith states: They traveled nearly a south-southeast direction until they came to the nineteenth degree of north latitude; then, nearly east to the sea of Arabia; then sailed in a southeast direction, and landed on the continent of South America, in Chili, thirty degrees south latitude.

With regard to the course of Mulek and his company we are left entirely in the dark; all we are told is that they landed in the northern continent. There is an understanding among the Latter-day Saints that this party traveled westward from Jerusalem. Some think they went first to Egypt under the guidance of the Prophet Jeremiah; then by the Mediterranean Sea either to Spain or Morocco, thence by ship across the Atlantic. Others fancy they went direct by ship from Palestine.

Reference is made in the Book of Mormon to many lands, places and cities on the eastern continent. Among the best known lands mentioned are Assyria, Babylon, Egypt, Ophir, Cush, Elam, Syria, Bashan, Galilee, Samaria, Palestina, Edom and Moab. Among cities—Jerusalem, Nazareth, Damascus, Sodom and Gomorrah;—of mountains Sinai, Horeb and Lebanon; the Red or Egyptian sea; and of peoples—the Medes, Chaldees, Midianites and Arabians.

CHAPTER LXX.

RELIGION OF THE NEPHITES—IT IS STATED BY NEPHI—THE PRIESTHOOD AND ORDINANCES THEREOF—BAPTISM—CONFIRMATION—ORDINATION—THE SACRAMENT—SPIRITUAL GIFTS.

THE religion of the Nephites was the gospel of our Lord and Savior Jesus Christ. It embraced, before his advent, those offerings and sacrifices typical of his life and death, the observance of which was enjoined upon the house of Israel by the law of Moses. As soon as he was offered upon the cross at Calvary these sacrifices ceased, as the law was fulfilled and its intent and purpose was accomplished.

Nephi epitomizes the religious faith of his people in the following graphic and comprehensive language:

For we labor diligently to write, to persuade our children, and also our brethren, to believe in Christ, and to be reconciled to God; for we know that it is by grace that we are saved, after all we can do.

And notwithstanding we believe in Christ, we keep the law of Moses, and look forward with steadfastness unto Christ, until the law shall be fulfilled;

For, for this end was the law given; wherefore the law hath become dead unto us, and we are made alive in Christ, because of our faith; yet we keep the law because of the commandments:

And we talk of Christ, we rejoice in Christ, we preach of Christ, we prophesy of Christ, and we write according to our prophecies, that our children may know to what source they may look for a remission of their sins.

Wherefore, we speak concerning the law, that our children may know the deadness of the law; and they, by knowing the deadness of the law, may look forward unto that life which is in Christ, and know for what end the law was given. And after the law was fulfilled in Christ, that they need not harden their hearts against him, when the law ought to be done away.

Here are a hundred sermons in a few sentences, and every sentence is pregnant with the force and glory of God's eternal truth. Again, how concisely the plan of salvation is explained in the following passages:

O how great the holiness of our God! For he knoweth all things, and there is not anything, save he knows it.

And he cometh into the world that he may save all men, if they will hearken unto his voice; for behold, he suffereth the pains of all men; yea, the pains of every living creature, both men, women, and children, who belong to the family of Adam.

And he suffereth this, that the resurrection might pass upon all men, that all might stand before him at the great and judgment day.

And he commandeth all men that they must repent, and be baptized in his name, having perfect faith in the Holy One of Israel, or they cannot be saved in the kingdom of God.

And if they will not repent and believe in his name, and be baptized in his name, and endure to the end, they must be damned; for the Lord God, the Holy One of Israel, has spoken it.

The priesthood of the Nephites was the same as ours. We read of High Priests, Elders, Priests and Teachers, in their church, but Evangelists, Bishops and Deacons are not mentioned. They also had numerous Prophets minister to them the pleasing or awful word of God, as their condition warranted or their lives deserved. But the spirit of prophecy is not confined to any particular grade of the priesthood, those holding none of its powers being frequently endowed with this most precious gift.

The Twelve special witnesses whom Jesus chose on this continent, of whom Nephi was the first, are never called apostles in the Book of Mormon, but always disciples; the word apostles is only used in that book when applied to the Twelve who ministered with the Savior in the land of Jerusalem.

The Nephite church when fully organized in the ages before the visit of the Redeemer, was always presided over by a High Priest. He held to them the keys of the Holy Priesthood. Whether these keys remained with the Nephites at all times is doubtful. But many of their presidents were undoubtedly thus empowered. The Lord made covenant with Nephi, the son of Helaman, with his own voice as follows:

Blessed art thou, Nephi, for those things which thou hast done; for I have beheld how thou hast with unwearyingness declared the word which I have given unto thee, unto this people. And thou hast not feared them, and hast not sought thine own life, but have sought my will, and to keep my commandments.

And now because thou hast done this with such unwearyingness, behold, I will bless thee forever; and I will make thee mighty in word and in deed, in faith and in works; yea, even that all things shall be done unto thee according to thy word, for thou shalt not ask that which is contrary to my will.

Behold, thou art Nephi, and I am God. Behold, I declare it unto thee in the presence of mine angels, that ye shall have power over this people, and shall smite the earth with famine, and with pestilence, and destruction, according to the wickedness of this people.

Behold, I give unto you power, that whatsoever ye shall seal on earth, shall be sealed in heaven; and whatsoever ye shall loose on earth, shall be loosed in heaven; and thus shall ye have power among this people.

And thus, if ye shall say unto this temple, it shall be rent in twain, it shall be done.

And if ye shall say unto this mountain, be thou cast down and become smooth, it shall be done.

And behold, if ye shall say, that God shall smite this people, it shall come to pass.

And now behold, I command you that ye shall go and declare unto this people, That thus saith the Lord God, who is the Almighty, except ye repent ye shall be smitten even unto destruction.

What greater powers than these has God ever given to man?

The churches in the various lands or districts appear to have each been presided over locally by a High Priest, as the different stakes of Zion are in these days. In this and other respects a close resemblance can be perceived between the organization and government of the ancient Nephite church and the Church of Jesus Christ of Latter-day Saints. As an example of these local High Priests we refer to the case of Ammon, the son of king Mosiah, who held this office among the Christian Lamanites in the land of Jershon at the time that Alma was the presiding High Priest over the whole church.

The duties, responsibilities and powers of the various orders of the priesthood were evidently identical with those possessed by the same officers in the church of God in these latter days. Were we arguing from a doctrinal standpoint we should claim that this must necessarily be so because of the unity of the church of the Lamb in all ages; but we are now simply affirming that which appears from the statements, historical and otherwise, that are to be found in the Book of Mormon. The fact of this identity of duties and powers is apparent in the instructions which are recorded as being given regarding the ordinance of baptism, the bestowal of the Holy Ghost, the administrations of the Sacrament of the Lord's supper, the ordination of Priests and Teachers, etc.

Not only was the priesthood identical but the ordinances of the church were the same. The same words were spoken in the baptism of converts as are used now. The same mode of baptism was observed. The same persons—the penitent believers—were baptized. The baptism of little children was forbidden in the most energetic language.* When Jesus instructed his disciples on the subject of baptism he said: On

---

*And their little children need no repentance, neither baptism. Behold, baptism is unto repentance to the fulfilling the commandments unto the remission of sins.

Little children cannot repent; wherefore it is awful wickedness to deny the pure mercies of God unto them, for they are all alive in him because of his mercy.

And he that saith, That little children need baptism, denieth the mercies of Christ, and setteth at naught the atonement of him and the power of his redemption.—MORMON.

this wise shall ye baptize; and there shall be no disputations among you.

Verily I say unto you, that whoso repenteth of his sins through your words, and desireth to be baptized in my name, on this wise shall ye baptize them: behold, ye shall go down and stand in the water, and in my name shall ye baptize them.

And now behold, these are the words which ye shall say, calling them by name, saying,

Having authority given me of Jesus Christ, I baptize you in the name of the Father, and of the Son, and of the Holy Ghost. Amen.

And then shall ye immerse them in the water, and come forth again out of the water.

The words spoken by the Elder or Priest who blessed the bread or the wine in the administration of the sacrament, were word for word, identical with those that we use; and the officers who officiated in the blessing of the emblems, Elders and Priests, were the same.

In ordinations to the priesthood a similar form was employed to that used in this dispensation, and men were ordained to the same calling. It is written:

The manner which the disciples, who were called the Elders of the church, ordained Priests and Teachers.

After they had prayed unto the Father in the name of Christ, they laid their hands upon them, and said,

In the name of Jesus Christ I ordain you to be a Priest: (or, if he be a Teacher, I ordain you to be a Teacher,) to preach repentance and remission of sins through Jesus Christ, by the endurance of faith on his name to the end. Amen.

It must be remembered that their various ordinances, so far as we have the record, were all performed in the name of Jesus Christ, except that of baptism, which was done in the name of the Father, Son and Holy Ghost.

With regard to the manner of conducting their meetings we are told, And their meeting were conducted by the church, after the manner af the workings of the Spirit, and by the power of the Holy Ghost; for as the power of the Holy Ghost led them whether to preach, or exhort, or to pray, or to supplicate, or to sing, even so it was done.

The same parallel between the two churches can also be found when we consider the subject of spiritual gifts. The Savior, when giving his charge to the Twelve Nephite disciples, said: Go ye into all the world, and preach the gospel to every creature,

And he that believeth and is baptized, shall be saved, but he that believeth not, shall be damned.

And these signs shall follow them that believe; in my name they shall cast out devils; they shall speak with new tongues; they shall take up serpents; and if they drink any deadly thing, it shall not hurt them, they shall lay hands on the sick and they shall recover.

And whosoever shall believe in my name, doubting nothing, unto him will I confirm all my words, even unto the ends of the earth.

Moroni, treating on this same subject, states:

For behold, to one is given by the Spirit of God, that he may teach the word of wisdom;

And to another, that he may teach the word of knowledge by the same Spirit;

And to another, exceeding great faith; and to another, the gifts of healing by the same Spirit.

And again, to another, that he may work mighty miracles;

And again, to another, that he may prophesy concerning all things;

And again, to another, the beholding of angels and ministering spirits;

And again, to another, all kinds of tongues;

And again, to another, the interpretation of languages and of divers kinds of tongues.

And all these gifts come by the power of Christ; and they come unto every man severally, according as he will.

And I would exhort you, my beloved brethren, that ye remember that every good gift cometh of Christ.

From these two quotations all can perceive that the gifts of the Spirit were the same in the Nephite church as among the ancient saints in Jerusalem and the people of God in these days.

CHAPTER LXXI.

MIRACLES AMONG THE NEPHITES—THE MIRACLES OF CHRIST—JOHN AND THE THREE NEPHITES—TRANSLATIONS.

THE subject of spiritual gifts leads us to the kindred one of miracles. The Book of Mormon teaches in very strong language that God is a God of miracles. Were it not so he would cease to be an unchangeable Being. He would be a partial God, blessing one people more than another.

Such is the teaching of the Book of Mormon on this point; and we find in the history of the Nephite people many remarkable manifestations of the marvelous power of God, either shown through the instrumentality of his acknowledged servants, or by the direct interposition of divine power.

Some of the miracles recorded in the annals of the Nephites bear a strong resemblance to others narrated in the Bible. There is nothing extraordinary in this: it is altogether reasonable to believe that in the healing of the sick, for instance, there would be incidents in common in many cases. Nor are the miracles of the Book of Mormon any more difficult of belief than those of the Bible. In fact, we are of the opinion that had the people of this dispensation been taught as persistently to believe the Book of Mormon as they have the Bible, the miracles of the first-named book would require less faith or explanation than some found in the latter.

The miracles of the Book of Mormon consist largely in the healing of the sick, the deliverance of God's servants, and the punishment of the wicked. Some of them are given in great detail, others are referred to in the most meagre language. Among those of which we have spoken at length in earlier portions of this work are the judgments that came upon the impious anti-Christs Sherem* and Korihor;† the deliverance of Alma and Amulek from the prison in Ammonihah;‡ the restoration of the lawyer Zeezrom to health;§ the deliverance of Nephi and Lehi; and the baptism with fire and the Holy Ghost of the Lamanites in the prison in the city of Lehi-Nephi;|| the famine caused and terminated by Nephi's prayer;¶ and the wonders that attended the ministrations of Ammon and his brethren during their mission among the Lamanites.** Of these we shall make no further mention. Nor shall we again review the miraculous signs and wonders that attended the earthly birth†† and death‡‡ of the Messiah. Neither do we think it necessary to take more than a passing glance at the miracles performed by Christ during his visits to the Nephites and the other wonders that glorified those days. But we will now refer, at slightly great length, to a few miraculous circumstances that do not come so prominently into view in the historical narrative.

---

*Chapter vi.
†Chapter xxvi.
‡Chapter xxiv.
§Chapter xxv.
||Chapter xxxvii.
¶Chapter xxxviii.
**Chapter xix.
††Chapter xl.
‡‡Chapter xli.

In the Book of Alma reference is made to an occurence which reminds us strongly of Daniel at the court of king Belshazzar. What is said is very brief and leaves the reader in entire darkness as to when and where the event took place. But from the context we are led to the conclusion that it took place in the land of Nephi, and certainly not later than the days of the first Mosiah. The Prophet Amulek, in the opening of his address to his fellow citizens of Ammonihah, to prove his standing in their midst, refers to his ancestry. Among his forefathers was one Aminadi, a Nephite, who interpreted certain writing, written by the finger of God upon the walls of a temple. Nothing more is told us of this exceedingly interesting and important event, and we are left to conjecture as to what circumstances led to this divine interposition, and whether the words so miraculously written were of instruction, comfort or reproof (*Alma x.* 2.)

The raising of Timothy to life by his brother Nephi after he had been stoned to death, is another miraculous circumstance which is only casually mentioned. Both these brothers were afterwards chosen by Jesus among the Twelve whom he selected as his disciples. The raising of the dead in the name of Christ manifested how great must have been the power with heaven possessed by this Nephi, as it was doubtless by others of his family—notably his father—before the time of the ministration of the Savior to this people.

The miracles that attended the ministry of the Savior on this land were, many of them, of the same character as the wondrous works he performed among the Jews; only frequently more marvelous and more glorious, on account of the greater faith of the Nephites. He healed the sick, cast out devils, raised the dead in Bountiful as he did in Judea and Galilee. But there were other manifestations that were somewhat different; that, so far as the record goes, were entirely dissimilar. In the land of Jerusalem Jesus miraculously fed five thousand by increasing the store of loaves and fishes that had been provided; in Bountiful he administered the emblems of his body and blood when neither the disciples nor the multitude had brought either bread or wine. Angels ministered to men during his labors among the Jews; they did so more abundantly during his visits to the Nephites. Again, though we are told in the Bible of the holy Redeemer blessing little children, we nowhere read therein of the glorious manifestations, the outpouring of the Spirit, the ministry of the angels, the baptism of fire that took place when the risen Redeemer condescended to bless the little ones of the Nephites.

Great were the wonders that attended the labors of the three Nephite disciples who were to tarry on earth unto the end. Death had no power over them; they passed through the most terrible ordeals unhurt. Swords would not slay them; fire would not burn them; savage beasts would not harm them; prisons could not hold them; chains could not bind them; the grave could not entomb them; the earth would not conceal them. No matter how much they were abused or maltreated they triumphed over all their persecutors.

The age in which the three ministered was a peculiar one. Under ordinary circumstances the superhuman powers shown by them would have brought the wicked to repentance. But the happy age of peace and innocence that had followed the Savior's ministry was fast passing away; the people were hardening their hearts; they were relapsing into iniquity with their eyes open; they were sinning knowingly and understandingly. Angels from heaven would not have converted them; they had given themselves up to Satan, and every manifestation of the power of God in behalf of his servants only made them more angry, and more determined upon the destruction of those who sounded in their ears the unwelcome message of divine wrath. The hurricane might demolish the dungeon; the earthquake overthrow the walls of the prison; the earth refuse to close when the disciples were cast into it; these protests of nature simply caused their hardened hearts to conjure up fresh methods of torture and devise new means to destroy those whom they so intensely, and yet so unwarrantably, hated. But they ever failed; the three Nephites still live.

Of what change passed upon John, the Apostle, or how it was brought about that he should not taste of death, we are not told; but so far as the three Nephites are concerned we are informed that they were caught up into heaven, and there experienced a change that is not explained; and that they there saw and heard unspeakable things. Mormon, writing about them, says:

And now behold, as I spake concerning those whom the Lord had chosen, yea, even three who were caught up into the heavens, that I knew not whether they were cleansed from mortality to immortality.

But, behold, since I wrote, I have inquired of the Lord, and he hath made it manifest unto me, that there must needs be a change wrought upon their bodies, or else it needs be that they must taste of death;

Therefore that they might not taste of death, there was a change wrought upon their bodies, that they might not suffer pain or sorrow, save it were for the sins of the world.

Now this change was not equal to that which should take place at the last day; but there was a change wrought upon them, insomuch that Satan could have no power over them, that he could not tempt them, and they were sanctified in the flesh, that they were holy, and that the powers of the earth could not hold them;

And in this state they were to remain until the judgment day of Christ; and at that day they were to receive a greater change, and to be received into the kingdom of the Father to go no more out, but to dwell with God eternally in the heavens.

In the Bible we read of two men who lived before the

Savior's advent—Moses and Elijah—who did not taste of death; we also read in the Book of Mormon of two—Alma and Nephi—who were translated.

CHAPTER LXXII.

THE PROPHECIES REGARDING THE SAVIOR—THEIR COMPLETENESS AND DETAIL—NAMES AND TITLES GIVEN TO CHRIST.

ONE of the most noteworthy things connected with the ancient Nephite church was the great plainness and detail with which the incidents of the birth, life and death of the Lord Jesus Christ were understood and prophesied of by the servants of God who dwelt on the earth before he tabernacled in mortality. Among other things it was declared of him that:

God himself should come down from heaven among the children of men and should redeem his people.

He should take upon him flesh and blood.

He should be born in the land of Jerusalem, the name given by the Nephites to the land of their forefathers, whence they came.

His mother's name should be Mary.

She should be a virgin of the city of Nazareth; very fair and beautiful, a precious and chosen vessel.

She should be overshadowed and conceive by the power of the Holy Ghost.

He should be called Jesus Christ, the Son of God.

At his birth a new star should appear in the heavens.

He should be baptized by John at Bethabara, beyond Jordan.

John should testify that he had baptized the Lamb of God, who should take away the sins of the world.

After his baptism the Holy Ghost should come down upon him out of heaven, and abide upon him in the form of a dove.

He should call twelve men as his special witnesses, to minister in his name.

He should go forth among the people, ministering in power and great glory, casting out devils, healing the sick, raising the dead, and performing many mighty miracles.

He should take upon him the infirmities of his people.

He should suffer temptation, pain of body, hunger, thirst and fatigue; blood should come from every pore of his body by reason of his anguish because of the abominations of his people.

He should be cast out and rejected by the Jews; be taken and scourged, and be judged of the world.

He should be lifted upon the cross and slain for the sins of the world.

He should be buried in a selpuchre, where he should remain three days.

After he was slain he should rise from the dead and should make himself manifest by the Holy Ghost unto the Gentiles.

He should lay down his life according to the flesh and take it up again by the power of the Spirit, that he might bring to pass the resurrection of the dead, being the first that should rise.

At his resurrection many graves should be opened and should yield up their dead; and many of the saints, who had beforetime passed away, should appear unto the living.

He should redeem all mankind who would believe on his name.

In the above list we have not inserted those prophecies with regard to the Savior that related to this continent and were fulfilled hereon. These were referred to in their place in the historical portions of this work. Nor have we mentioned the sayings of Isaiah and other Jewish prophets, which are inserted in the Book of Mormon, but which also appear in the Bible.

Among the names and titles given to Christ in the Book of Mormon are: Savior, Mediator, Messiah, Redeemer, Shepherd, Great and True Shepherd, Lamb, Lamb of God, Son of Righteousness, Son of the Eternal Father, Only Begotten of the Father, Creator, The Eternal Father of Heaven and Earth, King, King of Heaven, Heavenly King, King of all the Earth, God of Israel, God of the whole Earth, Most High God, Lord Omnipotent, Lord God Omnipotent, Mighty God, Holy One, Holy One of Israel, Mighty One of Jacob, Wonderful Counselor, Prince of Peace, and several others.

CHAPTER LXXIII.

NEPHITE APOSTATES—THE ORDER OF NEHOR—AMALEKITES—AMALICKIAHITES—AMULONITES—ABINADI'S PROPHECY—THE GADIANTONS.

NO PEOPLE seem to have been more given to apostasy from the truths of the gospel than were the Nephites in certain periods of their history. In the historical portions of this work we have drawn attention to the defections of Nehor, Amlici, Korihor, Zoram and others; therefore we need not go over that ground again. Yet there is one thing that stands out very prominently in the annals of all these backslidings. It is that the heresies of Nehor, the murderer of Gideon, were more or less adopted by succeeding false teachers, and that those who embraced his teachings and became associated therewith were always among the most bitter and vehement, the most bloodthirsty and hardened of all the enemies of the church of God. They are often spoken of as being after the order of Nehor; and we imagine to belong to that order required the Nephite to conform to certain unholy covenants and make certain vicious and immoral oaths. Many, if not all, of the Amlicites, Amalekites, Amulonites, Ammonihahites and Zoramites belonged to this iniquitous order.

Of the apostate sects, of whom we have previously said but little, the most prominent were the Amulonites and Amalekites.

AMALEKITES: A sect of Nephite apostates whose origin is not given. Many of them were after the order of Nehor. Very early in the days of the republic they had affiliated with the Lamanites and with them built a large city not far from the waters of Mormon, which they called Jerusalem. They were exceedingly crafty and hard-hearted; and in all the ministrations of the sons of Mosiah among them only one was converted. They led in the massacres of the Christian Lamanites or people of Anti-Nephi-Lehi; and in later years the Lamanite generals were in the habit of placing them in high command in their armies because of their greater force of character than the real descendants of Laman, their intense hatred to their former brethren, and their more wicked and murderous disposition. In the sacred record they are generally associated with the Zoramites and Amulonites.

AMALICKIAHITES: The followers of Amalickiah in his efforts to destroy the church, to uproot the Nephite commonwealth and establish a monarchy in its stead. Their leader, finding that they were not as numerous as those who wished to maintain the republic, and that many of them doubted the justness of their cause, led those who would follow him towards the land of Nephi, with the intention of joining the

Lamanites. Moroni, the general of the Nephites, by rapid marches reached the wilderness, where he intercepted them in their flight, when Amalickiah and a few others escaped to the Lamanites, while the greater majority were taken prisoners and carried back to Zarahemla. The Amalickiahites were then given the opportunity to make covenant to sustain the cause of liberty or be put to death. There were but very few who denied the covenant of freedom.

AMULONITES: The descendants of Amulon and his associates, the corrupt priests of king Noah. They were Nephites on their father's side and Lamanites on their mothers', but by association and education were of the latter race. Many of them, however, were displeased with the conduct of their fathers, and took upon them the name of Nephites, and were considered among that people ever after. Of those who remained Amulonites, many become followers of Nehor, and were scattered in the lands of Amulon, Helam, and Jerusalem, all of which appear to have been limited districts in the same region of country. In later years the sons of Mosiah and their fellow-missionaries preached to them, but not one repented and received the gospel message; to the contrary, they became leaders in the persecutions carried on against the suffering people of Anti-Nephi-Lehi, and were those who, with the Amalekites, slew the greater number of that unoffending people who suffered martyrdom. In the succeeding war with the Nephites (B. C. 81), when Ammonihah was destroyed, nearly all the Amulonites were killed in the battle in which Zoram, the Nephite general, defeated the Lamanites. The remainder of the Amulonites fled into the east wilderness, where they usurped power over the people of Laman, and in their bitter hatred to the truth caused many of the latter to be burned to death because of their belief in the gospel. These outrages aroused the Lamanites and they in turn began to hunt the Amulonites and to put them to death. This was in fulfillment of the words of Abinadi, who, as he suffered martyrdom by fire at the hands of Amulon and his associates, told them, What ye shall do unto me, shall be a type of things to come, by which he meant that many should suffer death by fire as he had suffered.

And he said unto the priests of Noah, that their seed should cause many to be put to death, in the like manner as he was, and that they should be scattered abroad and slain, even as a sheep having no shepherd is driven and slain by wild beasts; and now behold, these words were verified, for they were driven by the Lamanites, and they were hunted, and they were smitten.

GADIANTONS: Of all the factions that separated themselves from the Nephites none worked so much injury to that people as did the bands of Gadianton robbers. The very fact of their organization shows the deplorable condition of Nephite society, while their continuance and growth proclaim yet more loudly and emphatically how debased the community had become.

The Gadiantons were at first (B. C. 52) apparently a band of robbers and murderers bound together by the most horrible oaths of secrecy and satanic covenants to aid and shield each other in whatever sins and iniquities they might commit. These covenants did not originate with Gadianton or any of his crew. They were as old as the days of Cain, into whose ear the son of perdition whispered these bloodthirsty and infernal suggestions. These same secret societies flourished among the antediluvians; and had place with the Jaredites and other peoples of antiquity. In the end they invariably wrought ruin and destruction wherever they found a foothold. To their abominations can be traced the fall and extinction of both the Jaredite and Nephite races.

As time went on, the Gadiantons among the Nephites aspired to rule the republic. When, by their combinations, they could not carry their points at the elections, they would murder, or attempt to murder, any judge or other officer who was distasteful to them, and place a more acceptable man in his seat. So fell more than one of the Nephite chief judges. But they frequently had no need to do this, for as the people increased in iniquity they could easily carry the majority or the voice of the people with them. In this way several of their number were elected to the chief judgeship.

After the times of the conversion of the Lamanites by Lehi and Nephi (B. C. 30) the Gadianton robbers took their place in the history of ancient America. The divisions then became the righteous Nephites and Lamanites on one side, and the Gadiantons on the other. And, strange as it may appear, these robber bands received greater encouragement and attained to greater power among the Nephites than among the Lamanites; but the fact is, that at that era the Lamanites were a growing race, while the Nephites were a decaying one.

Many wars ensued between these two divisions, ending sometimes in the temporary suppression of the robbers, as in the year B. C. 17. But they soon reappeared, as they did five years after the instance here mentioned (B. C. 12). The most momentous of all these wars was the one that was waged during the earthly life of our Savior. It virtually commenced in the second year of his mortal existence and continued with slight intermissions until the twenty-first. So powerful and arrogant had the robbers grown in that age that Giddianhi, their leader, in A. C. 16, wrote an epistle to Lachoneus, the chief judge, calling upon the Nephites to submit themselves to the robbers and their ways; to accept their oaths and covenants; and in all things become like unto them. The presumption of the robber-chief does not appear to have been without foundation, for so desperate had the condition of the people become that Lachoneus devised and carried out the stupendous movement of gathering all, both Nephites and Lamanites, to one land, where they would be safe by consolidation, and be able to wear out the robbers by masterly inactivity. In this he succeeded, and the robber bands were destroyed by privation, famine and sword.

After the days of Jesus the Gadiantons again appeared when iniquity began to prevail; and by the year A. C. 300 they had spread over all the land. To their baneful influence may be attributed many of the atrocities and abominations that disgraced the last wars between the Nephites and Lamanites.

At certain periods of their history the Jaredites, Lamanites and Nephites were all idolaters. The Lamanites, as early as the days of Enos, are represented as bowing down to idols. This statement is repeated with regard to those of the times of Zeniff and of Ammon. The Nephites are sometimes called an idolatrous people, when the inference seems to be that they worshiped their gold and silver and the vain things of this world. On the other hand, it appears that some of them were actual worshipers of idols. Such a charge is plainly made against the Zoramites in the land of Antionum; and we are of the opinion that they were not the only ones.

In later times, during the final series of wars between the Nephites and Lamanites, the latter were idolaters, and had descended so far into savagery as to offer human sacrifices. They were in the habit of offering up in this way the Nephite women and children they captured in war. Special mention is made of this fact at the taking of the cities of Desolation and Boaz.

Still more horrible was the fate of some of the Lamanite women who fell into the hands of the Nephites; and it would seem that before the war was finished both peoples had sunk to the degradation of eating human flesh. Well might the prophet say: There never had been so great wickedness among all the children of Lehi, nor even among all the house of Israel, according to the words of the Lord, as were among this people.

CHAPTER LXXIV.

CHURCH DISCIPLINE AMONG THE NEPHITES—TREATMENT OF THE UNREPENTANT—THE WORD OF THE LORD REGARDING TRANSGRESSORS—THE TESTIMONY OF MORONI.

AS IN other things, the methods adopted in the Nephite church in the treatment of those who turned from righteousness were identical with those pursued in such cases in the church of God in other lands and in other ages. The erring ones were first labored with by the officers of the church in the spirit of love and reconciliation; they were visited by the Priests and Teachers; and if they repented they were continued in the fellowship of the Saints; but if they were obdurate and impenitent they were severed from the communion of the church. This course was pursued throughout their history from the days of Alma, the elder, to those of Moroni.

In the land of Zarahemla, when Mosiah was king and Alma was high priest, there was much hard-heartedness and evil doing in the midst of the Nephites. It may be remembered it was at this time that the sons of Mosiah, and the younger Alma, were leaders among those who were opposing the church and persecuting its members. The iniquity that existed with those who had made covenant with God, or were their children, caused Alma much pain and anxiety. The Priests and Teachers labored frequently in vain, and the presiding priesthood were in doubt with regard to the best course to pursue with the wicked. They had no precedents to guide them, for such a state of things had never before existed among the Nephites.

Alma applied to the king, but he refused to judge the offenders. He would not meddle in matters of church discipline, that he left to Alma; and to him he returned those who had transgressed the law of the Lord. In this dilemma Alma appealed with all his heart to the Lord, and inquired what he should do in the matter: for he was most desirous to do right in the sight of heaven. Then the voice of the Lord came to him, blessing him, because of his sincere inquiries concerning the transgressor, and instructing him that whosoever transgressed against God should be judged according to the sins which he had committed; and if he confessed his sins before the Lord and Alma and repented in the sincerity of his heart he should be forgiven, and God would forgive him also. The Lord adds: Yea, and as often as my people repent, will I forgive them their trespasses against me.

And ye shall also forgive one another your trespasses; for verily I say unto you, He that forgiveth not his neighbor's trespasses, when he says that he repents, the same hath brought himself under condemnation.

Now I say unto you, Go; and whosoever will not repent of his sins, the same shall not be numbered among my people; and this shall be observed from this time forward.

The sacred historian continues:

And it came to pass when Alma had heard these words, he wrote them down that he might have them, and that he might judge the people of that church, according to the commandments of God.

And it came to pass that Alma went and judged those that had been taken in iniquity, according to the word of the Lord.

And whosoever repented of their sins and did confess them, them he did number among the people of the church;

And those that would not confess their sins and repent of their iniquity, the same were not numbered among the people of the church, and their names were blotted out.

In this revelation we have the word of the Lord to guide the Nephite church throughout all its dispensations.

The same spirit is manifested in the instructions given by the Redeemer in his teachings to the Nephites.* They are full of love, mercy, and patience. On the other hand, they show that the church of God must not be defiled by countenancing iniquity or permitting that which is holy to be handled by the unworthy. Nearly four hundred years later, Moroni, speaking on church government, says:

And they were strict to observe that there shold be no iniquity among them; and whoso was found to commit iniquity, and three witnesses of the church did condemn them before the Elders; and if they repented not, and confessed not, their names were blotted out, and they were not numbered among the people of Christ;

But as oft as they repented, and sought forgiveness, with real intent, they were forgiven.

From these quotations we perceive that the spirit of the ancient church on this continent, with regard to offenses and offenders, was uniform in all its dispensations and identical in its methods with those of the latter days.

---

*See Chapter xlvi.

CHAPTER LXXV.

THE DISCOVERY OF THE JAREDITE RECORDS—CORIANTUMR—ETHER—THE DISPERSION AT BABEL—THE JOURNEY OF THE JAREDITES—ATLANTIS.

LET us return to the year 123 B. C. At that time the Nephites in the land of Nephi were suffering sore afflictions at the hands of the Lamanites. In this extremity Limhi, their king, sent a company of forty-three men, with instructions to discover, if possible, their brethren in the land of Zarahemla, that peradventure they would bring them succor and deliverance. The expedition was unsuccessful, so far as its immediate object was concerned. The company missed the land of Zarahemla, pushed northward into Central America, and how far beyond we cannot tell. At last they discovered the remains of an ancient people who had apparently been destroyed in battle. Among other things they found twenty-four plates of gold, covered with engravings. This treasure, with some other relics of the vanished race, they took back to king Limhi.

When, shortly after, this section of the Nephite people escaped from their Lamanite taskmasters and returned to Zarahemla, the twenty-four golden plates were presented to king Mosiah, the younger, and he being a seer, translated them by the aid of the Urim and Thummim.

These plates were found to contain the history of the world from the creation to the time of the building of the

Tower of Babel, and of the race whose remains had been found by the people of Limhi scattered on the land northward.

This was, however, not the first intimation that the Nephites had of the existence of this extinct people; for in the days of the elder Mosiah a large engraved stone was brought to him that had been discovered by the people of Zarahemla. It gave a very brief account of this same race, known to us as the Jaredites, but more particularly referred to its last ruler, named Coriantumr; who had himself been known to the Zarahemlaites; for he had, previous to his death, resided in their midst for nine months.

The history that we have of this remarkable people, as given in the Book of Mormon, is Moroni's abridgment of the record contained on the twenty-four plates of gold. It commences with the dispersion of the human family at Babel. Interspersed with the narrative are many interpolations of Moroni's, in the shape of reflections, prophecies and explanatory remarks. As these additions or notes are inserted in the body of the work, and not as foot notes, the reader of this abridgment has to use care in its perusal, or his ideas may become confused; and he is troubled to account for statements which grow perfectly plain when it is understood they were written nearly four hundred years after the advent of the Savior.

The history of the Jaredites is called the Book of Ether, because the twenty-four plates from which it is taken were hidden by a Jaredite prophet of that name, in the place where they were afterwards discovered by the people of Limhi.

The ancestors of the Jaredites were engaged in the attempt to build the Tower of Babel. It is probable they were of the family of Shem, as they were worshipers of the true God, and he conferred upon them his priesthood. How far they had wandered from the tower, if at all, when the Lord commenced the revelation of his will to them, is not apparent from the sacred text. They were commanded by him to go "*down* into the valley which is northward," and as the expressions up and down, when they occur in the Book of Mormon in connection with geographical locality, are always used with great exactitude, we may venture two surmises: that Jared and his friends had already wandered into some not far distant hilly region, or that the valley into which they were commanded to descend sloped towards the north, the flow of its waters, if any, being in that direction.

The valley into which the Lord led the Jaredites was called Nimrod, after that mighty hunter of the early postdiluvian age. Here they tarried for a time, while they prepared for the long journey which was before them. Their flocks and herds they had with them; they now went to work and snared fowls; they carried with them hives of honey bees (known to them by the name of Deseret); and prepared a vessel in which they transported the fish of the waters. Everything that could possibly be of use to them they appear to have collected. They were going to a land that had been swept clean by the waters of the Deluge; it had been bereft of all its animal life; the seeds of grains and fruits no longer germinated in its soil; and the colony had to replenish the continent with the animal and vegetable life, necessary for their comfort and sustenance, as though it was a new earth.

When in the valley of Nimrod the Lord came down and talked with the brother of Jared. But the brother of Jared saw him not, for the Lord remained concealed in a cloud. He directed that the company should go forth into the wilderness, into that quarter where man had never yet been. As they journeyed the Heavenly presence went before them in the cloud and instructed them and gave directions which way they should travel. In the course of their journey they had many waters—seas, rivers, and lakes—to cross, on which occasions they built barges, as directed by the Lord. It must have been an arduous labor, requiring much time and great patience to transport their flocks and herds, with all the rest of their cumbrous freight across these many waters.

We shall not attempt to trace the wanderings of the company on their way to the promised land. The account given in the Book of Ether is entirely too meagre for that purpose.

Some suppose that they went as far north as the Caspian Sea, which they crossed; then turning eastward slowly journeyed along the central Asia plateau; thence to the Pacific seaboard, most probably on the coast of China. These suppositions may be correct; the writer does not know enough to either affirm or deny them; but one thing is certain, the journey must have been a very long and tedious one. The region through which they passed was one in which no man dwelt, they could purchase no supplies, and if they did not live entirely on wild fruit, fish and small game, it is probable that they tarried now and again, at favorable points, long enough to plant and reap a crop. As they advanced to a great distance from the center of population in western Asia it is possible that they traveled beyond the limits to which the larger animals had, by that time scattered; and if so, they were entirely without the aid of the food obtained by the chase; on the other hand, it is probable that the fish in the lakes and rivers formed a valuable source of food supply; yet it must also be remembered they carried fish in a vessel with them.

Through their prayers and faith the founders of the Jaredite nation obtained many precious promises of the Lord. Among these was the assurance that their language should not be confounded, and that the Lord himself would go before them and lead them into a land choice above every other land. And again, that the nation that they should found there should be none greater upon all the face of the earth. The history of their descendants proves how fully this last promise was realized. The contemporary nations on the eastern continent—Egypt, Chaldea and Babylonia—were insignificant when compared with the vast extent of territory held and filled by the Jaredites; they were the sole rulers of the whole western hemisphere, and possibly the originals, whence arose the stories of the greatness and grandeur of the fabled Atlantis; for we have no account in the sacred records that God shut them out from the knowledge of the rest of mankind when he planted them in America, as he afterwards did the Nephites; and late research has shown that the geographical knowledge of the ancients was much greater in the earlier ages than at the time of the Savior and a few hundred years previous to his advent.

CHAPTER LXXVI.

MORIANCUMER—BUILDING THE BARGES—THE FINGER OF THE LORD—THE APPEARING OF THE SAVIOR—THE VOYAGE.

LED by the Lord personally, instructed by his own mouth, protected by his presence, the colony, of which Jared's brother appears to have been the prophet and leader, at last reached the borders of the great sea which divides the continents. To the place where they tarried they gave the name of Moriancumer. Here they remained for a period of four years, at the end of which time the Lord again visited the brother of Jared in a cloud and chastened him and his brethren because of their neglect to call upon his name. Repentance followed this reproof, and on their repentance their sins were forgiven them.

The brother of Jared was then commanded by the Lord to build eight barges, after the same pattern as those he had previously constructed. This command he obeyed with the assistance of the company. The vessels were small, light in construction and water tight. As they were dark in the in-

APPEARANCE OF CHRIST TO THE BROTHER OF JARED.

terior, by reason of being without windows, the Lord, at the entreaty of the brother of Jared, touched sixteen small white stones, which the latter had moulten out of a high mountain called Shelem; and after the Lord touched them they shone forth and gave light to the vessels in which they were placed. When the Lord put forth this finger to touch these stones, the veil was taken from the eyes of the brother of Jared and he saw the finger of the Lord; and it was as the finger of a man, like unto flesh and blood. Then the brother of Jared fell down before the Lord, for he was struck with fear, and because of the faith which the brother of Jared possessed the Lord not only permitted him to see his finger but showed himself to him.

Furthermore, he said, Behold, I am he who was prepared from the foundation of the world to redeem my people. Behold, I am Jesus Christ. I am the Father and the Son. In me shall all mankind have light, and that eternally, even they who shall believe on my name; and they shall become my sons and my daughters. And never have I showed mysef unto man whom I have created, for never has man believed in me as thou hast. Seest thou that ye are created after mine own image? Yea, even all men were created in the beginning, after mine own image. Behold, this body, which ye now behold, is the body of my spirit; and man have I created after the body of my spirit; and even as I appear unto thee to be in spirit, will I appear unto my people in the flesh.

All things being prepared, Jared and his people, with their animals, fishes, bees, seeds and multitudinous other things, went on board; a favorable wind wafted them from shore, and they gradually drifted to the American coast. At the end of the voyage of three hundred and forty-four days the colony landed on this continent. It is generally understood that the place where they landed was south of the Gulf of California and north of the isthmus of Panama.

CHAPTER LXXVII.

THE LAND OF PROMISE—A MONARCHY ESTABLISHED—THE KINGS OF THE JAREDITES FROM ORIAH TO OMER—AKISH—THE DAUGHTER OF JARED.

WHEN the members of the little colony set their feet upon the shores of America, they humbled themselves before the Lord, and shed tears of joy because of the multitude of his tender mercies over them. Then they went forth and began to till the earth, and soon grew strong in the land, being a righteous people, taught directly from on high.

Before long the question of government arose, and the people desired a king. This thing was grievous to their divinely inspired leaders, for they saw that it would lead to captivity; but perceiving the determination of the people, they consented. It was difficult to find any suitable man who would consent to occupy the royal position; at last the youngest son of Jared, named Orihah, consented, and he was anointed king.

It appears altogether probable that this choice was taken as a precedent, for among this people there seems to have prevailed a custom entirely opposite to that of most other nations—that of having one of the younger, generally the very youngest son, instead of the eldest, succeed his father on the throne. As the Jaredites were a very long-lived race, full of vitality, often having sons born to them to the end of their days, the number of generations mentioned during the period embraced in their history is much fewer than the general average for the same number of centuries, notably so where the eldest son succeeds to the rank and title of his sire.

The kings of the Jaredites, in the order of their succession were Orihah, Kib, Corihor, Kib restored, Shule. In the days of Shule, the kingdom was divided, Noah, the son of Corihor, establishing a separate monarchy over a portion of the land. After his death he was succeeded by his son Cohor, who was slain in battle by Shule, when the whole kingdom again returned to its allegiance to the last named.

Shule was succeeded by his son Omer, who was deposed and imprisoned by his son Jared, but two other sons afterwards defeated Jared and restored the kingdom to their father. In this civil war between Omer and his son Jared, when the latter had been defeated by his brothers, they only spared his life on condition that he recognize the right of his father to the throne.

Jared became very sorrowful at his defeat, as he had set his heart upon being king. While in this state of mind, his daughter, who was exceedingly fair, came to him, and, learning the cause of his discontent, made a most extraordinary and villainous proposition to him, which showed she was as conscienceless as her father. It was that he should invite a friend, named Akish, to visit him; when he came she would dance before him and use her charms to captivate his heart. If her plan succeeded and Akish desired her to wife, Jared was to grant his request on condition that Akish brought him the head of his father Omer. To enable him to accomplish this, the daughter of Jared reminded her father of the signs and covenants of the ancients, whereby they entered into compact, one with another, for mutual aid and protection in carrying out any great wickedness they might desire to commit.

Her plan was accepted and proved in every way a success. After the manner she suggested, Akish gathered his kinsfolks, and persuaded them to swear, with terrible oaths, that they would be faithful to him in all that he might require of them. By these wicked combinations the kingdom of Omer was overthrown. But he, being warned of the Lord, escaped to a distant land called Ablom. Then Jared was anointed king, and he gave his daughter to Akish for a wife.

But Akish was not satisfied; he plotted with his associates, and they slew Jared, as he sat on the throne, and Akish reigned in his stead. But after committing these crimes, he became suspicious of his partners in sin, and grew jealous of one of his own sons, whom he shut up in prison and starved to death. Before long other sons of Akish seduced the people from their allegiance to their father, a civil war of the utmost magnitude ensued, which ceased not until all the people were slain except thirty, and those who had fled to Omer in the land of Ablom. After this, Omer returned and reigned over the few souls that remained.

CHAPTER LXXVIII.

THE KINGS OF THE JAREDITES FROM OMER TO CORIANTUMR—THE MATERIAL PROSPERITY OF THIS RACE.

OMER was succeeded by his son Emer; he by his son Coriantum; Coriantum by his son Com. Com was slain by his son Heth, who took possession of the kingdom after having murdered his father.

In the days of Heth there was a great famine which destroyed the greater portion of the people, among them the king himself. He was succeeded by Shez, Shez by his son Riplakish, who was dethroned by Morianton, whose son Kim afterwards followed him in the kingly power. Kim was brought into captivity, through rebellion, and it was not until the next reign, that of his son Levi, that the usurpers were driven from the throne. Then follow the reigns of Corom,

Kish, Lib and Hearthom. The last named was deposed after reigning twenty-four years, and was held in captivity all the remainder of his days. So also were his son Heth, his grandson Aaron, his great grandson Amnigaddah, and the latter's son Coriantum.

We are not informed what were the names of the kings of the usurping dynasty, who reigned while the royal family served in captivity; but in the days of Coriantum's son Com, the reigning prince was named Amgid. Com went to war against him, overthrew him, and gained possession of the throne of his ancestors. Shiblon, the son of Com, succeeded his father, but was slain, his son Heth being made captive and thus held all his days.

In the next generation, Ahah, Heth's son, regained the throne and reigned over the whole people for a short time. Few and iniquitous were his days. Ethem, called a descendant, and also the son of Ahah, was the next king. His son Moron succeeded him; in his days there were renewed rebellions, which ended, as had been so frequently the case before, in the captivity of the king. Moron was a captive all the rest of his life, and his son Coriantor passed his whole earthly existence in captivity.

Ether, the prophet, was the son of Coriantor. The king in his day was named Coriantumr, the last of his race, for the wars that desolated the land in his reign culminated in the destruction of the Jaredites. This very short sketch of the reigns of their kings shows how thoroughly were the fears of Jared and his brother realized, that the anointing of a king would lead to captivity.

Like their successors, the Nephites, the troubles of the Jaredites grew out of their iniquities. Many mighty prophets ministered to them, but they were only occasionally listened to. Like the Nephites, in another phase of their existence, they owed many of their misfortunes to cherishing the secret bands of Gadianton-like assassins, who, bound by infernal covenants, perpetrated the most unnatural and bloodthirsty crimes. In the days of Omer, the daughter of Jared (who in more than one respect reminds us of the daughter of Herodias) was the instrument in first introducing these soul-destroying confederacies with Satan among the Jaredites; and in after ages they dwindled or flourished, according to the amount of faith and faithfulness in the people.

Materially the Jaredites were wonderfully blessed. It could scarcely have been otherwise; they had all the treasures of this most choice land at their disposal. In the days of Emer, the inspired historian describes them as having become exceeding rich, having all manner of fruit, grain, silks, fine linen, gold, silver, and precious things; and also all manner of cattle, sheep, swine, goats, and also many other kinds of animals which were useful for the food of man; and they also had horses, and asses, and there were elephants and cureloms and cumoms; all of which were useful to men, and more especially the elephants, cureloms and cumoms.*

CHAPTER LXXIX.

THE JUDGMENTS OF GOD ON THE JAREDITES—THE EXTINCTION OF THE RACE—THE HILL RAMAH—SHIZ AND CORIANTUMR—ETHER.

OWING to their gross and abounding iniquities, the Lord on several occasions visited the Jaredites with partial destruction. These judgments came in the shape of fratricidal war, pestilence, drought and famine. In the days of Heth there was a great dearth in the land, through which the in-

---

*Some suppose the cureloms and cumoms were alpacas and llamas, others that they were mammoths, the bones of which creatures, as well as those of the elephant, having been found on this continent.

ETHER FINISHING HIS RECORD.

habitants were destroyed exceedingly fast, while poisonous serpents came forth "and did poison many people." These serpents drove the flocks and herds south, and then congregating at the narrow neck uniting the two great divisions of the land, hedged up the way so that the people could not pass, thus adding another factor to their misery, for their crops were not only destroyed through the lack of rain, but the resource of animal food was taken from them. Thus they became a broken people, but when through their miseries they had sufficiently humbled themselves before the Lord, he sent the long desired rain, and there began to be fruit in the north countries and in all the countries round about. Other desolations at various times came upon them because of their defiant disobedience to the behests of Heaven.

The war which ended in the entire destruction of the Jaredite race was one of the most bloodthirsty, cruel and vindictive that ever cursed this fair planet. Men's most savage passions were worked up to such an extent that every better feeling of humanity was crushed out. The women and children armed themselves for the fray with the same fiendish activity, and, fought with the same intense hate, as the men. It was not a conflict of armies alone; it was the crushing together of a divided house that had long tottered because of internal weakness, but now fell in upon itself.

This war was not the work of a day; it was the outgrowth of centuries of dishonor, crime and iniquity. And as this continent was once cleansed of its unrighteous inhabitants by the overwhelming waters of a universal Deluge, and only eight souls left, so this second time, as a flood, through the promises of the Lord to Noah, was no longer possible, instead thereof the wicked slew the wicked until only two men remained, the king and the historian: the one to wander wounded, wretched and alone, until found by Mulek's colony; the other to record the last dreadful throes of his people for the profit of succeeding races, and then to be received into the loving care of his Father and his God. Both the Nephites and ourselves are indebted to him for our acquaintance with the earlier history of this continent, which otherwise would have been entirely shut out from our knowledge.

Some four or more years before the final battles around and near the hill Ramah, otherwise Cumorah, two millions of warriors had been slain, besides their wives and children. How many millions actually fell before the last terrible struggle ended, and Coriantumr stood alone the sole representative of his race, it is impossible to tell from the record that has been handed down to us, but we think we are justified in believing that for bloodshed and desolation no such war ever took place before, or has occurred since in the history of this world; if the annals of any nation have the record of its equal, it is not known to us.

The duel between the leaders of the two contending hosts, Coriantumr and Shiz, when their followers were all slain, was a unique and horrible one, for when all had fallen except these two Shiz had fainted for loss of blood. Then Coriantumr, after having taken a short rest, raised his sword and smote off the head of his foe. Shiz raised himself on his hands, fell, struggled for breath and died. Then, utterly exhausted, Coriantumr dropped to the ground and became as though he had no life.

Coriantumr, when he regained consciousness, wandered forth, aimlessly and alone, the last of his race. A whole continent lay around him, but there was nothing, in any place, to invite him either to tarry or depart. Companions he had none; every creature in the image of God, save himself, had moistened the soil with his life's blood. All had been swept into unsanctified graves or poisoned the air with their unburied bodies. The savage beasts alone remained to terrify him with their hideous calls as they held high carnival over the unnumbered slain. Weak from loss of blood, he staggered on, placing as great a distance as his failing powers would permit between himself and the horrors of the last battle ground. He passed onward through each deserted valley, each tenantless town; in neither was there any human voice to greet or chide him; the homes of his own people and those of his enemies were alike—a silent desolation; all the land was a wilderness.

How long he thus wandered to and fro, wretched, comfortless and forlorn, we know not; but at last he reached the southern portion of the northern continent, thousands of miles from Ramah, and there, to the great astonishment of both, he found the people of Mulek, who had been led by the hand of the Lord from Jerusalem. With them he spent his few remaining days, and when nine moons had grown and waned he passed away to join the hosts of his people in the unknown world of spirits.

All this was in fulfillment of the prophecies of Ether, who, years before, had been sent by the Lord to Coriantumr with the fateful message that if he and all his household would repent, the Lord would give unto him his kingdom, and spare the people; otherwise they should be destroyed, and all his household, save it were himself, and he should only live to see the fulfilling of the prophecies which had been spoken concerning another people receiving the land for their inheritance; and Coriantumr should receive a burial by them; and every soul should be destroyed save it were Coriantumr.

But Coriantumr did not repent, neither his household; and all the words of the Lord, through Ether, came to pass; not the least of them remained unfulfilled.

BOOK OF MORMON CHRONOLOGY.

THE events marked † are those about which the record does not appear sufficiently explicit to make the year certain. It is occasionally difficult to decide whether the circumstance narrated took place near the close of one year or in the commencement of the next.

The four dates marked thus ** are based upon the supposition that Zeniff re-occupied the land of Nephi B. C. 200. This may not be the exact year, but it is approximate.

The three dates marked thus * are based upon the idea that the "young man," Alma, was twenty-five years old when Abinadi was martyred.

The Book of Mormon appears to furnish no clue to the date of Lehi's colony landing in South America. It is supposed to have been about twelve years after its departure from Jerusalem.

B. C. signifies before the birth of Christ; A. C. after Christ; N. A. signifies Nephite Annals, or years after the departure of Lehi from Jerusalem; Y. J. years of the Judges, or of the Republic.

	B.C	N.A.	YJ.
Lehi and colony leave Jerusalem, and journey to the valley of Lemuel, by the Red Sea. The sons of Lehi return to Jerusalem and obtain the sacred records.	600	1	
Lehi and colony reach the land Bountiful, in Arabia, where Nephi commences to build a ship.	592	9	
Mulek, son of king Zedekiah, with a colony, leaves Jerusalem. Lehi and his colony reach South America.	590	11	
A temple built, Jacob and Joseph consecrated priests, etc., before	571	30	
Wars and contentions between the Nephites and Lamanites, during ten years previous to	561	40	
Nephi transfers the records to Jacob. The book of Jacob opens	546	55	
Jacob, having given the records to his son Enos, the latter transfers them to his son Jarom. Many wars between the Nephites and Lamanites during the days of Enos.	421	180	
The Nephites have increased and scattered much over the land; they strictly observe the law of Moses and are prospered. The Lamanites, much more numerous than the Nephites, often invade the Nephite lands.	401	200	
Jarom transfers the records to Omni. Many wars and contentions during Jarom's days.	362	239	
Omni has frequent wars with the Lamanites.	324	277	
Omni transfers the records to Amaron.	318	283	

	B.C.	N.A.	Y.J.
The more wicked part of the Nephites destroyed. Amaron transfers the records to Chemish.	280	321	
**About this date Zeniff leaves Zarahemla to reoccupy the land of Nephi. He makes a treaty with king Laman, and obtains the lands Lehi-Nephi and Shemlon.	200	401	
**The Lamanites make war with the people of Zeniff, but are repulsed with a loss of 3043 men.	183	418	
Alma, the elder, born in the land of Nephi.	173·	428	
**King Laman having died, his son attacks the people of Zeniff, but is driven back.	161	440	
*Zeniff confers the kingdom on his son Noah.	160	441	
Mosiah II. born in the land of Zarahemla.	154	447	
*The prophet Abinadi appears in the land of Nephi, and reproves Noah and his subjects for their iniquities.	150	451	
*Abinadi again appears, prophesies, and is martyred.	148	453	
*Alma establishes a Christian Church at the waters of Mormon, and afterwards, because of king Noah's persecutions, removes with his people to Helam.	147	454	
First Christian Church established in Zarahemla by king Benjamin, who also consecrates his son Mosiah king.	125	476	
A company sent by Limhi, son of Noah, to find Zarahemla, wander into the north country and discover numerous relics of the Jaredites.	123	478	
King Benjamin dies. A company under Ammon start from Zarahemla to find their brethren in the land of Nephi. They succeed, help them to escape from the Lamanites, and bring them safely to Zarahemla.	122	479	
Moroni, commander-in-chief of the Nephite armies, born.	99	502	
Alma, the elder, dies, aged eighty-two. Mosiah II. dies, aged sixty-three. Alma, the younger, elected Chief Judge of the Republic. The sons of Mosiah, with other Elders, start on a mission to the Lamanites in the land of Nephi. Priestcraft first introduced among the Nephites by Nehor. Nehor slays the aged patriarch, Gideon; is tried, condemned and executed. †King Lamoni and his household converted by Ammon.	91	510	1
Priestcraft spreads among the Nephites; pride and contention develop in the church. †A church established by Ammon in the land of Ishmael.	90	511	2
Continued peace among the Nephites, notwithstanding persecution and increased wickedness.	89	512	3
Amlici, a disciple of Nehor, desires to be king and to destroy the true church; his pretensions are rejected by the voice of the people; he raises a rebellion, and is consecrated king. Amlici's forces are defeated by the			

	B.C.	N.A.	Y.J.

Nephites under Alma, at the hill Amnihu. The Lamanites invade Zarahemla, are joined by the Amlicites; the united armies are defeated by Alma, on the west bank of the Sidon. Another invading Lamanite army is defeated on the east of the Sidon, and driven back to their own lands. Peace restored. Aaron and other missionaries imprisoned by the Lamanites in Middoni. — 87 / 514 / 5

The Nephites, because of their afflictions, are humbled; many are baptized. †Ammon and Lamoni proceed to Middoni, to release Aaron and his brethren; they meet Lamoni's father; he attempts to slay Ammon. †Antiomno, king of Middoni, releases the captives. — 86 / 515 / 6

3500 Nephites baptized into the church. Great peace and prosperity among them. †Lamoni's father, king of all the Lamanites, baptized. He issues a proclamation in favor of the Nephite missionaries. — 85 / 516 / 7

Pride increasing in the Nephite church causes envyings, malice, strife and persecutions. — 84 / 517 / 8

Alma, on account of increasing iniquity, resigns the chief-judgeship, and nominates Nephihah as his successor, who is accepted by the voice of the people. Alma devotes himself entirely to the work of the ministry. He sets in order the churches in Zarahemla and Gideon. — 83 / 518 / 9

Alma, as presiding High Priest, visits and administers to the people in Melek and Ammonihah. Amulek visited by an angel; he receives Alma into his house. They preach to the people of Ammonihah; are imprisoned and abused. Zeezrom, the lawyer, converted; afterwards healed of a fever and baptized. Those who accept the gospel are cast out of Ammonihah, while others, men, women and children, are martyred by fire. Alma and Amulek delivered, by the power of God, from prison; the prison is destroyed, and with it their persecutors. Massacre of 1005 believing Lamanites. — 82 / 519 / 10

The Lamanites, as foretold by Alma, destroy Ammonihah, with all its people, but are afterwards disastrously defeated by Zoram. — 81 / 520 / 11

The church greatly increases during this and two following years. — 80 / 521 / 12

†Second massacre of the people of Anti-Nephi-Lehi. — 79 / 522 / 13

†The people of Anti-Nephi-Lehi arrive in the land of Zarahemla. — 78 / 523 / 14

The people of Anti-Nephi-Lehi established in the land of Jershon. The Lamanites pursue the Ammonites; are defeated by the Nephites with great slaughter. — 77 / 524 / 15

	B.C.	N.A.	Y.J.

Korihor, the anti-Christ, struck dumb, and afterwards killed in a city of the Zoramites. Alma and others proceed to Antionum and minister among the Zoramite dissenters; the majority reject their words, and afterwards cast out their believing brethren. The latter flee to the land of Jershon, while the unrepentant ally themselves with the Lamanites and prepare for war. — 75 526 17

The Ammonites remove to Melek. The Zoramites become Lamanites; the united armies occupy Antionum and attempt to invade Manti. They are defeated by Moroni and Lehi near the hill Riplah. The Lamanites make a covenant of peace and return to their own lands. The record of Alma closes. — 74 527 18

Alma transfers the records to his son Helaman; leaves Zarahemla, as if to go to Melek, and is never heard of more. Dissensions arise in the church; the dissenters endeavor to make Amalickiah king. Moroni rears the "Title of Liberty," the people rally thereto, and Amalickiah retreats into the wilderness; the greater portion of his followers are slain; he escapes to the Lamanites, rises in power, poisons General Lehonti, kills the king, marries the queen, and is proclaimed king. Moroni fortifies the Nephite cities. The Lamanites invade Ammonihah and Noah; are repulsed with great loss and return home to their own lands. — 73 528 19

Moroni commences his line of defense along the southern line of the Nephite possessions. The Lamanites driven out of the east wilderness. The foundations laid of Moroni, Lehi, Nephihah, and other cities. — 72 529 20

Never was a happier time among the people of Nephi. — 71 530 21

Contention between the people of the cities of Morianton and Lehi. The former flee northward; their flight arrested by Teancum, who defeats and slays their leader. The difficulty is settled, and both people return to their own possessions. Nephihah, the second chief judge, dies; his son, Pahoran, succeeds him. — 68 533 24

Great contentions between the "king men" and "free men." The people decide in favor of the continuance of the republic, upon which the monarchists revolt; they refuse to take up arms against the invading Lamanites, but are defeated by Moroni, 4000 slain, and the rest cast into prison. Amalickiah captures the Nephite cities of Moroni, Nephihah, Lehi, Gid, Morianton, Omner, Mulek, etc., on the Atlantic coast. He is defeated by Teancum. Teancum enters the Lamanite camp at night and slays Amalickiah. — 67 534 25

	B.C.	N.A. Y.J.

The Lamanites retreat into Mulek. Ammaron, brother of Amalickiah succeeds him as their king, and takes command of their armies on the Pacific Coast. Moroni visits the Nephite forces in the southwest. Teancum fortifies the land Bountiful and the Isthmus of Panama. The Ammonites desire to assist in the war, but because of their oath are not permitted; but 2000 of their sons, under Helaman, join the Nephite armies in the southwest, where they find that the Lamanites have captured the cities of Manti, Zeezrom, Cumeni and Antiparah. — 66 535 26

Moroni re-enforces Teancum in Bountiful. The Nephite forces in the south-west finish fortifying the city of Judea. †Tremendous battle in the wilderness north of Judea; the Lamanites defeated, but Antipus, the Nephite commander, is slain. — 65 536 27

Mulek recaptured by Moroni, Lehi and Teancum. Jacob, the Lamanite general, killed. Lehi placed in command at Mulek. The Lamanite prisoners compelled to dig a ditch around and fortify the city Bountiful. The city of Antiparah vacated by the Lamanites and reoccupied by the Nephites. — 64 537 28

Pachus revolts and endeavors to establish a monarchy. Moroni recaptures Gid, and releases large numbers of Nephite prisoners. Six thousand men, from Zarahemla, join the Nephite armies in the south-west. The Lamanites surrender Cumeni. The Nephites drive the Lamanites eastward to the land of Manti. They are afterwards driven out of that region by Helaman. Helaman writes an epistle to Moroni, complaining of want of reinforcements. — 63 538 29

Pachus drives the chief judge out of Zarahemla; he seeks safety in Gideon. Pachus opens a treasonable correspondence with the Lamanites. Moroni, having received Helaman's epistle, writes twice to Pahoran; on receiving the latter's reply, he gathers up troops and goes to his aid. The united forces of Moroni and Pahoran defeat Pachus, who is slain, and the rebellion is put down. The Lamanite troops, driven out of the south-west, capture the city of Nephihah. — 62 539 30

Provisions and 6000 men sent to the relief of Helaman; the same to the commanders in the east. A battle fought on the road between Zarahemla and Nephihah. 4000 Lamanite prisoners make a covenant of peace, and are sent to join the Ammonites. Nephihah surprised and captured by Moroni. Lehi and several other cities on the

	B.C.	N.A.	Y.J.

Atlantic coast recaptured by the Nephites. Teancum slays Ammoron in the city of Moroni, and is himself slain by Ammoron's servants. The city is captured by the Nephites, and the Lamanites are driven to their own lands. — 61 / 540 / 31

Moroni fortifies the southern border of the Nephites, and transfers the command of his forces to his son Moronihah. Helaman and his fellow-laborers re-establish the church; great humility of its members. — 60 / 541 / 32

The Nephites begin to recover from the demoralization and disorganization incident to the protracted war. — 59 / 542 / 33

Helaman dies. †Shiblon takes charge of the sacred plates. — 57 / 544 / 35

Moroni dies, aged 43. — 56 / 545 / 36

Five thousand four hundred Nephites, with their families, leave Zarahemla to colonize the north country. Hagoth establishes ship-building yards on the pacific side of the Isthmus. — 55 / 546 / 37

Large migration northward. Two of Hagoth's ships never again seen after leaving port. — 54 / 557 / 38

Shiblon dies; the sacred records, etc., transferred to Helaman, the younger. Some Nephites dissent and go over to the Lamanites; the latter invade Zarahemla, but are driven out by Moronihah. Pahoran dies. The Book of Alma closes. — 53 / 548 / 39

The Book of Helaman opens. Tubaloth king of the Lamanites. Three of Pahoran's sons contend for the judgment seat. The people choose Pahoran, the younger. His brother Paanchi rebels, for which he is condemned and executed. One of his adherents, Kishkumen, assassinates Pahoran. Pacumeni chosen chief judge. The Gadianton bands organized. — 52 / 549 / 40

The Lamanites, under Coriantumr, invade Zarahemla, capture the city, slay Pacumeni, and advance northward. Later the Nephites, under Moronihah and Lehi, destroy the invading army. Coriantumr slain. — 51 / 550 / 41

Helaman elected chief judge; Kishkumen attempts to assassinate him, but is himself slain. Gadianton and his band flee into the wilderness. — 50 / 551 / 42

Much contention among the Nephites. Many emigrate north, as far as the great lakes. — 46 / 555 / 46

Great contentions. Helaman fills the judgment seat with justice and equity. — 45 / 556 / 47

The contentions measurably cease; the church is greatly prospered; tens of thousands baptized. The Gadianton robbers secretly increase in the more thickly settled portions of the land. — 43 / 558 / 49

| | B.C. | N.A. | Y.J. |

Pride increases: the more humble members of the church persecuted.   41   560   51

Helaman dies; his son Nephi chosen chief judge.   39   562   53

Contentions and bloodshed among the Nephites; the rebellious affiliate with the Lamanites.   38   563   54

More dissenters go over to the Lamanites, who are all the year preparing for war.   36   565   56

The Lamanites invade Zarahemla; the Nephites, owing to their dissensions and wickedness, are everywhere driven before them.   35   566   57

The Lamanites overrun all the Nephite possessions as far as Bountiful. The Nephites fortify the Isthmus.   34   567   58

The Lamanites obtain possession of all South America.   33   568   59

Moronihah reconquers the most northern portions of South America.   32   569   60

The Nephites regain about half their possessions, Zarahemla remaining in the hands of the Lamanites. Under the preaching of Nephi, and others, the Nephites commence to repent.   31   570   61

No more Nephite successes on account of their lack of faith. Nephi delivers up the judgment seat to Cezoram. Nephi and Lehi, having preached to the Nephites, go over to the Lamanites in Zarahemla; 8000 of that people are baptized. They then proceed to the land of Nephi, where they are imprisoned, but delivered by marvelous manifestations from heaven. The voice of the Lord is heard by those assembled at the prison, and they are surrounded by fire. The greater part of the Lamanites are converted and they surrender all the lands they had taken from the Nephites.   30   571   62

The Lamanites exceed the Nephites in righteousness; their missionaries preach in Zarahemla and the land northward; Nephi and Lehi also go north. Universal peace prevails throughout the continent, and Nephites and Lamanites travel, unrestrictedly in all parts.   29   572   63

An era of great prosperity. Much preaching and prophecy by the servants of God.   27   574   65

Chief Judge Cezoram slain by a Gadianton robber; his son and successor suffers the same fate.   26   575   66

The Nephites again growing exceedingly wicked, the greater part unite with the Gadianton robbers; they also build up to themselves idols of gold and silver.   25   576   67

The Lamanites grow in righteousness, while the Nephites increase in iniquity. The Gadianton bands are utterly destroyed from among the Lamanites, but are so greatly

STORY OF THE BOOK OF MORMON. 375

	B.C.	N.A.	Y.J.
encouraged by the Nephites that they obtain sole management of the government.	24	577	68
Chief Judge Seezoram assassinated by his brother, Seantum. Nephi, rejected in the north, returns to Zarahemla; he notifies the people of the murder of Seezoram, is arrested as an accessory, but afterwards released. The Lord makes a covenant with him, and directs him to continue his ministrations.	23	578	69
Nephi, preserved by the miraculous power of God, preaches from land to land.	22	579	70
Division, even to bloodshed, prevails among the Nephites.	21	580	71
Contentions and wars throughout all the land.	20	581	72
The internal wars, originating with the Gadianton robbers, still continue. To stay the bloodshed, Nephi prays for a famine; his prayer is answered.	19	582	73
The famine continues and spreads.	18	583	74
The whole land, both among the Nephites and Lamanites, smitten with the famine: thousands die of hunger and pestilence. The people, in their extremity repent; they exterminate the Gadianton bands.	17	584	75
The Lord sends rain; and the earth brings forth abundantly. Nephi is reverenced as a servant of God by all the people.	16	585	76
The people rapidly increase; the major part of both peoples belong to the church.	15	586	77
Slight contentions on doctrinal questions.	14	587	78
The controversies increase; Nephi and Lehi receive many revelations and put an end to the disputes.	13	588	79
Dissenters search out the ancient abominations, re-establish the Gadianton bands and commence war.	12	589	80
The robbers grow strong; defy the armies of the Nephites and Lamanites; commit depredations and carry off many prisoners. Great loss of life on both sides.	11	590	81
The Nephites again begin to forget the Lord. The Lamanites remain faithful.	10	591	82
The people wax strong in iniquity.	9	592	83
The people do not mend their ways.	8	593	84
The people grow in wickedness and ripen for destruction.	7	594	85
Samuel, the Lamanite, prophecies on the walls of Zarahemla; some attempt to kill him, others believe. The latter seek Nephi and are baptized. Samuel escapes to his own land. Nephi performs many miracles.	6	595	86
The greater portion of the people remain in their pride and wickedness, the lesser portion walking more circumspectly before God.	5	596	87
The people grow more hardened.	3	598	89

	B.C.	N.A.	Y.J.
The words of the prophets begin to be fulfilled; signs and wonders appear, betokening the coming of the Savior; angels are seen by many; yet the people still harden their hearts. The Book of Helaman closes.	2	599	90
The Third Book of Nephi opens. Nephi departs out of the land, and is never again seen. Lachoneus, chief judge and governor.	1	600	91
	A.C.		
The promised signs of the Redeemer's birth appear, to the joy of believers. The two days and one night of constant light; a new star appears. The majority of the people join the church. The Nephites reckon their time from the Messiah's advent.	1	601	92
The Gadianton robbers commit many murders; the people not strong enough to overpower them.	2	602	
Dissensions increase, owing to many joining the robber bands, especially among the young.	3	603	
Wickedness and unbelief greatly increase.	4	604	
Evil continues to gain strength to this time. Gadianton bands grow so numerous that both Nephites and Lamanites take up arms against them.	13	613	
The robbers driven into their secret fastnesses in the mountains and the wilderness.	14	614	
Owing to dissensions, the robbers gain many advantages.	15	615	
Giddianhi, the robber chief, writes an epistle to Lachoneus, calling upon the Nephites to surrender. Gidgiddoni chosen commander of the Nephite forces. Lachoneus decides to gather all the Nephites from both continents into the lands of Zarahemla and Bountiful, and fortify against the attacks of the robbers.	16	616	
The people, with all their movable substance and seven years' provisions, gather at the appointed place.	17	617	
In the latter part of the year the robbers leave their hiding places and occupy the lands deserted by the people.	18	618	
The robbers, under Giddianhi, attack the Nephites. The slaughter more terrible than in any previous battle among the children of Lehi; Giddianhi is slain, the robbers are defeated and pursued to the wilderness.	19	619	
The robbers do not venture to again attack the Nephites. Zemnarihah made chief of the robber bands.	20	620	
The robbers surround and ineffectually besiege the Nephites, who make many sorties and slay tens of thousands of them; the robbers attempt to concentrate in the north but are cut off, their armies destroyed, and thousands taken prisoners; among whom is Zemnarihah,			

	B.C.	N.A.Y.J.

who is afterwards hanged. The Nephites greatly rejoice in their marvelous deliverance.   21   621

All the Nephites believe the words of the prophets; righteousness prevails. They preach to their prisoners; all who make a covenant to murder no more are released, those who refuse are punished according to the law.   22   622

The Nephites all return to their own lands on both continents.   26   626

The laws revised according to justice and equity; great order throughout the land.   27   627

Many new cities built and old ones repaired; numerous other improvements made.   28   628

Disputings and contentions re-commence; pride and other evils increase.   29   629

Lachoneus, the younger, governor. The church broken up, except among a few Lamanites. Many prophets testify and are persecuted; some are executed contrary to law. The officers committing these crimes, on being called to account, rebel and seek to establish a monarchy, with Jacob as king. The chief judge is slain, and the ancient iniquitous combination re-introduced. The Nephite Republic is broken up, and the people divided into numerous tribes. Jacob leads his band into the northernmost part of the land.   30   630

The various tribes more fully regulated. Nephi performs many miracles; among others, raises his brother Timothy from the dead. But few are converted.   31   631

Nephi continues his preaching and ministry; a few accept his message.   32   632

Many join the church.   33   633

On the fourth day of the new year the signs of Christ's crucifixion commence. An unparalleled storm rages for three hours, convulsing the land and destroying many cities. It is followed by three days' darkness. The voice of the Lord is heard proclaiming the destruction that had happened. Jesus appears to the people in the land Bountiful. He preaches his gospel, performs many mighty works, and chooses twelve disciples. Nephi, the son of Nephi, takes the records.   34   634

All the people are converted, and the church becomes universal. The believers have all things in common.   36   636

The disciples of Jesus work many wonderful miracles.   37   637

The people again becoming numerous. Zarahemla and other cities rebuilt.   59   659

	A.C.	N.A.Y.J.
All the original twelve disciples, except the three who were to tarry, have died by this date.	100	700
The first generation in Christ have passed away. Nephi dies, and his son Amos takes charge of the records.	110	710
Amos dies. In his days a few apostatize and become Lamanites. His son Amos takes charge of the records.	194	794
All the second generation have passed away, except a few.	200	800
Pride appears in the church; its members have their goods no more in common, and sects arise.	201	801
Many churches established opposed to the true church.	210	810
The wicked increase; the disciples and saints persecuted. The three Nephites perform many miracles, from the last date to	230	830
The people divided into Nephites and Lamanites.	231	831
The more wicked portion of the people have grown much the stronger.	244	844
The wicked build up many expensive churches to their false faiths.	250	850
The members of the true church, or Nephites, begin to grow proud and sinful. The Gadianton iniquities are again developed.	260	860
Both Nephites and Lamanites have grown very wicked; none are righteous except the three disciples. The Gadianton robbers have spread over all the land.	300	900
Amos transfers the records to his brother Ammaron, and dies.	306	906
Mormon born.	311	911
Ammaron hides up the records in the hill Shim.	321	921
Mormon, the father of Mormon, takes his son to Zarahemla. War commences between the Nephites and Lamanites; a number of battles fought in which the Nephites prevail. Mormon's record opens.	322	922
The three Nephites cease to minister among the people, because of their iniquities. Things hidden in the earth become slippery. Mormon endeavors to preach, but his mouth is shut. War recommences, and Mormon is chosen general of the Nephites.	326	926
The Nephites retreat before the Lamanites to the north countries. The Lamanites capture Angola.	327	927
†The Lamanites drive the Nephites out of the land of David into the land of Joshua.	328	928
†Revolution and carnage throughout all the land. The Nephite warriors gather for battle into one place.	329	929
The Lamanite king, Aaron, defeated by Mormon.	330	930

	A.C.	N.A.Y.J.
Great sorrow among the Nephites, because of their pitiable condition.	331	931
Mormon obtains the plates, as Ammaron directed.	335	935
Wars, with much slaughter, until	344	944
The Lamanites drive the Nephites to the land of Jashon, thence northward to the land of Shem. The Nephites fortify the city of Shem.	345	945
Mormon, with 30,000 Nephites, defeats 50,000 Lamanites in the land of Shem; he pursues and again defeats the enemy.	346	946
The Nephites regain the lands of their inheritance by the end of the year	349	949
The Nephites as one party, and the Lamanites and Gadiantons as the other, make a treaty, by which the Nephites possess the country north of the Isthmus, and the Lamanites that south of it. Ten years' peace follows.	350	950
By the command of the Lord, Mormon preaches repentance, but the Nephites harden their hearts, during the ten years ending	360	960
The Lamanite king declares war; the Nephites gather at the land Desolation.	360	960
The Lamanites march to Desolation, are defeated and return home.	361	961
The Lamanites make another invasion and are defeated. Mormon refuses to lead the Nephites any longer.	362	962
The Nephites invade South America, and are driven back. The Lamanites capture the city of Desolation.	363	963
The Lamanites besiege Teancum, are repulsed, and the Nephites recapture Desolation.	364	964
The Lamanites re-commence war; they capture the cities of Desolation and Teancum, but are afterwards driven entirely out of the lands of the Nephites.	367	967
The Lamanites again commence war. A fierce battle is fought in the land Desolation. The Lamanites capture Desolation, Boaz and other cities. Mormon takes up all the records from the hill Shim.	375	975
Mormon resumes command of the Nephites, the Lamanites twice attack the city of Jordon, and are repulsed. They burn many Nephite towns.	379	979
The Nephites disastrously routed.	380	980
†Mormon writes to the Lamanite king, asking to be allowed to gather all his people to the hill Cumorah, and there give battle. His request is granted.	382	982
At the end of this year all the Nephites are gathered at the hill Cumorah.	384	984

	A.B.	N.A.Y.J.
Mormon hides all the records in Cumorah, save the abridged ones, which he gives to Moroni. The final battle, in which all but twenty-four Nephites are killed, and a few who escape to the south. Mormon closes his record.	385	985
Moroni records the death of his father and the extinction of his people, also the Lamanites are at war with each other all over the land.	400	1000
Moroni closes his record.	421	1021

APPENDIX.

THE COMING FORTH OF THE BOOK OF MORMON IN THE LATTER DAYS.

IN THE course of nature, Moroni died, and in the Lord's due time he was resurrected.* The sacred records, with the other holy things that he had buried in Cumorah, still remained in his care. On him the duty fell to watch that no unsanctified hands disturbed their rest. When the time set in the councils of heaven for their translation came, he delivered them to the instrument chosen by the Holy Ones on high. He, having accomplished his work, returned them to Moroni, who still keeps ward and watch over these treasures.

But was there any fear that the records would be disturbed by unholy hands? We believe there was. It must not be forgotten that the Lamanites of the days of Moroni were not the benighted savages of earlier centuries. They were not the pure blood of Laman and his associates. They were dissenters from the Nephites, apostates from the true church; and they were as well acquainted with the fact that the records existed as the prophet himself. In the days of Mormon he removed the plates from the hill Shim, for the very reason that he feared the Lamanites would get hold of and destroy them. There were the same reasons for fear should they discover their resting place in Cumorah.

---

* Joseph Smith's answer to the question, How and where did you obtain the Book of Mormon?—Moroni, who deposited the plates (from whence the Book of Mormon was translated) in a hill in Manchester, Ontario County, New York, being *dead and raised again* therefrom, appeared unto me, and told me where they were, and gave me directions how to obtain them. I obtained them, and the Urim and Thummim with them, by the means of which I translated the plates, and thus came the Book of Mormon.

The tradition of the existence of these records remained for long ages with the Lamanites; undoubtedly growing fainter and fainter and more confused as the centuries rolled by, but still not entirely extinguished. Indeed the remembrance is not utterly obliterated in the minds of some of Lehi's children to this very day.

So strong was this recollection in earlier days, that we are told of a time when a council of wise men, with royal consent, made an attempt to rewrite them. How successful they were we have no means of telling; but this we know, that when the Spaniards conquered Mexico the land was full of sacred books. These so much resembled the Bible of the Christians that the Catholic priests came to the conclusion that it was a trick of the devil to imitate the holy scriptures, and in this way lead the souls of the Indians to perdition. In their bigoted zeal they burned every copy of these books or charts that they could find, and inflicted abominably cruel punishments upon those who were found concealing them. In this way almost every copy of these valuable works were destroyed.

Though the original records were hidden by the power of God, it is quite possible that many copies of the scriptures remained in the hands of the Lamanites when the Nephites were destroyed. In the Book of Mormon frequent reference is made to the abundance of these copies. No doubt in the last desolating wars between the Nephites and Lamanites but little care was taken of these scriptures. Both peoples had sunken deep in iniquity; they cared nothing for the word of God, and probably, as we may infer from Mormon's apprehensions, the Lamanites destroyed all the copies of the holy books that they found. Still, it is not improbable that some few of these works remained untouched; and when the Lamanites had gotten over their first overwhelming bitterness in civilization, they would search for these records, if for nothing else than as valued curiosities; though we think they sometimes prized them much more highly.

The plates having been guarded by the power of God, were translated by the same power. No book was ever translated more accurately; none, by human wisdom, as faultlessly as the Book of Mormon.*

Joseph Smith, the youth whom God honored by making him the instrument in His hands of restoring these precious records to the knowledge of mankind, was born in the town of Sharon, Windsor County, Vermont, on the 23rd of December, 1805. When about ten years of age his parents, with their family, moved to Palmyra, in the State of New York, in the vicinity of which place he lived for about eleven years; the latter portion of the time in a village called Manchester. Joseph helped his father on the farm, hired out at day-work, and passed his years very much after the manner common to young men in the rural districts. His advantages for obtaining anything beyond the rudiments of education were exceedingly small: he could read without much difficulty, write an imperfect hand, and had but a very limited understanding of arithmetic.

The circumstances attending Joseph's first vision in the early spring of 1820, when he saw the Father and the Son, have been so often published, and must necessarily be so familiar to our readers, that with this bare reference to the fact we will pass them by. It is sufficient for the purpose of our present research to know that this marvelously important event did happen. Then and there the corner stone was laid of the vast fabric to God's glory of which Joseph was the master builder, when mortal beings alone are considered.

---

*In council with the Twelve Apostles, Joseph Smith said, I told the brethren that the Book of Mormon was the most correct of any book on earth, and the keystone of our religion, and a man would get nearer to God by abiding by its precepts, than by any other book.

On the evening of the 21st of September, 1823, he retired to his bed in a serious and contemplative state of mind. He shortly betook himself to prayer to the Almighty for a manifestation of his standing before Him, and endeavored to exercise faith in the precious promises of scripture. We will continue in his own words; he says: On a sudden a light like that of day, only of a far purer and more glorious appearance and brightness, burst into the room, indeed the first sight was as though the house was filled with consuming fire; the appearance produced a shock that affected the whole body; in a moment a personage stood before me surrounded with a glory yet greater than that with which I was already surrounded. This messenger proclaimed himself to be an angel of God,* sent to bring the joyful tidings, that the covenant which God made with ancient Israel was at hand to be fulfilled, that the preparatory work for the second coming of the Messiah was speedily to commence; that the time was at hand for the Gospel, in all its fullness, to be preached in power unto all nations, that a people might be prepared for the millennial reign. I was informed that I was chosen to be an instrument in the hands of God to bring about some of His purposes in this glorious dispensation. I was also informed concerning the aboriginal inhabitants of this country, and shown who they were, and from whence they came; a brief sketch of their origin, progress, civilization, laws, governments, of their righteousness and iniquity, and the blessings of God being finally withdrawn from them as a people, was made known unto me. I was also told where there were deposited some plates, on which were engraved an abridgment of the records of the ancient prophets that had existed on this continent. The angel appeared to me three times the same night and unfolded the same things.

The next day after this glorious appearing Joseph went

---

* Moroni.

to the place which the angel had designated. There he found the plates and the other holy things. But he was not permitted by the angel to remove them. They must remain in the stone box in which Moroni had placed them until the time determined, by the heavens, for their removal had arrived. But he was instructed to visit the spot, open the box, and look at the records, on precisely the same evening of each succeeding year until he had liberty given him to take them in his charge. This Joseph did; and on each occasion the angel met him and gave him such instructions, light, and intelligence as the youthful seer needed.

At length the time arrived for obtaining the plates, the Urim and Thummim, and the breastplate. On the twenty-second day of September, 1827, having gone as usual, at the end of another year, to the place where they were deposited, the same heavenly messenger delivered them up to him with this charge, that he should be responsible for them; that if he should let them go carelessly or through any neglect of his, he should be cut off; but that if he would use all his endeavors to preserve them, until he, the messenger, should call for them, they should be protected.

The same night that Joseph obtained the plates marvelous things appeared in the heavens. It would seem as though all eternity was stirred by the greatness of the events that were about to take place. The powers of light and of darkness were at war; the hosts of heaven were marshaled; Satan's kingdom was tottering; the time had arrived for the commencement of the preparatory work that would usher in the reign of Christ as King over all the earth.

The late President Heber C. Kimball relates that on that eventful night he saw a white smoke arise on the eastern horizon, which formed itself, with a noise like that of a mighty wind, into a belt, as it uprose: eventually forming a bow across the heavens from the eastern to the western horizon. He further says: In this bow an army moved, commencing from the east and marching to the west; they continued marching until they reached the western horizon. They moved in platoons, and walked so close that the rear ranks trod in the steps of their file leaders, until the whole bow was literally crowded with soldiers. We could distinctly see the muskets, bayonets and knapsacks of the men, who wore caps and feathers like those used by the American soldiers in the last war with Britain; and also saw their officers with their swords and equipage, and the clashing and jingling of their implements of war, and could discover the forms and features of the men. The most profound order existed throughout the entire army; when the foremost man stepped, every man stepped at the same time; I could hear the steps. When the front rank reached the western horizon a battle ensued, as we could distinctly hear the report of arms and the rush.

Thus with signs upon earth and wonders in the heavens was the record of the mighty dead of this continent brought forth again by the power and wisdom of God.

www.ingramcontent.com/pod-product-compliance
Lightning Source LLC
Chambersburg PA
CBHW022334230426
43664CB00040B/483